Reflections on the Tasmanian Landscape

C J Binks

ECHO BOOKS

First published in 2006 by Barrallier Books.
Registered Office: 35-37 Gordon Avenue, West Geelong, Victoria 3220, Australia.
This paperback edition was published in 2014 by Barrallier Books
Reprinted in 2017 by Echo Books

Copyright © Chris Binks 2006
National Library of Australia Cataloguing-in-publication
Author: Binks, C. J., author.
Title: Hills of the west wind : reflections on the Tasmanian landscape / Chris Binks.
ISBN: 9780992444860 (paperback)
Notes: Includes bibliographical references and index.
Subjects: Tasmania--History.
Dewey Number: 994.6
www.barrallierbooks.com

CONTENTS

Page

Acknowledgements
Illustrations v
Maps vii

INTRODUCTION

Section I
SHAPING AN ISLAND
1   In the beginning: the formative forces   5
2   After the storms: a profile   11
3   A place of wonders   21

Section II
A VARIED TAPESTRY
4   The mountain kingdom   41
5   Coasts of contrast   65
6   Bluestone walls and hillside farms   81
7   The magic of the Tiers   101
8   A world apart: The Central Plateau   109
9   Valleys wild and gentle   131

Section III
ABORIGINES AND THEIR LAND
10   Kinship and management: Aborigines and the land   159

SECTION IV
TWO CENTURIES OF PROGRESS: ASPECTS OF EUROPEAN SETTLEMENT
11   Two Centuries of Progress   187

SECTION V
POWER OF A MYTH: THE PRACTICAL TRADITION
12   Builders and craftsmen   233
13   Living with the land   241
14   Skills of the land-users   259
15   A practical people   275
16   Living with the myth   283

SECTION VI
THE COUNTER-CULTURE: A LAND TO BE CHERISHED
17   The artists' view   295
18   A process of recognition   313
19   The personal quest   325
20   Values in conflict   341

SECTION VII
LANDSCAPE OF THE FUTURE
21   The Landscape of the Future   357
Notes   369
Bibliography   381
Index   387

ILLUSTRATIONS

Page

SECTION I

Glaciated country in the Tyndall Range	8
Cradle Mountain in winter	12
Cawood on the Ouse River	22
Changing weather in the Meander Valley	28

SECTION II

Mount Gell, from Calder's Lookout	45
Paddy's Lake, Black Bluff	62
Fortesque Bay, Tasman Peninsula	66
Tasman Passage	68
The basalt soil and timbered hills of the north-west	83
Dairy Plains and Quarmby Bluff	84
Cottage at the foot of the Western Tiers	102
Rainforest stream, Western Tiers	104
The Central Plateau in winter	115
Junction Lake	122
Near New Norfolk, Van Dieman's Land	133
Lake Pedder	140
White Gums, Forth valley	147

SECTION III

Middlesex Plains   173

SECTION IV

Redlands, Plenty, an island of English tree   191
Timber Tram, Don Valley c1870   194

SECTION V

View of Launceston, c1900   234
Lees Paddocks, the upper Mersey valley   246
Trapper's hut, Wurragarra Creek   249
Tree fellers Don Valley c1870   269
Railway bridge at the foot of Montezuma Falls, 1900   278

SECTION VI

John Skinner Prout: Waterfall, near Mount Wellington   300
Grass Tree Bend, Gordon River   317
Lake Windermere 1898   321
Johnny Arbherg: Ferryman of the Pieman River   328
James and Jessie Wilson of 'Steppes'   330
Deny King of Port Davey   332
Gustav Weindorfer of Cradle Mountain   334

PAINTINGS

	Page
John Glover: *Cawood on the Ouse River* (TMAG)	22
Francis De Wesselow: *Near New Norfolk, Van Diemens Land October 14th '48* (TMAG)	133
John Skinner Prout: *Mount Wellington, Hobarton, 1846* (TMAG)	300

MAPS

	Page
Tasmania (Map supplied by TASMAP)	xii–xiii
Mountains and Plains (Louise Radloff)	36
Rivers and Valleys (Louise Radloff)	108

ACKNOWLEDGEMENTS

The author is indebted to many people who have offered advice and encouragement, or have contributed to the drafting and publishing of this work. The publisher, Ian Gordon of Barrallier Books, has accepted the spirit of the book, and has taken great pride in its production. He has contributed generously and expertly to its clarity and comprehensiveness with his work on maps and his close attention to the detail of the text.

Also of particular importance is the work of the designer, Louise Radloff, for her creation of the dustjacket and book design.

My wife Mary, who shares my love of this island, has provided encouragement and companionship in the preparation of this book, and has assisted me in clarifying many perceptions.

Among those whose assistance has been of value, the following are warmly acknowledged:

Archives Office of Tasmania
Raymond Arnold, Queenstown
Christine Burgess, Brisbane
Gerard Castles, Hobart
Hobart Walking Club Inc., Hobart
Simon Kleinig, Hobart
Brenton Knott, Perth WA
Cathy and Terry McCullagh, Canberra

Queen Victoria Museum & Art Gallery, Launceston
Royal Society of Tasmania, Hobart
State Library of Tasmania, Hobart
Tasmanian Museum & Art Gallery, Hobart
TASMAP and Michael Harding, DPIWE, Hobart
Luke Waldon, Devonport
Lynda Warner, Hobart

Permission to quote from various books and journals has been sought in all cases. However, it has not been possible to contact all publishers or authors. The sources of all quotations have been fully acknowledged.

ABBREVIATIONS

AOT	Archives Office of Tasmania
BP	(years) before the present
HEC	Hydro Electric Commission
P&P	Papers and Proceedings
PP	Parliamentary Papers
QVMAG	Queen Victoria Museum & Art Gallery (Launceston)
RST	Royal Society of Tasmania
SLT	State Library of Tasmania
THRA	Tasmanian Historical Research Association
TMAG	Tasmanian Museum & Art Gallery (Hobart)
UTA	University of Tasmania Library (Archives)
VDL	Van Diemen's Land
VDL Co	Van Diemen's Land Company

I
INTRODUCTION

INTRODUCTION

Australians are now at a critical point in their relationship with their own country ...

AUSTRALIANS have long been aware of issues affecting Tasmania's landscape. Since the 1960s there have been conflicts on a national scale, notably the flooding of Lake Pedder, the Franklin blockade and the conflict in the Southern Forests, as well as others less well publicised. Many have visited, and most have seen in graphic photographs, the stark, denuded hills of Queenstown or recall the devastating wildfires of 1967 which blackened much of the south-east of the state. Beyond the headline-catching events, however, Australians are also aware of the beauty and variety of an island which draws many thousands from all states every year to enjoy its quiet countryside, explore its history and walk its mountain tracks. Because of its compact area, the vivid colours of its fields, hills, beaches and seas, and the breathtaking range of its features, the Tasmanian landscape has an intensity, an impact upon people, found nowhere else in temperate Australia. It is this intensity that determines the way in which different groups relate to it: the artists and writers who respond to its qualities, the visitors who have come to know and value its quiet beauty, perhaps even those who see in its forests and mountains the resources to fuel major industries. This very intensity brings people into conflict over land issues, for it is a land which one comes to care about passionately. In this, Tasmania has become a focus for Australia as a whole: so many Australians are familiar with Tasmania's landscape that they feel a sense of its belonging to them, even those who live in very different surroundings. As well, its compactness and variety have narrowed and sharpened issues which are just as relevant throughout the country, creating an urgency and tension which have only regional focus elsewhere. But the issues are the same: the relentless urban invasion of open countryside and woodland, the steady alienation of coastline, the degrading of fine streetscapes through inappropriate building, the fate of the remnant of original native forests. Much of Australia's landscape has been changed and its value lost over the past two centuries. This has been especially marked in the period since 1950 which has seen an acceleration in this process, not because of necessary resource development, expansion of settlement and population growth, but because we have not cared sufficiently about the land and our relationship with it to ensure that development proceeds with sensitivity while landscape and ecological values are protected.

Why should this matter? Many consider landscape loss an inevitable price of 'progress' and that the ultimate benefits of development outweigh the destruction of field, forest and coast. It matters for a number of reasons, about which there will always be disagreement.

Like all other creatures we belong to the earth, and our natural environment is still profoundly important to us, whether or not we are conscious of it. There must always be places in which we can see the unaffected natural form of the world. Similar feelings are created by the built environment: the grace and proportion of the buildings, streetscapes and other elements of our man-made surroundings have a direct bearing upon the quality of our lives. We need the unspoiled natural world as a source of our own spiritual replenishment. That world has its own rights. Western society has always assumed the right to use and dispose of the land and all it contains. Now that assumption is open to challenge. It is increasingly accepted that mankind has an obligation to care for the land and to maintain its natural features and systems. We degrade it at our peril.

Like Tasmania, continental Australia is an island, originally part of the supercontinent Gondwana. Together they drifted north, sometimes as one land, sometimes separated by a narrow strait, bearing a complex range of plant and animal species insulated from those of other lands. The island continent is also fragile, its thin soils, endemic animals and fire-prone forests finely adapted to an exacting range of conditions. Both have been groomed by Aboriginal fire management over thousands of generations and both have been drastically altered since European settlement. Fire frequency, soil disturbance and removal, the introduction of exotic plants and animals, the spread of settlement and the clearing of vegetation have all exerted widespread and profound influences. Tasmania is therefore a model of the changes and processes which affect the continent: a compact and focussed model where the drama of change has been played out on a smaller, clearer stage. In both Tasmania and across the continent as a whole the same re-shaping of culture, the same recognition of landscape and ecological values is required, before land qualities of inestimable value are lost.

Landscape subsumes all of the visual surroundings of a particular location: features such as hills and forests, altered areas such as farmland and plantations, and the built environment. All are important for the ways in which people relate to them and for the values which are conveyed by these relationships. Landscape values relate closely to particular cultures, to the history of people's contact with the land, and to the formulated expressions and images of the land as it has been perceived by the thinkers and creative spirits of a society. In addition, each person will develop responses to particular qualities of the land from personal and inherited experience. Every person has places to which he or she is attracted through some particular blend of qualities which please the eye and affect the spirit. The human association with landscape is a complex one: a large proportion of this country has been influenced by human actions over thousands of years. The awareness of this past interaction of people with the land can itself form a strong element in the viewer's response to a particular landscape. Because harmony with their surroundings is such a vital aspect of people's lives it is proper to take account of this in planning development, and in the long term treatment of the land. Aesthetic values are as important as practical considerations in reaching decisions about land, but however profoundly they affect the spirit, rarely do they enter discussion or gain priority.

Most non Aboriginal Australians still do not live at peace with this land; we are still aliens and may remain so for many more generations. We have always feared its vast spaces; we fear the power of mountains and limitless plains. Most of all, we fear its forests and the strength and majesty of tall trees. Nowhere is this seen more clearly than in the brief history of European settlement in Tasmania. Only in recent decades have there been indications that as a society we are beginning to come to terms with the land and to accept it spiritually. The issue of the preservation of landscape is therefore a source of continuing conflict. All land is subject to constant change, and cannot be rendered static. However, the quality of landscape may be retained, even when development is taking place, if there is sufficient sensitivity to its values. This is particularly so when it is a matter of preserving the ecological health of an area, or the integrity of the built environment. All planning requires a context, and such a context should include landscape values as a foremost element. Willingness and capacity to protect the land are a measure of the maturity of any society.

Australians are now at a critical point in their relationship with their own country, with two strong cultures in opposition, a situation readily apparent in Tasmania. For two centuries we have been colonists, settlers and developers, concerned to clear a space for ourselves, to build a society, to exploit the resources of the land. Our view of the land has so far been essentially that of settlers, assessing its 'property' or material value, its ability to sustain or enrich. As settlers and the descendants of settlers we have developed skills relating largely to its utilisation: to farming and mining, to harvesting forest and harnessing energy, to building and providing all the complex infrastructure of a modern state. Now we have the knowledge to recognise the mistakes we made in our past treatment of the land and to rectify many of them. As we gain the wisdom to see this country with a clearer vision and to value its ancient beauty, we are able to come a little closer to the spirit of the land and to begin to protect and care for it. Thus it is possible now to change our whole culture of land exploitation and to develop a far more sensitive relationship with our surroundings. If we succeed in this we will at last truly belong in this country.

The following discussion is neither a history nor an analysis of landscape values and judgements relating to them. Although it draws upon some historical events and people's responses to the land, it is largely concerned with processes of change in the Tasmanian landscape and with the values and attitudes which lie behind them. Above all, it is an appeal for the preservation of one of the most beautiful lands in the world.

HILLS OF THE WEST WIND

Section I

SHAPING AN ISLAND

1   IN THE BEGINNING: THE FORMATIVE FORCES

... Tasmania was alternately a long southern peninsula of the continent when sea levels fell during glacial intervals, and then an island again, separated by the shallow waters of what is now Bass Strait.

TASMANIA JUTS FAR DOWN on the globe, a lone, fragile island in the empty reaches of the Southern Ocean. For much of the past sixty million years it has remained a solitary outrider as the continent edged northward, a barrier to the great waves which sweep and surge between the warmth of northern lands and the remote polar regions. Colossal forces have wrought their changes on the island over a vast time-span as the continents moved and divided upon the face of the deep, shaping its surface into the profiles of the present day. In the process these forces have created its complex and finely balanced qualities: its form, its beauty and its character.

Four hundred million years ago, on a younger planet where the continents were all part of the huge supercontinent Pangaea, the bedrock of the island had already been laid. However, powerful stresses were still working on the plastic crust of the earth. By two hundred and eighty million years ago Pangaea had been torn apart; the Gondwana plate had separated from the mass and had drifted south across the Antarctic Circle. Huge ice sheets covered much of the land and the ancient rocks were torn and ground by their pressures. Ice still covered most of Gondwana fifty million years later, but the Permian world was changing in many ways. The debris of ice action and the alluvial deposits of the huge melt streams accumulated beneath shallow seas and compacted into thick sedimentary layers which would one day underlie Tasmania's mountains, becoming the shoulders and passes of a far gentler country. In the ice-free valleys primitive forests flourished, with masses of ferns and tall conifers which were the ancestors of present-day rainforest species. In time these forests reached beyond the sheltered valleys of the Triassic lowlands and in a warmer, kindlier climate they extended across the plains and plateaus following the retreating ice.

In the increasing warmth and dampness the yellow sandstone beds of the southern midlands were set in place. The land was softer and more level for a time but events which took place one hundred and seventy million years ago were to have a profound effect upon the future form and climate of the island. In a brief but turbulent interlude in the Jurassic period, molten rock poured from deep in the earth and spread across part of the Gondwana plate in a sheet a thousand metres thick, thrusting the overlying sedimentary beds high into the air. As it cooled and fractured the characteristic fluted columns of many of the island's dolerite mountains and sea cliffs took shape, as well as the high scarps of the central plateau. The soft sandstones and mudstones subsequently eroded away, leaving the dolerite surface exposed.

One hundred million years ago, in the forests of Cretaceous Gondwana, new and splendid forms of life were evolving. Flowering plants appeared, the first birds darted about the trees and below them early mammals foraged among the roots, many of them direct forebears of animals which now inhabit Tasmania's forests. Twenty million years later Gondwana itself began to break up and by forty million years ago a great rift had developed between the Australian and Antarctic plates. As the Australian plate drifted north in the mild, wet climate of the early tertiary, grasses, eucalypts and acacias slowly evolved and established themselves; temperate forest and rainforest began to cover the continent. In the late Tertiary, reaching forward to within two million years of the present time, the mega-fauna ruled the land: huge, slow-moving browsers and agile predators, many of which were cast in the forms of today's marsupials.

During the Australian continent's northward movement there had been no thrusting pressure from other plates and relatively little volcanic activity to throw up high mountains. The greater part of the land surface remained level, much of it formed from the sediments of ancient seas and the erosion of hills. However, in Tasmania there had been extensive faulting in some areas, with sections of the surface being lifted significantly. The exposed dolerite sheet which now forms the Central Plateau has been elevated several times, notably some seventy five million years ago when it attained its present altitude.

As sea levels fluctuated into the Pleistocene epoch, Tasmania was alternately a long southern peninsula of the continent when sea levels fell during glacial intervals, and then an island again, separated by the shallow waters of what is now Bass Strait. It shared the undulating landforms of much of the continent but the high, hard dolerite she et remained over a substantial part of its centre. It also shared the extraordinary variety of living forms which filled the continent during its long journey north. Being colder and wetter than other parts of Australasia, Tasmania harboured an even greater diversity of temperate rainforest plants, dominated by myrtle and sassafras, and it possessed a rich understory of shrubs and ferns. Much of Tasmania's land mass was relatively high and at latitudes in the 40s this provided a cool, stable alpine environment during interglacials for the many plants such as pines, heaths and mosses which had evolved in colder parts of the Gondwana landscape. The sheltered lowlands were ideal for casuarinas, eucalypts, acacias and the other species of the open woodlands. In a remarkably small area there existed a very rich array of plant communities.

The Pleistocene epoch, which lasted from two million to ten thous-

'The ice ... plucked out masses of rock ...'
Glaciated country in the Tyndall Range (author).

and years ago, was crucial in determining the final landforms and to a great extent the life-forms of Tasmania. This period was marked by interludes of prolonged cold and glaciation; Antarctic ice spread far into the Southern Ocean and much of the earth's surface water was frozen into the ice-caps, causing the sea to fall by as much as one hundred and fifty metres below its present level. Forested plains of inland Australia became open savannah and most of the centre dried into a cold desert. In the south-east of the continent the highlands were subjected to very harsh conditions, with small glaciers forming in the Snowy Mountains. The cold was particularly severe in the remote Tasmanian peninsula. In the most recent glacial period ice sheets up to one hundred metres thick covered the western part of the Central Plateau, the Cradle Mountain–Du Cane ridge and much of the West Coast Range, and cirque glaciers formed in the upland valleys.

The ice ground away the exposed dolerite, planing and smoothing the surfaces as it moved. It plucked out masses of rock to form steep cirques and headwalls, carving the flanks of the peaks and ridges into their present forms, and filled the deeper river valleys such as the Forth, Mersey and Mackintosh with glacial ice to a depth of nearly five hundred metres. The climax of this final period of glaciation occurred eighteen thousand years ago. During this time the continental shelf was exposed and an open plain, the Bassian Plain, extended north to the Australian mainland. It was at the beginning of the earlier of the last two ice ages, some fifty thousand years ago, that the first waves of migrant people crossed the exposed land bridges and narrow straits to enter the north of the Australian continent. At least thirty-five thousand years ago, having occupied much of Australia, they moved southward into the open, mountainous Tasmanian peninsula. Their descendants were still living there when, between twelve thousand and ten and a half thousand years ago, the glaciers and ice-sheets at last retreated and the sea rose to recreate the island.

For a long time the cold of Tasmania's southern latitudes formed a barrier, isolating the peninsula from the main mass of the continent. The highlands remained ice-bound for much of the past forty thousand years, forcing alpine plant communities to lower levels among the ice-free foothills, and the rainforest into the deepest and most sheltered valleys. There was little threat to plant species in this remote corner of Australia: wildfire was unknown on the cool savannahs below the ice, apart from Aboriginal firing, and the severe climate deterred potential invaders from the north. Those plants which had specialised and adapted to the cold, and which were therefore most vulnerable when the climate warmed, found a sanctuary in the peninsula. When the seas flooded across the continental shelf and the strait was filled again, the island's plant and animal communities were even more secure.

2 AFTER THE STORMS: A PROFILE

In any vision of the land, hills are the essential frame.

The west wind holds sway and dominates the land to an extent not normally experienced on a larger land mass.

AS A RESULT of the processes of long formative epochs, Tasmania has emerged as a quite distinctive part of Australasia. It has, compressed within a small land area, such a combination of natural features that it is unlike any other island in the world. This distinctive character is immediately evident in the extraordinary beauty of the island's landscapes; it becomes even more apparent as one moves amongst its mountains and valleys, its coasts, forests and heathlands, and begins to identify its range of environmental settings. It is an island which appeals not just to the mind and the senses, but also to the receptive spirit.

The variety of landforms within Tasmania reflects the changes of the past, to the extent that in places the presence of those forces which shaped the island can still be felt. This is not surprising: it is little more than ten thousand years since ice-sheets covered the western mountains.

Within a short distance there occur coastal dune systems, ancient rainforests, mountain peaks of fifteen hundred metres, an extensive highland plateau, grassy sheltered plains, open valleys and many types of eucalypt forest. Within these contrasting regions are numerous combinations of forest, soils and geological structures. Even after two hundred years of European settlement, clearance and exploitation, much of the land retains its diversity of species and its natural integrity.

Cradle Mountain in winter. The fluted dolerite columns are a characteristic feature of mountains in the central and eastern regions (author).

Of all the geographical features of Tasmania, it is the mountains which have the greatest impact upon the character of its landscapes. In every part of the island high hills, peaks, distant ranges or forested ridges are never far from sight or consciousness. In any vision of the land, hills are the essential frame. At times dramatic and dominant, at others ragged and unremarkable, balancing a vista of valley or undulating lowland; always there is a presence of hills, a presence which affects the awareness and even the subconscious perceptions of those who are close to them. The work of writers, artists, photographers and others who have portrayed the landscape over two centuries is a measure of the depth of this awareness.

Tasmania's peaks and ranges do not rise to alpine heights. None is permanently snow-capped. Their appeal lies rather in their profiles and proportions, and in the subtle complexity of their features. In the centre of the island stands the chain of dolerite crags which the glaciers shaped as the ice lay thick upon the highlands: the high blocks of Olympus, the fine spire of Mt Anne and the pointed ridges of Cradle. It is mountains such as these which define one of the major Tasmanian mountain forms, not only in outline, but in the detail of fluted cliffs and boulder-fields, dolerite monoliths, and the sweeping lines of timbered slopes dropping into the valleys.

The peaks of the West Coast Range are different in character and in the impressions they convey. The sculptured gray slabs and pinnacles of Mt Murchison and the red conglomerates of the Tyndalls could belong to mountains of a different country from the dolerite cliffs of the Eldons, rather than close neighbours.

The gray-green ranges of the south-west create another landscape again, typified by the fine array of bluffs and peaks of the Arthur and Frankland ranges, or the remote beauty of Frenchmans Cap rising above its dark, contorted range. The east of the island is gentler country, yet in the eastern highlands there are remarkable mountains such as the shapely peaks of Mt Victoria, a landmark across the entire north-east region, and the high plateau and bluffs of Ben Lomond.

A further chain extends along the east and south-east coastline, blending seascape, hills and woodland. The Freycinet group is formed from distinctive red granite, with smooth slabs and prominent rounded boulders. One very attractive landscape is formed by the series of timbered hills and mountain peaks rising to the west of the bays and reaches of D'Entrecasteaux Channel, the Snowy and Hartz ranges and Adamsons Peak often carrying winter snow.

The higher sections of many of Tasmania's valleys have been formed by glacial action as the mountains themselves were being shaped. The turbulent melt-streams of those times have also scoured them, so that most are steep and narrow, particularly amongst the central and western mountains. Once free of the mountains, the rivers move more slowly and the valleys widen; layers of silt deposited over millennia have become fertile farmlands. The Huon, South Esk, Derwent and Tamar valleys contain attractive rural landscapes set against a backdrop of hills. The valleys carry the tallest and richest forest across their flats and on their slopes. Rainforest which has been evolving since Cretaceous times clothes many of the mountain valleys where it found refuge during the ice ages, and reaches far up the tributary streams into the high country. Other valleys, and the hills and ridges above them, support giant eucalypts, many of which, in climax stands, have been growing for over four hundred years, their massive straight trunks rising seventy or eighty metres. The vista of forested ridges is one of the abiding visions of the Tasmanian landscape. The tops of big trees form the distant skylines, notching the sky as spreading crowns are thrust towards the light. On a rainforest slope there is a mosaic of tones ranging from the intense green of sassafras to the dark green of myrtle and the russets and browns of new myrtle tips, each tree a slightly different shade.

Eucalypts are more uniform in colour, though even they have variations of grays and greens, and in summer the reds and browns of new growth. Eucalypt forest is more broken, even in sheltered valleys, and few stretches of forest are without the stark white skeleton of a long-dead warrior or 'stag' which has yet to fall. In clearing weather a remnant of mist drifts through the treetops like smoke.

Valleys are never quiet. Always there is the distant sound of water over rock and shingle bank, and on all but the stillest night there is the soft rise and fall of wind passing through thousands of trees. In the afternoon light the low sun reflects sharply from the leaves, each one a tiny mirror against the deepening blue shadows, the trunks themselves outlined in light. It is the valley landscapes which are most vulnerable, as the effects of two hundred years of white settlement have shown.

A further consequence of both Tasmania's long periods of glaciation and of the great extrusion of dolerite in the Jurassic era was the formation of thousands of lakes, particularly in the central highlands. Most lie in depressions scoured by the movement of ice; others resulted from glaciers plucking their headwalls and carving deep defiles from mountainsides, or piling great morainal mounds of boulders across the courses of streams, effectively damming them. If the mountain ranges and valleys are the sculptured texture of the Tasmanian landscape, then it is the lakes which are its brilliant highlights. The high, exposed country on the northern and north-western sections of the Central Plateau is relatively level, and most recently affected by ice. It is here that the lakes are most thickly scattered, ranging in size from pools of a few square metres to sheets of water several kilometres in length. These lakes are shallow, blending perfectly with the harsh boulder fields, exposed slabs and low ridges of the Plateau.

Their surroundings are made less severe by stands of pencil pines,[1] low clumps of cheshunt pines,[2] resilient brown *Scoparia*[3] on the slopes and occasional snow gums[4] in the protected hollows. Drainage lines are often picked out by the vivid greens of cushion plants.[5] The water captures the cold of wintry skies, the flow of wind and the softness of drifting mist in an elemental world: a world of light, rock and water. The lakes of the lower country create a far warmer impression. Theirs is a more complex environment, where the hillsides offer shelter and the ice-worn rocks and screes have been hidden by a profusion of shrubs and ground-dwelling plants. Here the highland-adapted eucalypts such as snow gum and yellow gum[6] add grace, intricacy and a range of colours to the pattern. These are larger, deeper lakes; the surrounding hills drop steeply to rocky shores. Their waters reflect not only the rapid interplay of sunshine and cloud, but also the greens and blues of wooded hills and the slender trunks of trees along the shore. It was these lakes which fascinated the early colonial painter William Piguenit, who saw in them a major focus of the Tasmania landscape.

In an island with a varied, compact topography and where mountains and hills are dominant, the limited areas of level or undulating country on good soils are of prime importance, both economically and because they are ecologically distinct from the wetter and more mountainous regions. The farmlands are characterised by variety, colour and intricate detail, highlighting the contours and profiles of the land. They have a rich visual quality which in many places complements what remains of the original natural landscape. As most of this land lies in the drier, sheltered eastern half and had been kept open or lightly timbered by Aboriginal fire-grooming, the greater part of it was taken up for farming in the first thirty years of settlement. The landscapes of the lower country are at once more vivid and more complex than the muted tones of forest and highland. This is particularly so where there is a convergence of pasture or cropland, native trees, wooded hills and mountain backdrop. Such landscapes are to be found in many places from the far north-west to the Tasman Peninsula, but more extensively along the foothills of the Western Tiers near Westbury and Deloraine, and in the Kentish Plains beneath the gray battlements of Mt Roland. Dairy Plains and Stockers Plain are two of the most delightful corners of the countryside, the green farmland dotted with eucalypts and blackwoods[7] running to the foot of the mountains. In the north-west, the slopes of Flowerdale and Table Cape look out across rounded hills, farms and forest to the distant cone of St Valentines Peak. The north-east has a remarkable sense of space. Like the north-west, it has red basaltic soils, the most fertile in the island. The hill country is cut by narrow valleys, with high forested ridges breaking the patterns of cleared land. It is a country which is transformed by the varied play of colour and light; in the clear air the spurs of Blumont and Mt Maurice rise above the farms and patches of forest, and on a fine evening these and the more distant heights of Mt Barrow and Mt Arthur turn from deep blue to purple in the fading light. The south-east is the driest part of the island, with brown and gold the predominant colours. Although this is the oldest settled region, there is still some of the native forest remaining on the hills, though much of this has been degraded by logging and frequent fires. Here too there is variety in the landscape: the Wellington Range is a distant presence in much of the lower midlands, while to both east and west high timbered hills serve as a constant reminder that tranquil pastoral landscapes form only a small proportion of a mountainous island.

The changes of the past have left a coastline which is a study in contrasts. The evidence of fluctuations in sea level is still evident in the ancient dunes, wave platforms and terraces of old coastlines. During the ice ages the sea receded, exposing much of the continental shelf as a coastal plain. While the coast was several kilometres distant the major rivers cut their valleys through and beyond the present shoreline, so that when the sea rose these were inundated, becoming extensive estuaries and landlocked bays. The Tamar, Derwent and Huon estuaries were formed by this process. The great valley carved by the confluence of the Gordon, King and other western streams as they plunged from the mountains into the coastal plain was drowned to create the wide reaches of Macquarie Harbour, while the bays and inlets of Port Davey were formed from the valleys of south-western rivers.

The island's position in the path of the 'roaring forties' is in part responsible for the contrast between west and east coasts. The east is sheltered, apart from the occasional Tasman Sea storm; so sheltered that in some of the calm inlets tall eucalypts along the shore extend their branches far over the water. Swells break quietly upon clean, smooth beaches and there are no fierce currents or dangerous rips, although to the north where the eastward-moving Bass Strait waters flow through the narrow confines of Banks Strait and across the shoals beyond Franklin Sound, it is a different story. The west and south coasts are exposed to the full force of wind and sea, and the great rollers which build over a wind-fetch of thousands of kilometres thunder onto the western beaches and smash themselves in broad fields of foam below the south coast bluffs.

No coastline could be more dramatic, with the high sea cliffs of the Tasman Peninsula, the contorted reefs and rocky headlands of the south-west and the caverns, arches and grottos that the sea has carved. Yet few coasts can have the quiet appeal and tranquillity of the D'Entrecasteaux Channel, Wineglass Bay or Fortescue. The country bordering the coasts is as varied as the coastal formations themselves; climate, soil and geology have created a range from dunes to heathlands, forest to marsh, and mountain ridges which drop precipitately into the sea. Each area has its own individual quality and character. The open hills of Rocky Cape,

Badger Head or South Bruny support a wonderful variety of shrubs, ground-dwellers and wild flowers adapted to their dry, sandy soils. On the Tasman Peninsula tall eucalypt forests stretch down to the shore in many places, while some of the south coast headlands have such densely growing, wind-packed scrub cover as to make access almost impossible.

Tasmania's climate is an island climate. The west wind holds sway and dominates the land to an extent not normally experienced on a larger land mass. The location of the island in the westerly stream has had a profound effect upon vegetation and the distribution of species. The separation of the Australasian plate and other sections of Gondwana from the Antarctic continent opened an avenue for a continual wind and ocean stream to circle the globe at higher latitudes, and the journey north has left Tasmania in the path of this stream. Because the weather systems come predominantly from the west, the mountainous western and central sections are most strongly influenced by them, and are consequently wet, cool and windy, while the sheltered midlands and eastern areas are warmer and drier. Parts of the central west record over three thousand millimetres of rain a year, while the midlands receive as little as three hundred millimetres. This contrast is often noticeable even over a very short distance in the western highlands and Central Plateau. Mountains to the west as far as Black Bluff may be hidden by low, ragged cloud and subject to constant rain. Western Bluff and the western Plateau will have cloud on their higher levels and frequent showers. Further east, however, beyond Mt Ironstone, Great Lake and the eastern Plateau may well have a clear, windy day with sunshine and perhaps an occasional shower. West coast residents speak of driving into the 'wall of rain' at Hampshire as they return from the north-west.

Such a range of rainfall and temperature across the small area and complex landforms of the island has been a strong factor in sustaining a rich variety of conditions for plants and plant communities: a variety which would be rare in any other region of comparable area. Tasmania still retains some two hundred endemic species amongst its total of two thousand flowering plants. It is only during the past two centuries, the duration of European settlement, that this varied and valuable range of species has come under substantial pressure: pressure which will grow as the remaining unaltered areas of the island are increasingly exploited.

Even a brief profile suggests the complexity of the island, its topography and climate, and the conditions to which life-forms have become acclimatised. Its value can be perceived only when it is considered in its entirety: an island of extraordinary natural and ecological wealth. Its landscapes, created over such vast periods of time and by such diverse forces have so far survived human occupation and activity.

3   A PLACE OF WONDERS: TASMANIA IN 1800

*Free of external influences, humans, animal
and plant species lived within a total ecological system
which had been relatively stable for
four thousand years.*

AT THE TIME of white settlement, Tasmania was occupied by between three thousand and six thousand Aboriginal people, a race which had lived here for at least thirty-five thousand years. Although they had a significant effect upon the vegetation, particularly through the use of fire, the distribution of species of plants and animals and the nature of the land itself were largely determined by natural conditions over a long period of time.

White settlement brought about major changes in the use of land and its resources, in its ecological balances, and consequently in the island's landscapes. Agriculture required large-scale clearance of native forest, shrubs and grasses. This in turn affected the habitats of many animals and birds. Use of timber as fuel, in building and construction, mining and other industries as well as for export, led to the harvesting of forests on land beyond farming and grazing areas, a process which accelerated with

John Glover (1767–1849): *Cawood on the Ouse River*, 1835, oil on canvas, 75.5 x 114, Gift of Mrs G C Nicholas in memory of her husband, 1936, AG1, (TMAG).

advances in technology. Wildfire frequency increased: both accidental escapes and those lit to clear undergrowth for grazing or to open the country for access. Roads penetrated the countryside; cities, towns and villages spread; animals were hunted in large numbers for food and skins, and were fenced out of the grassed areas. Wetlands were drained, estuaries cleared and dredged, and stream and river flows altered. In two centuries much of the face of Tasmania was drastically changed.

It is still possible to form some impressions of the Tasmanian landscape of 1800. To some extent this can be done by projecting back from remaining evidence and by taking account of the processes we know were used by the settlers. It is also possible to gain insights into the early nineteenth century landscape from the writing of settlers and travellers such as G A Robinson, the journals of explorers and the work of the early artists. However, material from these sources remains at best general and selective. Any model of the island of that time must be largely speculative and it is rarely possible to arrive at a precise or detailed account of even a specific locality.

The most obvious difference in the appearance of Tasmania over two hundred years is the change in vegetation. At present about forty per cent of the island carries tree cover of some kind. In 1800 this would have been considerably higher, the major clearance having taken place in the eastern half and the north-west.

The midland plain consisted of open, grassy forest and grassland dotted with eucalypts. On lower and less well drained areas there were stands of swamp gum,[8] and on higher ground and hillocks clumps of black peppermint.[9] Light undergrowth, bracken and regrowth were present in some of these stands, while others grew on rocky ground or sheltered grassland. This was an area subject to regular burning in the north by the North Midland Tribe and further south by the Oyster Bay Tribe. The earliest travellers between Hobart and Launceston on horseback or with carts had little difficulty negotiating this country. Much of the south-east was also lightly forested. This included the Brighton–Richmond–Sorell district, extending up the Coal River valley. East of the valley the forest became thicker as was noted in the journals of Louisa Meredith.

In the north the Tamar Valley carried good forests of brown top stringybark[10] as well as black peppermint. This was also a well-used hunting area of the North Midland people and sections of the valley would have been kept free of undergrowth by fire. Colonel Paterson's settlers at the mouth of the Tamar found open ground along the river, though the more marshy streams would have been flanked by thickets of paperbarks.[11] The Norfolk Plains, now the Longford–Cressy district, were lightly timbered like the main midland plain, and a chain of clearings stretched westward below the scarp of the Western Tiers, almost as far as the Mersey. West of the Tamar the hilly country carried very tall eucalypt forest and myrtle,[12] sassafras[13] and other rainforest species grew in the deeper gullies where remnants survive today. Towards Port Sorell there were some natural openings around the shores of the shallow estuary and on the eastern side, with heathland rising into the northern end of the Asbestos Range and tea-tree[14] covering the flats which were later cleared for the earliest farms in the north-west. Along the north-west coast, firing by the North Tribe as they travelled had preserved openings such as Northdown Plain, but further inland the Sassafras district carried tall timber with high manferns[15] and thick understorey. It was here that the Merediths became lost on a picnic in one of the dark fern glades. The clearings under the Western Tiers provided a ready-made stock-route for the settlers moving west in the 1820s and there were also clearings along the middle reaches of the Mersey, reported by Captain Rolland in 1823.[16]

The north-western forests were described in some detail, initially by coastal explorers such as Hardwicke in 1823 and Hobbs in 1824.

Hardwicke's report on the country west of the Mersey is often referred to, with his gloomy assessment that the land between the Mersey and Rocky Cape was '... mountainous, extremely barren, and totally unfit for habitation'.[17] Both sides of the Mersey he described as 'thickly wooded'. The red basaltic soils of the north-west certainly produced very high forest; the dead white trunks of trees ringbarked by the first settlers stood in many places for over seventy years, an ever-present source of danger to people working the ground beneath them. The Van Diemen's Land Company's Advance Party, in the winter of 1826, made slow progress following the course of the Rubicon ('Avenue') River from Elizabeth Town to Port Sorell, though this area did not carry the very tall timber and dense undergrowth encountered later south of Emu Bay. *Amygdalina* and *obliqua* probably dominated the original north-west forests, with stands of *ovata* and mountain ash.[18] In the higher country further south *delegatensis* would have been dominant. The Van Diemen's Land Company's Chief Surveyor, Henry Hellyer, left a detailed account of the forest south of Emu Bay in his record of a small party cutting the Hampshire Hills road in July–August 1827. He measured one fallen white gum[19] at one hundred and ninety-two feet to the break in its trunk and estimated that it might have been eighty to one hundred feet higher. 'Who will doubt that there are trees in this island 300 feet high?'

Beneath these trees stood large manferns which almost shut out the daylight, while nearby Hellyer recorded stands of blackwood, with giant myrtle beside the Emu River.[20] Van Diemen's Land Company records indicate that there were extensive native grass plains in the Hampshire and Surrey Hills, running as far west as Knole Plain, south-west of Waratah. Aboriginal people of the North Tribe kept these plains open by regular burning as they provided fine hunting grounds. After the failure of the Company's grazing attempts and the removal of the Aboriginal population in the 1830s, the plains began to revert to forest. Blackwoods were plentiful in the north-west forests, many reaching a considerable size. They rarely formed pure stands, though in the high rainfall area south of Smithton there were large numbers associated both with wet eucalypt forest and with rainforest. The initial settlement of the Van Diemen's Land Company in the north-west was encouraged by the discovery of open country at Circular Head and by the extensive heathlands towards Cape Grim, where the Woolnorth station was established.

Most of the inland areas of the north-east carried eucalypt forest, though a network of openings ran across the high Mathinna Plains west of Mt Victoria, linking the South Esk Valley with the Ringarooma district. The coastal plains of the north-east were more open than those of the wetter north-west, with extensive heathlands and tea-tree flats. These were burned periodically by the North-east Tribe. Broad belts of heath extended beyond Cape Portland, past Eddystone Point and the significantly named Bay of Fires.

Much of the central highlands was timbered but some of the valleys were kept relatively free of undergrowth. The valleys of the Clyde, Ouse (the 'Big River') and the Shannon were hunting land for the Big River Tribe and were affected by hunting fires, as was the Plateau as far north as Great Lake and Lake Augusta. However, the higher northern sections of the Plateau appear not to have been burned before white settlement: here the stands of dead pencil pine remain as monuments to the fires of the past century. There is evidence that the button grass plains in the Mt King William–Lake St Clair district were periodically fired by the Aborigines so that new growth would attract game, though this is as far west as the hunting parties would have travelled. At times these fires spread into the surrounding hills.

Many of the west coast ranges and valleys retained their dense forests into the prospecting and mining era of the last two decades of the nineteenth century, particularly the western slopes of the West Coast Range itself. The coastal plain, however, was a movement corridor and hunting area for the North-west and South-west tribes who, at the time of white contact, did not penetrate far inland. The coastal area was kept open by burning which restricted forest to protected gullies. Fires spread periodically over the slopes of the Norfolk, Heemskirk, D'Aguillar, Lawson and other ranges adjacent to the coast and must often have swept far inland across the Frankland River country and the plains south of the Gordon, though in the Gordon Valley and the valleys of its main tributaries the deep rainforests were rarely sufficiently dry for forest debris to burn. Even in these forests damage from occasional fires was not permanent; in the absence of eucalypts, rainforest species will regenerate and re-establish the forest after fire. Rapidly growing tea-tree, heaths, acacias and other hardy species were best adapted to conditions near the coast. Most of the button grass flats and slopes of the west and south-west were much as they remain today, their location determined more by soil and drainage and by fire frequency in the dry period following the last Pleistocene glacial. In the protected valleys and on sheltered slopes of the ranges were forests which had stood unchanged for thousands of years: Huon[21] and King Billy[22] pines, myrtle, *pandani*[23] and other rainforest trees which had survived in these refuges through successive ice ages. The bleached skeletons of some of these old pines still stand on the slopes where prospectors' fires blazed a century ago.

The landscapes of Tasmania's northern and eastern coasts would have been substantially different before white settlement. Some coastal forest in the south-east reached the shoreline itself in sheltered bays, with tall eucalypts growing right to the water's edge, but with very little undergrowth. The first white visitor, Abel Tasman, left an account of the eastern side of Forestier Peninsula after a boat's crew from his ship the *Zeehaen* had spent a few hours ashore south of Cape Paul Lamanon, at a place which has probably changed little over the intervening three hundred and fifty years:

> ... the country is generally occupied with trees, which stand so thinly scattered that you may pass through everywhere and see to a far distance ... as it is unencumbered by thick wood or underwood.[24]

'Many of the early arrivals expressed their astonishment at the beauty of the Tasmanian landscape.'

Changing weather in the Meander Valley (author).

Tasman's men also observed smoke from the Oyster Bay people's fires on this occasion and regular burning had kept much of the forest free of undergrowth along the east and north coasts. In areas clear of forest there was low scrub consisting of species such as *Banksia*,[25] boobyalla[26] and tea-tree, often in dense thickets, and heathland with low tea-tree, Mimosa[27] and other resilient cover.

There were, in 1800, many more coastal swamps and lagoons: wetlands which were soon drained for pasture, their paperbarks cleared and burned. Around river mouths and estuaries were tidal flats and marshes which supported large populations of waterbirds. Many rivers had shallow sand bars similar to those that still form at the mouths of the west coast streams. Rivers such as the Mersey, Forth and Leven had a depth of water on their bars of only two to three metres at low water. Littering the shallows of the estuaries were masses of logs which had been washed down from inland forests and lay for decades rotting in the mud.

With far greater forest cover on the island prior to white settlement, it is likely that rainfall was higher than present levels. Certainly the drainage and water retention patterns were different over much of the country. The drier regions in the east and midlands retained more surface water than now through long native grasses, undergrowth and tree root systems slowing run-off. Watercourses which have now become eroded, silted or obstructed by introduced plants such as willows, were then running clearly and evenly, their banks and verges protected by trees and undergrowth which filtered and regulated drainage from their surroundings. On steeper hillsides and mountain ranges the forests and highland shrubberies also retained water, even after heavy rains or rapid thaws, so that major flooding in the river systems would have been less common than it is today.

In the wide range of undisturbed habitats of 1800 there were large numbers of animals and birds, a great diversity of species and a complex set of balances and interrelationships between them which had developed over many thousands of years. The Aborigines hunted wallabies, possums, ducks, swans, seals and mutton-birds periodically, but their relatively small numbers, regular patterns of movement within tribal areas and the preference of coastal tribes for shellfish, ensured that animals were not placed under pressure for survival in any region. Large animals such as the Forester kangaroo[28] had a wider range than they do at present. This fine animal was spread across the north and northern midlands and into the north-west, whereas it has since become restricted to the far north-east. Large birds of prey, including the wedge-tail eagle[29] and white-breasted sea eagle[30] were common, as were the smaller hawks, sustained by plentiful numbers of small animals, birds and reptiles. Other predators such as the thylacine,[31] Tasmanian devil,[32] native cat[33] and tiger cat[34] had a controlling influence upon animal populations. The dingo was never introduced to Tasmania, having spread across continental Australia about four thousand years ago, well after the flooding of Bass Strait. This barrier thus ensured the survival of many animal species which would otherwise have fallen prey to the dingo or failed to compete with it, as was the case with the mainland thylacine. The Tasmanian emu[35] was not plentiful at the time of settlement, but was reported occasionally as late as the 1820s, notably in the north-west.

In Tasmania's varied, isolated and secure conditions, animal and marine life flourished, many species exhibiting characteristics which differentiated them from their mainland counterparts. Fur seals[36] came in to the coasts and basked on offshore rocks and islands. Bennett's wallabies,[37] bettongs,[38] pademelons[39] and potoroos[40] made their pathways through the undergrowth. Wombats[41] tunnelled among the tree roots and grazed the flats from sea level to the high mountain country. In the canopy of eucalypt forests were both brush-tailed[42] and ring-tailed[43] possums, as well as the beautiful little sugar gliders[44] and pigmy possums.[45] Echidna[46] were well established in most regions, while living by streams and marshes were platypus,[47] swamp rats[48] and water rats.[49]

From the alpine plateaus to the seashores and lagoons, the forests, heathlands and reed beds were home to very large numbers of birds of many species. They ranged from tiny pardalotes, finches and wrens to colourful honeyeaters and noisy wattlebirds; from robins and thornbills to rosellas and cockatoos. The lake margins, wetlands and estuaries were particularly rich in waders and sand-dwellers. There were no droughts to affect breeding patterns and few predators beyond the native snakes, quolls and raptors to threaten nesting sites.

Even the Central Plateau with its long, severe winters was not too harsh a habitat for the tiger snake[50] and whip snake,[51] as well as for several species of skinks and lizards, while the lower country in all parts of the island supported a quite large snake population. There were ample food sources for them in the numbers of frogs inhabiting the stream and swamp verges and the bird and insect numbers. Snakes also had few predators, though the young were attractive to birds of prey. The streams and lakes carried native fish, blackfish and the galaxias, as well as the remarkable *syncarids*, freshwater lobsters whose burrows may be seen in damp situations in most areas, and *anaspides* of the mountain pools, which differed very little from their ancestors of the Carboniferous period. These may have been far more widespread even in lower level streams.

Both animals and plants had benefited from Tasmania's long period of isolation. Although the island is small, they had developed across a very broad range of ecological conditions, finding niches which would not have been so readily available elsewhere, and refuges in time of stress. A number of plant species have been in Tasmania for as long as twenty-two million years. Although variations of climate, temperature and altitude are considerable, the island is generally temperate and lacks the extremes of cold, heat and aridity that might have lessened the chances of some species' survival. Tasmania has no major internal barriers which could inhibit interrelationships within species: there are few substantial waterways in the hinterland and the Central Plateau extends across only a small proportion of the land surface. Consequently, species had the opportunity to develop across their whole range and to diversify. It is these conditions which presented such a rich diversity of life to the first white settlers.

The first European explorers and settlers to set foot in Tasmania found a veritable wonderland. It was not an island where change was absent: nature is never static and changes had been taking place throughout the entire course of its history. What was remarkable was that a relative equilibrium had been established within a defined location with its own integrity. Free of external influences, humans, animal and plant species lived within a total ecological system which had been relatively stable for four thousand years. When changes did take place they were on a time-scale in which populations could adapt to them. There was a natural harmony: not the imagined paradise of the European Romantic, but one which rested upon a complex series of balanced relationships.

Many of the early arrivals expressed their astonishment at the beauty of the Tasmanian landscape, sensing in it far more than the pleasing outward form of what they saw. Some, like Louisa Meredith, wrote extensively not just of its scenic beauty, but of the details of trees, birds and animals. An English visitor, Augustus Prinsep, arrived in the Derwent from India in 1829 ill and fatigued; he had little more than a year to live. In a penal colony he expected to find a harsh, unattractive landscape matching the human blight, but instead was overwhelmed by the view of mountain, forest and river, even though the scene was strange to a taste attuned to the English countryside:

> The view from the harbour would make the most magnificent panorama in the world, were a painter to give the deep brown and purple tints to the foliage which clothes the hills; ... these dark woods form a rich background to the town as you view it from the water; they are principally formed of gum trees, ... when united in groups, they form a mass of dark leaves enlivened by their white irregular trunks. They are evergreens, or rather everbrowns, which in this clear atmosphere, up the wild glens of Mt Wellington, deepen into the richest purple in the distance.[52]

The accompanying illustrations by Prinsep and his wife Elizabeth also capture the freshness and colour of the landscape, with wooded hills close by. The description, like those of many other early travellers, expresses the writer's response to the essential elements of the newly settled country: mountain and hill, forest, clear atmosphere, the absence of intrusive effects of settlement upon the land, and the spell of the landscape upon the spirit. It is these elements which have, ever since, impressed themselves upon those who visit the island. Coming as they do with a fresh vision, newcomers perceive, perhaps even more clearly than those who spend their lives here, the unique value of all that Tasmania represents.

Section II

A Varied Tapestry

Mountains and plains referred to in the text
(map by Louise Radloff).

There is still time and the possibility of a way of life suited to the rhythms of the land.

THE MOST VALUABLE single attribute of the island of Tasmania is its landscape. This concept embraces the qualities of its topography and all of those features which together create its unique and characteristic presence: plants and animals, the range of habitats and ecological systems, plant communities, coastline, farmland and aspects of the built environment. Inescapably, a vital element of landscape is its human involvement. Interactions with physical surroundings are deeply subjective; they must inevitably be coloured and qualified by the knowledge of past associations and by present activities. People are part of the history and mythology of any landscape. An exceptional convergence of factors gives to the Tasmanian landscape its particular quality. Even the light differs from that elsewhere: the sun is relatively low for much of the year, emphasising shape, contour, highlight and shade, texture of surface, colour and tone. Topography is varied across short distances; the scale of the island is small so that variations of landform are compressed. Vistas are clear, often softened by a moist maritime atmosphere. The constant and frequently rapid changing of weather creates skies of great depth and movement.

Though the land has been changed it has not yet been spoiled. Much of the built and altered landscape is itself attractive and adds a further dimension to the quality of the whole. There is still space: not emptiness but a sense of uncrowded, uncluttered land which allows the spirit its freedom. There is still time and the possibility of a way of life suited to the rhythms of the land.

There are many kinds of landscape in the island but all of them recognisably and uniquely Tasmanian. That is why there is in one sense a larger Tasmanian landscape; it is a varied tapestry with a strong underlying design, an interrelated whole reflecting not only the image of the island but also its spiritual dimension.

Just as there are many facets of the Tasmanian landscape, there are few places which are typical and which embody all of the features that characterise the whole. It is possible to examine individual features of a remarkable island and in doing so to identify some of the elements that create its essential quality. Features of any landscape have their own particular blend of components which change with time and with prevailing conditions. A lake or valley glimpsed through a rift of storm cloud or drifting flurries of snow creates an entirely different set of impressions from those of the same scene on a still, sunlit morning: the essential qualities remain though the subjective response will alter. In fact the experience of place is heightened by the interplay of these variations. Because interaction with landscape is both intensely subjective and active on different imaginative levels, all manner of factors have a bearing on one's responses. All perceptions are dependent upon the tastes, cultural background, values and experience of the observer and particularly upon the quality and intensity of the relationship he or she has with the land itself. James Calder could be awed by the great untouched forests of northern and western Tasmania which he helped to explore, yet lament with the voice of his time the absence of human industry in their midst.

Landscape is dynamic and complex; it does not possess simply a photographic quality. Therefore there is not a solely visual experience but one which at different times may be social and cultural, and certainly spiritual. To know a land intimately and to care deeply about it is to come closer to its spiritual force.

4   THE MOUNTAIN KINGDOM

... the beauty of the scene lay in the surrounding hills chequered in the moon's rays, at one time bright as day, and in the next moment steeped in shade.

Black Bluff gives depth and space to the landscape of much of the north-west, complemented by the forested hills of the Dial Range and the ranges north of the Leven.

MOUNTAINS COMMAND the Tasmanian landscape to such an extent that they create much of its character. Some, like Mt Gell, Wylds Craig and Mt Roland, stand in pivotal positions, perhaps at the boundaries of different regions or where people passed along natural pathways over many generations. By studying a particular mountain such as Mt Gell in some detail, the general qualities of the familiar dolerite peaks can be seen. A glance at several others can then define the range of distinguishing features which mark the characters of other mountains. This process of selection can also suggest something of the nature of the contact of people with mountains and of their responses to them. Little is known of the relations of the Aboriginal people with particular mountains, though every feature of the land was important in the spiritual frame of their lives. With the flow of travellers through the countryside since white settlement, there are records of the different activities which have taken place upon and around them. Some of these provide insights into the ways in which those people have responded to the presence of a mountain, its form and vistas. Each of the six mountains has its own individual character; each represents the values of mountain landscape in this island in its own particular way.

Mt Gell stands as a guardian over the young Franklin River as it cascades down from its headwaters in the Cheyne Range and turns southwest towards Frenchmans Cap. The mountain is one of the western ramparts of the great dolerite sheet which extends across the centre of the island. With its neighbours the King William Range to the south and the Cheyne Range to the north, it marks a dramatic change in the appearance of the country: between the open highlands and brown dolerite peaks of the centre and the rainforest valleys, quartzite bluffs and gray-green ranges of the west. Its extensive flanks of forest and screes form one of the island's characteristic and important landscapes, one which has strongly influenced white people's interaction with the western mountains.

Seen from the mountains to the north-east, Gell does not capture the interest and imagination at once, as do some of its neighbours: the shapely cone of Goulds Sugarloaf, the abrupt bluff of Hugel, or even the fine triple peak of King William I. Standing well away from the other heights, it appears as a prominent square summit capping a smooth ridge which slopes gently north-west into a high saddle before joining the Cheyne Range, really an extension of Gell. The gaze is inevitably led beyond, to the white spire of Frenchmans Cap. Gell is one of the great array of ranges and crests extending southward; many would not readily identify it.

In winter the mountain is more prominent, its shoulders and high ridge holding the snow even after all but the deepest drifts have disappeared from the surrounding peaks.

It is when Gell is approached from the Franklin Valley to the west, or when it swings into view as one crosses the pass of Mt Arrowsmith that the full impact of the mountain is felt. Here it turns a different face to the traveller, a slope whose ridges ascend in one great sweep of over a thousand metres from Wombat Glen to the summit. Unbroken forest clothes the side of the mountain from the Franklin to the brown screes below the summit. Rainforest fills the Franklin Valley and the deep gullies which run far up into the slopes. On the ridges are eucalypts, giving way at higher altitude to low, dense alpine vegetation. From the summit a rocky buttress juts towards the south-east, sharp-edged and carved into pinnacles, giving rise to one of its early local names 'The Twelve Apostles'. The summit crags and boulder-fields carry the heaviest of the winter snow, plastered and frozen onto them by south-westerly winds. When the clouds break after a heavy fall, the upper section of the mountain is a dazzling snowfield surmounting the dark, forested ridges.

The eastern slopes of Gell are clearer and reveal plainly the effects of glaciation. The mountain was close to the edge of the Pleistocene ice-cap which over-rode the central highlands. As the ice flowed along Gell's eastern flank it planed the surfaces of the ancient pre-Cambrian quartzes and filled the upper valley of the Franklin. The ice-sheet, or small glaciers which remained, gouged the depressions now filled by Lake Australia and its unnamed neighbour on the south-eastern shoulder and formed several lakes in the valley, including the beautiful Lake Undine. The same powerful flow of ice had carved the great basin of Lake St Clair, ten kilometres to the north-east. When the ice retreated it left piles of morainal rocks in the valleys, forming small ridges and penning back the waters of the Franklin in Lake Dixon.

The Franklin is a pleasant highland stream in this open valley, dashing across rock bars, overhung by low, spreading eucalypts, its current slowing in deep pools stained brown by peat. Where it drops into the lower country around the foot of Mt Gell the river has cut a narrow gorge three hundred metres deep.

Gell is similar in form to many other dolerite mountains. A high craggy peak dominates the southern fall but the ridge leading north, now called the Cheyne Range, is broad and open, dotted with more glacial tarns and lakes such as Lake Hermione. The range was known as the Gell Plateau until the 1960s and is essentially part of the mountain's structure. On this upland are many alpine communities. Extensive banks of *Richea scoparia* blaze red in early summer. Snow gums cluster around tiny pools sheltering groves of *Richea pandanifolia* and there are soft pastures of pineapple grass and *Gleichenia alpina*. Amongst the rocks and in protected corners golden *Helichrysum*, gentians and many other alpine flowers create tiny flashes of colour.

Before white settlement the open country around Lake Dixon was visited in summer by occasional hunting parties of the Big River Tribe, and there is evidence that Aboriginal bands were forced into this country and beyond in the late 1820s by the pressure of settlement.

For nearly one hundred and seventy years a tide of activity has swirled about the pass between Mt Gell and the King William Range: an open plateau known generally as Mt Arrowsmith, which has been the key to the route westward from the settled country since William Sharland first used it in 1832. Convicts escaping from Macquarie Harbour crossed the pass on their way to the havens of stockkeepers' huts in the upper Derwent Valley. Tracks, prospecting ventures, a main highway, railway surveys and sawmilling have all concentrated upon this narrow corridor through the mountains. The commanding position has brought to many travellers a fine mountain landscape, but its constant use has also posed considerable threats to the area from fire, scarring and degrading its scenic and natural values. The many different developments have themselves given the mountain and its pass a cultural focus.

In 1841 James Calder marked a track from Lake St Clair across the button grass of the Navarre and Burns plains, over the high ground north of Mt Arrowsmith, crossing an open spur which since that time has been known as Calders Lookout. This track was cut to allow Sir John and Lady Franklin and their party to travel to the Gordon River near Macquarie Harbour

*Mt Gell from Calders Lookout:
a key point, both for landscape and human activity (author).*

in April and May 1842. Franklin wished to investigate the possibility of constructing a road over this route to Macquarie Harbour and re-opening Sarah Island as a probation station. He could see at once that the country traversed was quite unsuitable for such a road, though had Calder retraced the escape route of at least one party of convicts and used the Collingwood and King River valleys, a road would have been perfectly feasible. The cutting of Calder's track through the rough country south of Frenchmans Cap was one of the epics of western exploration and Calder accomplished it with the work of seven assigned convicts who had come straight from Port Arthur. Calder paid tribute to their effort and perseverance, writing later that 'better men were never placed under a master'.[1]

Calder had named the high mountain to the north of the pass 'Cheyne's Mountain' in honour of the Director of Roads and Bridges, but Franklin renamed it after his future son-in-law, the Rev J P Gell, just as he scattered names upon many other features along the track. The button grass plain east of Arrowsmith he named Burns Plain, at Lady Jane's suggestion, as a compliment to the chronicler of the journey, David Burn. Franklin had a perceptive eye for landscape, and he was particularly impressed by Mt Gell's 'naked soaring peak', and by the other heights which rose on all sides, as well as the wonderful vista from the highest point of the track where it crossed Calders Lookout, then known as 'Fatigue Hill'. The widely travelled Franklin declared that 'it had never been his fortune to see so magnificent a picture as the one then before him'.[2] Calder himself disliked the monotony of unbroken forest, and longed for signs of human industry and habitation in the western valleys. Even so, he classed the panorama from the Lookout as 'quite unequalled ... in all Tasmania for magnificence'.[3] He recommended that any traveller in the region should visit this vantage point:

... from whence on a clear day he views, if not the fairest, at least the sternest landscape in Tasmania. So varied is the immense panorama that lies before him that his feelings must indeed be obtuse if he can contemplate it without excitement ... In almost every quarter of the horizon immense mountains form the background of this picture, and nothing can exceed the ruggedness of the outline of these stupendous barriers.[4]

A grazier named Clark who owned a property at Bronte on the Nive, pastured sheep on the plains in the 1840s and 1850s, his shepherds building huts near the foot of King William I and at Lake Dixon. The sheep grazed on patches of native grass on the edges of the timber but also, to Calder's surprise, adapted to button grass. Clark's shepherds gave the name 'The Sisters' to the two prominent quartz outcrops near the head of the pass, which are now known as 'The Beehives'.[5]

Calder's track was used during the 1850s by naturalists such as Dr Milligan, R C Gunn and P E de Strzelecki in their examination of the western mountains. In this decade prospectors tramped westward across Calders Lookout hoping to find gold in the foothills of Frenchmans Cap, which stood invitingly close across the intervening valleys. In 1859 William Tully maintained a camp high on the western slope of Arrowsmith for nine weeks while parties of prospectors probed the country to the west, sampling quartz outcrops and sinking shafts in the gravels in a vain search for gold. Like Calder, Tully was deeply impressed with the landscape of the Gell region, but it was not only the drama of the sweeping panorama of mountains which he recalled. He also found the open plains and stands of timber to the east near Lake Dixon to have their own particular appeal:

Belts of myrtle forest are also occasionally seen with the characteristic vegetation which is invariably found with it,–the darker hue of its foliage and the depth of its shade, afford an agreeable contrast to the gayer green of the gum trees, and the wide plains which stretch away for miles, broken here and there by a line of picturesque trees. To an artist, no portion of the Island affords more variety–every description of scenery abounds–from the Arcadian to the Pyrenean, and the latter in its finest and grandest aspect. I have not seen anything more magnificent than the views breaking suddenly, when ascending Mt Arrowsmith; it is then the Frenchman Tier in its massive grandeur first appears; it is invariably a surprise,–the thoroughly alpine character of the mountains,–the rugged outline and the tortuous ravines,–have a novelty which charms the eye. Looking from an elevation of two thousand feet over a valley, bounded on the other side by that massive range, I do not think there can be a finer view in these colonies.

One bright moonlight night there was a thunderstorm, southward of the Cap; it was many miles off, but the flashes and streaks of lightning were plainly visible,–it was grand to see the horizon gleaming with yellow light, and two or three links of dazzling brightness connecting the clouds with the earth; at times the mountain caught the glare, and stood forth for an instant in its austere majesty, and then retired into gloom; but the beauty of the scene lay in the surrounding hills chequered in the moon's rays, at one time bright as day, and in the next moment steeped in shade.[6]

By the 1880s mining had commenced on the west coast and building a direct, practical access from Hobart to the new mines was essential. A high-level track had been pioneered by T B Moore in 1877 and in 1883 Moore marked out the first direct track, the Linda Track, using the early part of Calder's route over Mt Arrowsmith and following the valleys of the

Franklin, Collingwood and Nelson rivers through to the Linda Valley in the West Coast Range. Instead of plunging down the steep face of Fatigue Hill from Calders Lookout, Moore angled his track across the slope to gain a better gradient, turning it sharply onto the west face opposite Mt Gell. As a result, travellers going west came suddenly upon the prospect of the entire sweep of Mt Gell from the Franklin gorge to the summit and then a few steps further on gazed out at the broad panorama of ranges dominated by Frenchmans Cap. Many who travelled the Linda Track wrote of their impressions of this experience, few with greater force than J B Walker in 1887, when he was a member of C P Sprent's party visiting the west coast:

> ... the red crags of Mt Gell towering a thousand feet above us to the right, its lower slopes clothed in dense, dark myrtle forest running sharply down a thousand feet below us into the deep gorge of the Franklin River. Turning a corner of the descending zigzag, the enormous range of the Frenchman's Cap, near five thousand feet high, suddenly burst upon us in all its glory, its fantastic peaks crowned with cliffs of glistening quartzite, looking like snow but for the fact that it was the cliffs that were white ...[7]

Walker was impressed not only by the complete contrast in the short distance between the top of Arrowsmith and the Franklin, but also by the beauty of the ancient rainforest which extended from the river onto Mt Gell:

> The change of scenery was striking: we had now left the high uplands and entered the dense and beautiful scrubs of the western valleys, and we plunged into the very heart of a virgin forest of myrtle, a splendid study for a painter.[8]

One of the other members of Sprent's party was the painter W C Piguenit. He was so taken with Mt Gell, Frenchmans Cap and the beauty of this whole area that he and Colonel Legge left the others and remained here for several days, climbing, sketching and absorbing the qualities of the landscape. From the top of the track over Arrowsmith Piguenit sketched both Gell and Frenchmans Cap, later making paintings of each mountain. As Sprent's party crossed the Franklin they met the men who were at work upgrading the track. By then there were huts such as the Iron Store and Wooden Store, and light bridges over some of the streams. Part of the Linda Track may still be followed on Mt Arrowsmith today. A telephone line was erected in 1890–91, the first to link the west coast with the outside world. In winter the high, open country of Arrowsmith is often covered by deep snow, and the men who were employed to patrol and repair the line had a difficult and sometimes dangerous task. Until 1900 the linesmen had to go along most of the track between the Clarence and the Linda Valley on foot. They would frequently cover distances of up to forty kilometres a day, usually in weather which kept them wet through. When snow fell, the patrols had to be maintained and progress over Arrowsmith was very difficult, the men having at times to crawl on hands and knees across drifts estimated to be five metres deep. One linesman lost his life in the snow on the pass, and the two men with him were fortunate to survive.[9]

Several railway surveys were undertaken to connect the west coast with the south-east and two of these would have brought a railway right to the foot of Mt Gell. James Moore carried out a survey in 1890–91 to extend the Derwent Valley Railway to the west coast. This line was to commence at Ouse and run below the northern slopes of Mt King William I, sidling into the Franklin Valley at Wombat Glen, surprisingly achieving a gradient of one to fifty. The survey then followed the Collingwood Valley westward, crossing the West Coast Range through the Sedgwick Gap.[10]

In 1897–98 a preliminary survey was carried out for the Great Western Railway from Tyenna to Queenstown. This survey used the Vale of Rasselas, penetrating the King William Range through the pass north of King William II. It dropped gradually, using the northern slopes of the Surprise Valley and crossing below Mt Arrowsmith, where it swung north in a large loop up the Franklin flats to the very foot of Mt Gell, re-emerging to cross Wombat Glen and continue west along the line of Moore's survey to the Sedgwick Gap. About two kilometres of embankment for this railway was actually built before the plan was abandoned.[11] Other surveys for proposed railways made use of valleys further south.

The first major development close to Mt Gell in the twentieth century was the building of the west coast road: the Lyell Highway of 1932. The road followed the general line of Moore's Linda Track, but an easier grade was found down the southern slope of Mt Arrowsmith, where the formation was blasted out of the steep mountainside. With the road came accelerated activity which threatened drastic change to the landscape. As early as the 1860s the forest near the foot of Mt Gell was being burned. Tully himself started huge fires in the Collingwood Valley and the plains to the east of Arrowsmith were periodically fired to provide better herbage for sheep. With the road passing through the midst of this country the risk of major fires and of other destructive forces increased considerably. In the 1950s a fire swept across the Loddon Range from the Surprise Valley close to the highway; the white trunks of the forest destroyed in this fire will be visible on the slopes for another century.

In the 1930s the Lyell Highway provided access to the mountain forests. The Davie Brothers' tramway was laid across the flats of the Franklin River from Wombat Glen, a mill was established and a network of roads and snig tracks spread upwards into the rainforest towards the stands of ancient King Billy pine on the south-western and southern slopes of Mt Gell, twisting ever further into the ridge system of the mountain. The timbermen selected trees with sturdy, straight trunks reaching towards the canopy. These were felled with cross-cut saws and the logs cut into manageable lengths for haulage down the snig tracks. There were no bulldozers or chainsaws, and no chip-mills waiting for the less valuable timber. The debris was left to rot on the forest floor, and eventually the mill closed without scarring or noticeably changing the side of the mountain.

Trappers set their snare lines in the upper Franklin Valley and a small hut was built in the early 1930s a short distance north of Lake Dixon. Dick Reed was one who visited the area regularly at this time. A boat was kept beside the lake so that a crossing could be made when the Franklin was in flood.

In postwar years development has also come close to the mountain. The Hydro Electric Commission's Beehive Canal on Mt Arrowsmith and the Rufus Canal near Lake Dixon diverted local streams into the catchment of Lake King William; a branch of the Beehive Canal erased the remains of the old Iron Store on the Linda Track.

Mt Gell and its surroundings have had little protection over the years. It was not included in the Cradle Mountain–Lake St Clair National Park, and it is only its recent incorporation within the South-west World Heritage Area that has given this fine and prominent landscape a measure of security.

Each year thousands of people stop as they drive onto the King William Saddle and gaze across at the blue heights of Mt Gell, at the great tangle of ranges to the west and at the curved white spire of Frenchmans Cap. They are affected by this landscape, just as were Calder and Franklin, Tully and Piguenit. But no longer can they share Calder's reservation that this sweep of mountain and forest is wasteland because it lacks human industry and habitation. For unlike their forbears, the travellers of today come from a crowded, anxious world in which unchanged natural spaces are rare and diminishing, and in which the spirit yearns for such spaces in order to find its own dimensions and pathways.

There are many other mountains which, like Mt Gell, form landscapes that draw the eye and excite the imagination. Their structures and combinations of features differ widely one from another, but each has the same power to create a sense of space, of time which moves to another scale, of beauty and serenity. Some are already changed, and some are being altered by encroaching activity. Mountain landscapes are such a vital feature of the island's character that the loss or degrading of a single one lessens the quality of the entire design.

In its general structure, Wylds Craig bears a resemblance to Gell. It has a high peak terminating its ridge to the south, with an alpine plateau extending north-west for several kilometres. It too has heavily forested slopes dropping into the surrounding valleys. Although Wylds Craig is one of the most prominent mountains in Tasmania, it does not lie close to a major road or highway, and is not therefore part of a familiar landscape for most travellers.

The Craig is a high, shapely dolerite peak; its dramatic cliffs and southern ridges overlook both the Florentine Valley and Vale of Rasselas, as well as the tangled, forested Gordon and Tiger ranges which divide these valleys. Its open plateau is not as broad or complex as the Cheyne Range, and it has just the one major lake, Lake Daphne, with two other small tarns, the Twin Lakes, nestled high on its eastern slopes.

To travellers in the west throughout most of the nineteenth century the Craig was a guiding beacon, its distinctive sphinx shape for a time the only named and recognisable mountain of south-western Tasmania. Its early name, 'Peak of Teneriffe', suggests its special place, like that of the conspicuous Canary Islands peak which was the seamark to Atlantic voyagers.

The old name is still retained in the marshes at the western foot of the mountain. Wylds Craig can be seen clearly from the high plains and hill country above the Clyde and the Shannon and near Victoria Valley, the lands into which settlers pushed their flocks in the period of expansion from 1820. Selectors, shepherds, bushrangers, surveyors all were familiar with its well-defined outline and blue timbered flanks. Goodwin and Connelly, escapees from Macquarie Harbour, knew that once past it they were close to the settled lands and that their ordeal would soon be over.

The Craig stands alone. Wide gulfs separate it from the ranges to the east and west. This and its height give it prominence when seen from points in every direction. It also makes the peak itself one of the finest vantage points of the island. Surveyors have used its summit to map the western country since the 1830s. In 1833 John Darke and his party fought their way through the forests to the north and camped near Lake Daphne, relaxing in the clear evening light. The following morning they almost perished in wind and driving snow before clambering down to the shelter of the Teneriffe Marshes. Two years later, Surveyor-General George Frankland, leading the campaign to map the main river sources of the west and south, achieved his long-held ambition of gaining the summit and gazing across the wide panorama of range and valley, forest and plain, all of it then unmapped.

The Craig has several distinctive features: a sharply pointed crest, alpine plateau, lakes and sweeping ridges. But most remarkable of all was the great forest which grew upon its flanks and upon the ranges to the south and east; for these were among the tallest flowering plants in the world, *Eucalyptus regnans* towering to heights of a hundred metres, and the landscape of the peak when its forests were standing was without parallel. Its relative isolation was its surest protection. It was not until the late 1940s that timber roads began to penetrate the Florentine Valley to the south-east and approach the mountain and its outlying spurs. Steadily the high forest fell back year after year as the road network spread, until the coupes reached the foot of the peak itself.

The landscape of the dolerite mountains is frequently taken to be the characteristic highland setting of Tasmania. So often in the settled regions the eye is led to fluted cliffs, gray-brown screes and shaggy, timbered ridges. This is the character of Gell and Wylds Craig, as it is of a hundred other mountains from Precipitous Bluff on the south coast to Western Bluff in the north-west. These are the heights which tend to be seen and photographed and many are enclosed in national parks and reserves as the classic mountains of the island: Olympus and Pelion West, Cradle and the Eldons, Wellington, and Ben Lomond... Though they share certain features in their geological structure, their general form and their vegetation, they are all distinctive and individual, with their own personalities, intricate ridging and quirks of weather. Each has its own particular story of natural events and of human associations.

Many travellers are impressed by the sudden appearance of the western face of Mt Murchison from the highway on the saddle of Mt Black. The most dominant of the chain of conglomerate peaks which make up the West Coast Range, Murchison has, even to the casual glance, a completely different character and structure from the dolerite mountains. Its rocks are gray and folded and give the impression of age far more than does the warm, brown dolerite. Instead of the regular fluted columns there are great buttresses with contorted strata, and pinnacles sculpted by ages of weathering. No broad alpine plateau softens the form of this mountain; its narrow, exposed spine is swept bare by wind and snow above the level of wind-packed scrub. To the west the mountain plunges a thousand metres to the forests of the Stirling and Stitt valleys. Glaciers have carved its eastern flanks into sharp ridges, gullies and moraines which hold back the waters of several lakes. Towards the summit in the north the mountain has been shattered into peaks and chasms, with huge slabs of sharply tilted rock. Directly below the summit cone is a magnificent basin scooped by the ice, in which a shadowed lake reflects the vertical buttresses and ribs two hundred metres above. Low on the precipitous western side, Murchison still retains some of the dark forests of myrtle, sassafras and King Billy pine which reclaimed the slope after the ice-cap had melted. Fire does not seem to have touched it for centuries and much of the forest remains on this most majestic of mountains. But to the south-east the fires have struck. In the deeper gorges the ancient pines still stand but further up the slopes there is only the wet, tight regrowth of the west and the bleached skeletons of long-dead pines.

The mountain landscape of Murchison had been little affected by mining and other development until recent years. From the late 1890s the town of Rosebery gradually spread in its western foothills in a wet clearing close to the Stitt River. Timber was essential for the early mines and buildings, and logging tracks were soon cut into the rainforest. King Billy pine was especially valuable, being easily worked and durable and last century a timber tram was built to the Moxon Saddle which divides Murchison from Mt Read to the south, so that logs could be brought down from the higher slopes on horse-drawn trolleys. Other localities around the base of the mountain were prospected and by the 1890s there were mines in the Stirling Valley far below the summit cliffs and at Red Hills, a bare rocky outcrop to the south-east. A tramway ran from North Farrell (Tullah) to service the Stirling Valley Mine. In 1924 a transmission line was constructed from Rosebery to connect the new electrolytic smelter with its power source at Lake Margaret, the steel pylons striding up the south-west slope of the mountain and across Moxon Saddle. The successful processing of ore from the large Rosebery ore-body led to the extension of both the mine and the town, which soon covered the hillsides below Mt Black. Tailings ponds stretched eastwards towards the foot of Murchison. In the 1960s the Murchison Highway provided Rosebery, Tullah and other west coast towns with an outlet to the north, supplementing the Emu Bay Railway which since 1900 had been the only northern link. The new highway crossed the ridge between Mt Black and Murchison above the pass used by the old pack-track of 1898, bringing to public gaze a striking mountain vista.

The quiet, secluded valleys and foothills on the eastern flank of Murchison had escaped mining and other developments for a century. However, with the construction of the Henty–Anthony power scheme in the 1980s, the Murchison River gorge close to the northern scarp was penetrated by a road and the waters of the river were held by a dam some distance above the gorge. A further dam was built across the Anthony River at the south-eastern foot of the mountain, with its attendant canals and service roads. One of these roads was blasted from the side of Murchison to serve as a major link with the Henty construction site and ultimately as a shorter route for the highway to Queenstown. A second transmission line crossed high on the northern ridge above the Murchison gorge. Mountain valleys to the north and east have now been flooded. Bulldozed tracks and road cuttings intrude starkly into the fastness of the upland valleys and ridge-lines and diminish the grandeur of the great crags and buttresses which stand directly above.

In spite of the intrusive developments which have surrounded it, Mt Murchison has been fortunate to escape the devastation that has affected so much of the West Coast Range. This chain of mountains, which extends from north of Tullah to the shore of Macquarie Harbour, contains some of the finest mountain landscapes in the island: a line of imposing peaks with rock-faces of pink, white and gray conglomerate,[12] their western slopes once clothed in primitive forest. Little now remains of this forest apart from remnants in the Ring Valley, on Murchison and Mt Black and on the western and southern ridges of Mt Dundas. The old methods of prospecting and mining, particularly the large-scale firing of bushland and the increased frequency of wildfire, have drastically altered the appearance of the greater part of the range. There is still a wonderful grandeur about the West Coast Range; with its forests intact it would have been truly magnificent.

The quartzite ranges of Tasmania's south-west with their sharply defined gray peaks, white-flecked spurs and muted greens and browns give to that region of the island a wild, remote quality which has always set it apart. This distinctive landscape surprised and awed early exploring parties, so different was it from the other parts of the island. Surveyor James Scott wrote of his own response to its aloof beauty after he had seen for the first time the long line of fretted peaks of the Arthur Range from the foot of Mt Picton, on his journey to Port Davey in 1871:

> For my part I must confess that the beauty of the scenery, both in the grandeur of the mountain ranges, and the brightness and harmony of colouring, far exceeded my expectations. The country is almost destitute of timber, excepting narrow belts along the sides of the streams, and the effect from an eminence is that the spectator is looking over a vast extent of well grassed fertile valleys, bordered by precipitous rocky mountains, rising abruptly from the green plains, and towering up into sharp peaks and fantastic outlines, such as I never saw elsewhere in Tasmania. The mountains being of quartzite or some silicious stone full of quartz veins, the delicate tints of the rocks (from pure white to silver grey, or pink in the light, and a deep atmospheric blue in the shadow) made a splendid contrast with the vivid warm green of the button grass

plain, and the darker green of the timber, kept always bright by the moisture of the climate. The brilliant colours were not due to the temporary effect of sunrise or sunset, but were continuous and ever varying in outline throughout the day.[13]

Tasmania's mountain landscapes are characterised not just by the dramatic peaks and ranges of the west, south-west and centre. In many respects the familiar mountains which, like Mt Wellington, provide a background to the cities, towns and farmlands have a greater influence upon the lives of Tasmanians. Amongst these are the high scarps and bluffs of Ben Lomond which overlook the Fingal Valley and which were admired by the painters Glover and Simpkinson, and the well-known shapes of Mt Roland and Black Bluff, landmarks of the north-west.

Mt Roland is one of the best loved, most often painted and photographed of the island's mountains. Originally known as 'Rolland's Repulse', the name recorded the western extent of the exploration of Captain John Rolland in 1823, when he found that the relatively clear, promising land he had followed beyond Mole Creek terminated in steep hillsides and forests west of the Mersey. Far from being 'repulsed', Rolland was able to return to the lower Mersey Valley by exploiting the clear eastern shoulder of the mountain and climbing down to the Dasher River. The view of Roland from the lovely farmlands of the Barrington and Kentish districts is one of the prime delights of the island, especially when the slanting sun picks out buttress and gully in sharp relief and ever-changing cloud and mist wreaths its pinnacles. James Calder proclaimed Roland 'the handsomest mountain in Tasmania'.[14]

Calder made his second ascent from the Kentish Plains in the 1860s in order to gain a broad perspective of the mid north-west region and particularly to identify any open land, just as Hellyer and Curr had done when they made the first ascent in 1826. Calder's account of the climb was graphic. He had climbed many mountains as a veteran surveyor, and had cut tracks in the west and south-west, but he had never encountered difficulties such as Roland presented:

> ... we reached the base of the enormous black rock that constitutes the higher part of this mountain, and which, I should think, is little less difficult of ascent than the seaward slopes of Gibraltar themselves. These massive and gigantic cliffs extend round the whole of the east, north and western fronts of this great eminence, towering above the forests (that grow up to its very base) to the height of certainly little less than a thousand feet.[15]

So exhausted were Calder and his men that when they reached the small pool beneath the summit they pitched their tent, rolled into their blankets and slept the night through, 'though it commenced thundering enough to wake the seven sleepers'. Calder found nothing in the view to compensate for his effort, only 'one apparently boundless ocean of forests ... The immense and deep ravines of the Rivers Forth and Mersey, and others less prominent'.

He returned to camp 'confoundedly disappointed' and his party packed up their camp 'with all the haste of beaten and retreating soldiers'. But Roland had not finished with Calder. He could not identify the particular gully by which they had reached the summit ridge and attempted to descend the one closest to the summit, scrambling down for a considerable distance until they reached the edge of a vertical rock wall. This was repeated with three other gullies with the same result: each time they had to climb up again with their heavy loads of camping and surveying equipment. Calder was forced to spend a further night on the summit before he succeeded in finding a route through the cliffs.

Calder had first climbed Mt Roland in 1845, when Governor Eardley-Wilmot sent him to investigate the country along the course of the Van Diemen's Land Company's road from Deloraine to Emu Bay. On that occasion he had ascended the south-east ridge, a far less arduous climb than the steep northern gullies. What caught his attention then was the presence of smoke in the remote country at the head of the Mersey and Forth rivers, country which was not likely to be entered by white men at that time. This confirmed his view that isolated bands of Aborigines still lived in the west twelve years after Robinson's mission had been completed and three years after John Lanna's family had surrendered at Cape Grim. Calder was not aware that even then graziers from the Clyde had driven stock to the secluded plains of the upper Mersey.

The sea of forest which Calder observed in all directions from the summit has long since diminished before the settler's axe and timber cutter's saw. Even the thickly packed scrub which he found choking the gullies of the north face has been thinned by successive fires that have roared up the narrow chimneys in these cliffs. Fortunately, many of the plant species still thrive on the slopes and open plateau of Roland. Gustav and Kate Weindorfer, both devoted naturalists, found the mountain's variety of plants so rich and attractive that they spent their honeymoon camped on the plateau, adding to their collection and descriptions. It is also fortunate that the proposed road surveyed to the summit in the 1960s was not built. However, the forests have been logged to the base of the cliffs; clearings extend high onto the northern ridges and the houses are following.

Like Mt Roland, Black Bluff is now an island in the midst of developed land. Around it lie the farms of the Nietta plateau, the native grass grazing land of Middlesex and the Vale of Belvoir, and to the west the tree-farms of the Surrey Hills. The small extent of forest at its northern foot has dwindled steadily before axe and chain-saw, since a tramway penetrated to the base of Winterbrook Falls in the 1920s to haul out King Billy pine. Clear-felling near the Leven Canyon has been modified following public protest. The Bluff has little of the rocky drama of Roland; its high moors

Paddys Lake, Black Bluff.
The Bluff and its adjacent moorland are now almost surrounded by farmland and tree plantations (author).

are covered with button grass and alpine heaths, and it is the presence of its blue heights and its cleanness of contour that attract the eye. Because the slopes are so smooth and exposed, they hold the snow; the mountain in fact was a ski-field for a time in the 1920s. Long after a snowfall the north face and main ridge are flecked with deep drifts. It was the open moorlands which provided 'Philosopher' Smith with a direct route to the Middlesex Plains for his prospecting ventures in the 1860s, though the mountain's position and height attract the weather and many of his crossings must have been made in thick mist, wind and rain. In summer the moors are bright with heaths and wild flowers and the slopes above Paddy's Lake are carpeted with white gentians and golden helichrysums.

Black Bluff gives depth and space to the landscape of much of the north-west, complemented by the forested hills of the Dial Range and the ranges north of the Leven. When he ascended the Bluff in January 1828, Henry Hellyer could see no break in the huge forests of the north-west, except for the small natural clearing of Gunns Plains. Now it is the Leven Canyon that holds the attention in the northern panorama and to the south the array of peaks such as Cradle Mountain, Barn Bluff, Murchison and the Eldon Range.

There are delightful gems hidden in the folds of the rolling hill country, such as the dark little Paddy's Lake immediately beneath the northern cliffs of the summit ridge. The lake, hardly more than a pool, is surrounded by a fringe of low King Billy pines which by some miracle have escaped the fires and on a still day the peat-stained water reflects cliffs, ledges, sky and trees in perfect detail. The slim, silvery Winterbrook Falls drop from a moorland scarp into rainforest and can be seen from the Nietta farms in clear weather. Further south, the Cascades descend over dozens of rock ledges amid snow gum and yellow gum in a sparkling display as they wind towards the Lea River.

Tasmania is a mountainous island and mountains provide much of the appeal of its landscape. This appeal is derived not simply from the dramatic formations of the mountains, grand and splendid as these are, but also from the contrast which they afford to the familiar conditions of lowland life. They confront us with a sterner and more challenging aspect of the world and with uncompromising conditions. They draw the gaze and assert a presence, an influence and a point of reference in a particular locality with which people come to identify over time: a process which has no doubt taken place in this island for many thousands of years.

5   COASTS OF CONTRAST

There is no land in the world that appears more lovely than this Island, ... the stranger is at once captivated by the first glance of this - in very truth - most beautiful island.[16]

Port Davey has the quality of a fastness: of a world apart.

TASMANIA'S UNIQUE geographical position and geological complexity have given the island a wide range of coastal conditions, on a coastline of five and a half thousand kilometres: longer than those of Victoria or New South Wales. The west and south coasts are exposed to the full force of the west winds and the turbulent Southern Ocean, and are subject to frequent storms, creating wild and impressive scenes. On the more sheltered eastern side, by contrast, are quiet inlets and calm channels; tree-clad hills and farmland slope gently to the water's edge. Two hundred years have brought extensive changes to the coasts, but much as yet retains its colour and remote charm.

The Tasman Peninsula models Tasmania's immensely varied coastline. Within its compact area may be found almost all of the situations which

*Fortescue Bay, Tasman Peninsula:
A tranquil bay, where forests grow to the water's edge (author).*

make up the different coastal regions of the island, a range extending across wooded, sheltered bays and high sea cliffs, heathland and dunes, open beaches, tidal flats and settled lands. Much has changed due to activities dating from the early decades of European settlement, but the major part of the Tasman coastal landscape still possesses its original character

Fortescue Bay is a deep arm of the sea which swings back from the shattered ramparts of Cape Hauy into the hills of the Peninsula. Long Tasman Sea swells break on a firm, white beach, the sand setting off the clarity of the water. Close to the northern shore, floating kelp strands are the visible canopy of an undersea forest anchored to the seabed many metres below. Along the shores of Canoe Bay, eucalypts still stretch their branches over the water and ferns grow in the damp, shaded gullies only metres from the shore. On the hills which almost encircle Fortescue the forests are being steadily clear-felled and in the remainder the taller trees, *obliqua* and *regnans*, have long been removed. The timber-cutters were attracted to these hills almost as soon as the Peninsula was settled. When convict gangs had logged the areas close to Port Arthur they moved onto the high ground above Fortescue, hauling the logs away without mechanical assistance. A track provided access to the bay and its lagoon as early as the 1830s. On the slopes of Mt Fortescue there are still the stumps of trees cut down in 1838 to clear the view-field for the semaphore station. At the end of the century a mill was built on the shore of Canoe Bay, with bullock and snig tracks leading up the gully of Walkers Creek, the whine of the saw and hiss of steam cutting into the quiet of the bay. The milled timber was taken away in tiny ketches and schooners which ran the gauntlet of the stormy capes, beating westward towards the Derwent. The mill was transferred to the south side of Fortescue in later years. Where Mill Creek runs into the sea a small jetty was built for loading the ships, a tramway ran close to the shore, and a handful of paling huts clustered beside the bay until the 1940s. Except in the occasional south-east blow, the waters of Fortescue and its inlets are tranquil, reflecting the tones of a changing sky and leading the eye seaward to the commanding headlands of Cape Hauy and Dolomieu Point.

Beyond Fortescue Bay the Tasman coast is open and severe. The hills descend steeply to a rocky shore and are wooded, or in places such as Cape Hauy, covered with low, wind-packed scrub. The outstanding features of this coast are its cliff-lines and stacks. Cape Hauy itself has been cut by the sea in two great chasms which isolate The Lanterns and the slender rock towers of The Candlestick and The Totem. In Munro Bight the sea has

'... for generations of seamen ... the final seamarks in the approach to the Derwent.'
Tasman Passage, with Cape Pillar on the left and Tasman Island on the right (author).

carved soft rock buttresses into intricate grottos and passages. Further south stand the two great headlands that dominate Storm Bay with some of the highest sea-cliffs of the continent. The dolerite columns of Cape Pillar and Cape Raoul are reminiscent of the mountain formations of the high country, dropping sheer into the ocean from a height of three hundred metres.

The two capes have been for generations of seamen and travellers the final seamarks in the approach to the Derwent. They extend far into Storm

Bay, facing the south-westerly swells which in wild weather break around their bases in huge bursts of blown spray. Raoul thrusts forward sharply out of a cliff-bound promontory, its shape resembling from a distance the ram bow of an old-time warship. From close above or from the sea, however, the massive dolerite columns stand out, dark and dangerous, the sea swirling about them. Cape Pillar is the more complex of the two, with the spire of Cathedral Rock rising from its seaward base, the knife-edged ridge of The Blade poised high above its southern cliffs and the battlements of Tasman Island separated from it by a narrow passage. In storm time, waves forced into the passage break almost across its entire breadth in a welter of spray and churning sea. In calm weather fishing boats short-cut through this passage, known locally as 'the hole in the wall', as did some of the coastal trading vessels. Writer Patsy Adam-Smith recorded her experience of sailing through the 'hole' aboard the *Naracoopa* in the 1950s:

> The "hole in the wall" was ... spine-chilling ... On one side was Tasman Island, over three hundred metres of sheer cliff. On the other, Cape Pillar, just as big and craggy, and in between a narrow gap. The sea curled up at the base of the cliffs, was sucked back into the channel between, and swirled and fulminated there.[17]

On Tasman Island stands the tall white column of Tasman Light. The plateau of the island, once covered by a dense, wind-packed mixture of banksia, tea-tree, eucalypts and other shrubs, has been denuded over the years by lighthouse families seeking firewood, and there is nothing now but wind-swept tussocks. The strongly built keepers' houses were often damaged by the force of the gales once the protective vegetation had gone.

The bays on the western side of the Peninsula are sheltered, though the coast itself is open to the force of westerly winds and seas. Port Arthur, at the head of a deep inlet between the two capes, is built in one of the most tranquil and attractive settings imaginable. Blue, forest-covered hills rise across the water to the east, where the ridge-lines of Crescent Mountain and Arthurs Peak stand over five hundred metres above the bay. To the west, trees also notch the skyline, while along the shore beyond the settlement are the intense greens of well-watered fields. The old penitentiary buildings of yellow and gray sandstone now dream away the long years in peace. The penal settlement and its associations have always troubled those who view the bay, and even now continue to cast a shadow over the whole of this beautiful peninsula. Captain Stoney was intensely aware of the contrast between the prison and its setting when he described it on his visit in 1853:

> ... for it is, in very truth, a smiling valley ... As the equestrian gains the hill above the settlement and takes a last look over the tranquil bay, the clang of chain is no longer heard, and the beautiful little church peeps from amid the foliage with a lovely shrubbery surrounding it. The villas seem as gems in the view, with their rich gardens and verdant fields. The sad scene and remembrance of the prison-house is forgotten, and the hope rises ... but a yellow-jacketed gang is even now appearing ...[18]

Legend has preserved and magnified the sense of a 'stain', and it is customary now to denigrate the penal settlement as a place of unmitigated cruelty and suffering. The prison was, in fact, ahead of its time and based upon enlightened concepts. Its major purpose was the rehabilitation of hardened criminals and those who had re-offended in the colony. The Separate Prison was founded on the Quaker perception of bringing the prisoner to face his own conscience in a period of complete silence and isolation. The silence was not intended to torture or to punish, but to restore. This was followed by a graduated series of rewards, including payment and training as the prisoner responded. Floggings were rare after the first few years. The whole system was designed to return a man to society as a useful and settled member, and few were ever re-sentenced to the settlement.[19] Its faults are now clear, but for many Port Arthur was a place of hope. A penal experiment such as this, which was intended to avoid the brutality and degradation of prisons of the time, has to be judged in the context of its own time and society, and not by the criteria of a very different society one hundred and sixty years removed from it. It is unfortunate and unjust that perceptions of the settlement's past should still haunt its serene beauty today. The other shadow, that of the 1996 massacre, is characterised by its very randomness. It was not related to the historic past, nor to the setting. This event also will, in the future, yield to the healing beauty of hills and water.

The peace of the Peninsula may be felt in many other places, such as the arm of Wedge Bay on which the town of Nubeena clusters, the clean, open beach of North Bay which saw Tasman's ships draw in towards the land, and the far reaches of Norfolk Bay. It is Norfolk Bay of all the Peninsula landscapes that embodies its tranquillity, space and beauty. In the clear afternoons, cloud reflections hang in the still waters, and distant promontories and bays provide a perspective towards Frederick Henry Bay and the far blue lines of the Wellington Range. Sea and sky, shadows and reflections form a complex pattern with the closer trees and sandstone bluffs. The region has for long been remote; settlements are small and unobtrusive. The pleasant farmland is broken by streams, stands of trees and timbered slopes. The hills always stand close. The shorelines of the bay, still relatively free from human clutter, are vulnerable as increasing pressures on land for out-of-town development, together with the Tasman's natural features, draw more people and the houses spread.

It is this sense of space and distance, of an uncrowded, undeveloped coastline, that can be found in so many parts of the island but which, as on the Peninsula, is fragile and expendable. Much of the east coast shares the qualities of the Peninsula; the range of hills that rises just beyond the coastal plain has few prominent peaks or bluffs but has, nevertheless, an insistent presence, with its blue ridges a constant background to the quiet, clear beaches and rocky promontories of the coast. The profile of Cape Bernier and the distant heights of Maria Island provide colour, detail and quality of light which have been recorded by painters from Francis Simpkinson and Skinner Prout to Max Angus. The effects of light across Great Oyster Bay are just as striking: the peaks of The Hazards, Freycinet and Schouten change throughout the day, particularly in the low winter sun, with the light picking out the contours of ridge and gully and the warm flush of granite.

Open, unchanged coast may still be found in the far north-east and on Flinders Island. The appeal of the north-east lies in its surprising, hidden beaches, notably those near Cape Portland backed by finely shaped dunes which look seaward towards the distant shapes of the Furneaux Islands. It was to Cape Portland and the high ridge of Mt Cameron, clearly visible from Flinders in fine weather, that the Aboriginal people used to gaze from the hills above Wybalenna during the terrible years of their exile in the 1830s and 40s. Taken from the land which was their spiritual home, the tribal structure broken and their ceremonies and language forbidden, the survivors had little apart from those distant blue hills and their memories to cling to. Many at the Mission would have been members of the North-east Tribe, the area having supported a substantial Aboriginal population in the years before the sealers began to raid their camps. A century of alluvial tin mining has scarred many of the gullies inland from the Cape, the wounds being slow to heal, but the coast itself is still unspoiled and is largely free from the rash of housing development which has spread along much of the east coast.

Flinders Island has a granite landscape. Few places in the world of comparable accessibility can still enjoy the complete freedom from intrusive change of the island's beaches, red and gray outcrops, heathlands and ranges. On the eastern coast the beaches seem endless, with the distant hump of Babel Island nearly always in view. But the most remarkable section of the coast is Franklin Sound, the strait that separates Flinders from Cape Barren Island to the south. Here, island shapes and coastal landforms create a complex pattern, with a scatter of some twenty islands of different shapes and sizes. In the distance rise the mountains of Cape Barren, often cloud-capped and shadowed.

Woven into this landscape are the memories of shipwreck, the strange tales of the sealing bands, gang feuds and the colourful, independent personalities who roamed the islands in the 1820s. The shapely hull of the barque *Farsund* still lies as though riding at anchor off Vansittart Island at the eastern entrance to the Sound, close to where she struck the Vansittart Shoals in March 1912. Her presence is a reminder of the many ships which have foundered in the two centuries since seamen have tested their skills and courage against this meeting-place of rip tides. Beyond her the waters heave, surge and break in the confusion of the Shoals and of Pot Boil further north, whose shifting channels are used by only the most capable of island fishermen. Above all, there is behind this landscape the tragic story of the last days of the Aboriginal tribes. Many of their women were abducted by sealers, but by a chance of time and history these women ensured the survival of the descendants of the Tasmanian people. One of the most prominent islands in Franklin Sound is Vansittart, formerly known as Guncarriage Island, the second place after Swan Island to which the Tasmanian tribes were taken after Robinson's 'conciliation' mission had commenced. Since those days the islands have remained closely associated with the Aboriginal people, through their quest for land of their own where they can continue to live in the manner they developed over one hundred and seventy years, and sustain the culture of many thousands of years. Their skills as boatmen and hunters have given them a way of life amongst the islands as the Moonbird People, continuing the traditional harvesting of the short-tailed shearwater or mutton-bird. There is a still older story beyond the Flinders landscape, suggested by the scattered tools and other evidence, of the Aborigines who continued to live on this island for over four thousand years after the sea rose and isolated them from both the Australian mainland and Tasmania. Sadly, very little of their story can ever be known beyond the archaeological details.

The physical structure of the north-west coast has encouraged extensive ribbon development. In many sections the land rises steeply behind a narrow coastal plain. Road and railway follow the shoreline at times and settlement has spread close to the coast. There are fine coastal landscapes, in particular among the heathy hills and beaches of the Asbestos Range and Rocky Cape, both of which are protected. The dense forests which grew to the water's edge from the Mersey to Sisters Beach have long disappeared. Even on the farmlands that extend along the coast in places, the remnants have been carefully cleared. The woodland south of Sisters Hills provides some indication of the original cover, though even here none of the tall climax eucalypts remain. By remarkable good fortune the groves of gnarled old *Banksia serata* beyond Sisters Beach, the only occurrence in Tasmania, have survived the settlers' fires and are now within a national park. The ancient outcrop of conglomerate which extends through the Dial Range forms a splendidly sharp, rocky section of foreshore and an attractively forested range rising to six hundred metres which dominates the central coast. The range provides an island of native forest west of the Leven River which, in spite of the intrusions of the past century, still stands as a contrast and backdrop to the greens and browns of the north-western farms.

The west and south coasts are hostile, stormy and magnificent. During a run of westerly weather the great waves that have been created away in the Southern Ocean and have been built by the winds over thousands of kilometres, thunder onto the beaches and headlands with an impact which can be heard far inland amongst the mountains. During prolonged storms the sight of waves breaking on the rock-bound shore north of Trial Harbour is both exhilarating and frightening. Each hill of water moves in relentlessly, growing steeper as it nears the shore until it becomes a huge green wall, its crest toppling before it smashes upon the rocks with a shock that can be felt through the ground, filling the air with driven spray. Large fields of foam spread across the surface of each inlet, built steadily by the breaking seas. The open wastes of Ocean Beach present wild scenes in this weather, with many lines of breakers, the spindrift caught by the wind flying off each wave as it advances.

It is a coast hostile to ships. So many have foundered along this shore than no complete record of them exists: full-rigged ships, steamers, coastal traders, ketches, schooners, fishing boats ... The tragic losses continue year by year as men wrest a living from its waters. The broken green ranges of this coastal landscape match the harshness of the sea. Most are bare of timber, having been fired by Aborigines whose regular path lay along the coast, and later by prospectors seeking tin in the folds of the hills. On the slopes of Mt Agnew and in the valley of the Little Henty dense remnants of forest remain but most of the country is dour and windswept. Occasional white gravel tracks lace the ridges and a few deserted workings survive from the days of the South Heemskirk tin field, but much of the west coast retains its wild, aloof character.

From Mt Berry, a high point overlooking the entrance to Port Davey, the intricate pattern of bays, headlands and waterways of the drowned valley can be seen stretching eastwards into the far distance where Bathurst Harbour is partly hidden by the nearer bulk of Mt Rugby. To seaward the swells break upon the sheer sides of Big Caroline Rock, standing sharply out of the sea, and a line of headlands fades into the haze to the south, towards South West Cape. Names tell their stories: Payne Bay, Joe Page Bay, The Spring River, Bramble Cove, Settlement Point; ... many of the major features have associations with people, ships and events over the centuries since the people of the South-west Tribe ruled their own country. Matthew Flinders charted and named the northern entrance, Cape St Vincent, while Denis McCarthy claimed to have been the first to enter the harbour when his schooner *Geordy* was wrecked near the entrance in November 1815. It was left to two whaleboat explorers, Kelly and Hobbs, to examine the inner reaches of the complex waterway. Robinson had a first tentative meeting here with the Port Davey people, and Sir John Franklin further delayed his return from Macquarie Harbour to investigate its potential. After the Aborigines left, those who came to know Port Davey best were the whalers who used it as a base for nearly twenty years and the piners who worked the rivers to the north for over seventy years. For all this there is little evidence of the early activity. Foam edges the rocks of Breaksea Island and along the coast the heaths, gray outcrops and white beaches form a mosaic which has changed little since the sea invaded the valley.

Viewed from a lower level, the smooth, open ridges rise steeply from button grass plains, their sides flecked with gray screes and broken by white quartzite buttresses. Trees are low, crowding into sheltered gullies and along watercourses. The thin, gravely soil does not encourage timber. In valleys hidden between the ranges, where the soil is deeper and fires have rarely penetrated, there is a veritable jungle, with tall manukas, cutting-grass, *Bauera* and other densely growing species of the west predominating, making progress a frustrating and exhausting struggle.

The landscape is austere. Early visitors such as surveyors George Evans and John Oxley called it barren and saw it as a wasteland without any function or benefit to mankind. When skies are overcast, which is often, or in the frequent squalls which lash the hills, the bleakness of this country can be overwhelming. When the weather begins to clear and brief patches of sunshine skitter across the hillsides between squalls, life returns to the land. The endless dim gray of plain and ridge assumes a wide range of colours and tones: brown, russet, different greens, pink. Sunlight sparkles on the bays and channels and white-capped, wind-driven waves bring restless movement. On days when the air is still, this deep arm of the sea is transformed. The dark water, stained by the peaty soil of every stream catchment, reflects its surroundings perfectly. Clouds are mirrored, as are the shapes of Rugby, Mackenzie, Balmoral Hill and the other heights close to the shore. The Celery Top Islands provide a contrast of dark green vegetation, white lichen-covered rocks and deep blue water. But such intervals are brief: usually only an hour in the early morning.

James Scott spent a week investigating the complex arms and inlets of Port Davey, Payne Bay and Bathurst Harbour by boat and land on his second visit in March 1875. Like many others he came under its spell, considering it to be one of the most interesting and attractive regions of the island. He wrote:

> The greater portion of the country is open, consisting of broken ground or large flat plains between steep and lofty ranges, covered with button grass and intersected by belts of timber of various shapes and sizes; the timber is generally along the banks of streams,

or in gullies on the mountain sides, though some of the ranges are entirely wooded. The hills are steep and rugged, and show their white quartzite rocks bare at the top, which gives many the appearance of being snow-clad, and throughout the day they are ever assuming new forms and colours as the sunlight strikes them at a different angle. Thus the country is most picturesquely diversified by white rocky ranges, warm-coloured plains and sombre forest; and in fine weather looks both wild and beautiful.[20]

Port Davey has the quality of a fastness: of a world apart. In spite of its harshness and severity of climate and landform, this is a landscape that is immensely fragile. Every mechanical disturbance to its vegetation and its thin soil leaves a lasting scar as the tracks and mining areas of Cox Bight and airstrip amply demonstrate. Its remoteness and climate have given it only limited protection over the past two centuries. In the pining years, from 1815 onwards, activity depended upon tiny sailing vessels clawing their way around the south coast in the teeth of the westerlies and the long Southern Ocean swells. Three settlements were established, by whalers at Bramble Cove and by piners at Payne Bay and the Spring River, but these did not develop beyond a scattering of paling cottages and small slab huts or 'Badger Boxes'. At the time of Scott's visit in 1875 all three settlements were still standing. There were fifty people at Payne Bay, some families having cultivated productive gardens around their homes. Joe Page still lived at the Spring River and the Bramble Cove huts were intact, though by then unoccupied. The piners left evidence of their activity in the forests bordering the Davey, Frankland and Spring rivers, where flat-topped stumps thickly grown with moss can still be seen. A shipbuilding slip on the shore of Payne Bay was used for several years but no permanent roading or major facility was ever built. When pining ceased early this century the scrub soon reclaimed the settlement sites. Even the Huon Pine grave headboards have largely disappeared, most burned as firewood by visiting whalers. The remains of alluvial tin-mining are more obtrusive, though it was a tin-miner, Denis King, his parents and his family, who came to know and love the Port Davey area during the long years spent in it and who did a great deal to make its beauty known and have it protected. The scar of the airstrip, visible from most high points, survives as the most enduring evidence of human activity, a reminder that the isolation of this wonderful landscape has now diminished.

There are many sections of the western and south-western coasts which posses to varying degrees the qualities of remoteness and mystery, as well as the beauty, of Port Davey and Bathurst Harbour. The beaches and headlands south of Low Rocky Point, the 'corner' of South West Cape and its neighbouring ranges and bays, the great line of bluffs along the south coast and particularly Prion Bay and New River Lagoon are still relatively difficult to access. There are no roads, no airstrip. They are still unaffected by human intrusion. The protective status of the World Heritage Area is essential but such protection is never absolute. Even our love for these fragile places can bring harm to them. The fact that there are such remote parts of the island's coasts, places which it may always be difficult to reach, brings a further quality to the landscape tapestry. There will never again be that sense of the unknown that belonged to the south-west when it could be visited only by sailing on a frail coastal craft or by journeys such as those of James Scott and his contemporaries, involving many days of walking across difficult country. Then this coast offered a challenge to the spirit. But something remains of this mystery; its remoteness is still a vital quality which, if ever we allow permanent facilities or easy access to destroy it, will be a significant loss to the island's landscape.

6   BLUESTONE WALLS AND HILLSIDE FARMS

Deloraine dreams quietly on its tranquil reach of the Meander, its bridge spanning the river close to the old ford.

The men who worked in these forests and their families in the paling cottages both feared and loved the trees.

TASMANIA IS A RURAL ISLAND. Much of its settled land is used for farming, and some of the more attractive parts of the island are those in which natural values have been complemented by agriculture. Its compactness brings rural land close to natural features, so that the remembered image is often of fields, ploughed land or orchard in close proximity to stands of timber, natural stream or riverbanks and the slopes of hills. In the same way, towns and villages are set in both rural and natural contexts, and even the two largest cities have surroundings which add balance and variety to their landscape qualities.

Dairy Plains is a farming district south of Deloraine, a lush, broad plain running along the foot of the Western Tiers. Extending east to Stockers Plain close to the township of Meander and west to Chudleigh in what was known as the Western Marshes, this country was regarded by the earliest settlers as a continuation of the wide Norfolk Plains and of the northern midlands. This had been the traditional hunting land of the Pallitore band of the Northern Tribe, though it was also crossed by others under careful treaty arrangements as it formed part of trade and access routes for the North Midland and Big River tribes.

Of particular importance was the nearby ochre mine on the southern side of Mt Gog, known to the early stockkeepers as the 'City of Ochre'.[21] The Big River bands generally moved down from the Central Plateau during the late summer by way of the Liffey and Meander valleys, routes which had been in use since the ice receded from the Plateau eight thousand years earlier.

By 1820 settlers had taken up land along the course of the Meander, the 'Western River', with the furthest permanent habitation at William Leith's run beside Quamby Brook where the property 'Westfield' is now located. In the mid 1820s, as the clearer and more accessible country was occupied, the land-seekers were forced ever further west, their rough stock track crossing the Meander at a stony ford near the present Deloraine bridge. The nearby low rise on which the older part of the town is built was long known as Ford Hill. Here the paths of the settlers diverged. Some, notably Captain Malcolm Laing Smith, turned north-west along the Rubicon, then called the 'Avenue', where the Van Diemen's Land Company's Advance Party cut their track to Port Sorell in 1826. Smith's property at Whitefoord Hills was described even then as being one of the best cattle runs in the island. Others, including David Gibson, Thomas Simpson, the Hobart merchant Robert Bostock, Lieutenant Thomas Ritchie and William Stocker, followed the chain of openings into the Western Marshes as far as Lobster Creek. Turning south along the course of the streams that flowed down from the Tiers, they found lightly timbered grassland right under the blue-forested wall of the mountains.

To these remote plains the settlers and their convict shepherds brought their small flocks and their stock, building up numbers year by year in slow drives along the muddy track from the Tamar. Their names are still remembered in stream, plain and hill in the locality. Landholders came and passed on. Some found the district too isolated to bring their families or to leave their valued property. They feared the Aborigines, thylacines, bushrangers, and they even distrusted their own servants and neighbours. Others were more adventurous. They sensed the potential

'Landholders came and passed on.'
The basalt soil and the timbered hills of the north-east (author).

of the well-watered native grass plains and knew that it would be only a matter of time before roads, villages and substantial houses spread across the north. Foremost among the adventurers was William Field, publican and cattleman. He was prepared to take risks and exploit opportunities, particularly in the fluid situation before the advent of fences, surveys and established pastures. His cattle followed the explorers' rough tracks westward. He bought promising runs from settlers who were giving up,

'... dominated across the south by the imposing line of bluffs and escarpment of the Tiers.'
Dairy Plains and Quamby Bluff (author).

and in time he created a small stock empire which extended across the north, through the Middlesex Plains, and even survived in the Surrey Hills where the Van Diemen's Land Company failed. Stockers Plains and Dairy Plains and the other clearings were rich little worlds on their own, bounded to the north by low hills, to the east by the loaf-shaped mass of Quamby Bluff, and dominated across the south by the imposing line of bluffs and escarpments of the Tiers. Huge stringybarks stood along the watercourses and on rocky outcrops, and a massive forest rose from the foothills of the mountains, clothing ridge and gully as far as the alpine screes. The main avenue of movement lay a few kilometres to the north, where the track forded the Meander. A Van Diemen's Land Company stock station was built at Retreat, east of the Meander ford. Here in April 1828 Joseph Fossey began to blaze and cut out the stock route, grandly called the Great Western Road, from the settled lands of the Meander to the Company's new grant in the Surrey Hills. The route was little used by the Company, but eventually it would greatly benefit William Field and his sons, linking many of their distant outstations.

As the flocks and herds were pastured in Stockers and Dairy Plains the keepers put up their simple huts. Most were slab-sided or paling, a few made from logs notched and chocked at the corners. Bark roof-strips were held down by saplings and floors were packed earth, covered with fine river gravel if a stream were close. Life was tenuous for stockkeepers and shepherds, just as it was for their animals. Early runs were unfenced and there was no protection for sheep, which had been pitched into completely wild country. Thylacines took a heavy toll, as did packs of feral dogs which had strayed from settlers' camps, so that few of the flocks increased for several years. The cattle also suffered from the extremely wet nature of the ground. In generations to come as the farms became established, a network of drains would be dug across sections of the plains, allowing the soil to consolidate and domestic grasses to gain a hold. With stands of timber and undergrowth intersecting and encircling the plains, cattle were easily lost. They strayed, joined other herds or went wild. William Field and his stockmen were not averse to rounding up a few of their neighbours' beasts in their own muster, a cause of much local resentment. Then there was the war.

By 1824 the Aborigines had lost many of their open hunting grounds as the flocks spread across the available clear land. Sheep and cattle competed for feed with wallaby and other native animals that formed the main food source for the inland tribes and clans. As well, the shepherds and stockkeepers themselves hunted wallaby to supplement their rations, creating resentment among the Aborigines. Yet the Aborigines could not comprehend why they were punished for spearing the new animals which had appeared on their own hunting grounds. There was no understanding by whites of the way in which the Aboriginal people saw this process, and no realisation that appropriate compensation was required by tribal custom for what had been taken. The Aborigines became desperate, striving to halt the advance of the settlers and to drive them from their lands. By this stage the tribal organisation had broken down under the whites' relentless land pressure and the high rate of losses sustained against the whites' guns. The Pallitore were joined by remnants of the North Midland and Big River people in making their stand. So developed a conflict which, given the blacks' small numbers, was deadly in its effectiveness. Huts were burned with fire-spears. Stockmen, shepherds and settlers were cut down with spear and waddy on their isolated selections. Aborigines were hunted by armed bands and bounty-seekers. Until Robinson's 'missions' of the early 1830s resulted in the Aborigines' agreement to be moved, no life was safe in these newly settled areas.

With the Aborigines removed from their land, the farms developed steadily. Runs were consolidated, the big trees on the plains were ringbarked and the undergrowth burned, extending the clearings along the foot of the Tiers and into the lower hills. More comfortable houses were built to provide for families, though paling and shingle still prevailed. So the landscape changed. Domestic English grasses which replaced the white native tussocks turned the clearings green. Runs were fenced and the flocks prospered and increased. From the 1840s this was no longer frontier territory. Substantial homes began to appear after mid-century in the Georgian and Victorian Gothic modes of the time, surrounded by the dark greens of oaks and elms and bright gardens of English flowers. Here and there in the fields and along the roads and lanes, many of the majestic old stringybark warriors still stood, survivors of the invasion, towering above the foreign trees.

Aloof, above the plains and the farms, rose the mountain escarpment. By the early twentieth century the bluffs looked down upon an altered landscape. The cries of hunting bands and the smoke of campfires beside bark shelters had long ago dissolved upon the air. On the plains the cycle of planting, harvesting and pasturing was an established pattern. The plains were drained, more timber was cleared, the stumps were laboriously grubbed out and the farms lost the appearance of pioneering ventures. Now the tracks of the timber-cutters climbed into the mountain valleys in search of the straight trunks of *delegatensis*, the logs hauled down by bullock team and snig cable to mills such as that of the Higgs family on Dale Brook. Eventually there came also the bulldozer, chain-saw and powerful motor transport, and the rate of harvesting in the tall forests escalated. Even the face of the mountains was vulnerable.

By good fortune, this final change has not proceeded on a broad scale. The long, blue line of forested bluffs endures, much as it was when the settlers arrived. To the east, the rounded outline of Quamby Bluff still dominates Stockers Plain with its timbered foothills, its extensive boulderfields warm brown in the afternoon sun. Closer, the shapely, elegant peak of Mother Cummings, referred to by Hellyer as the 'Grand Mountain Top', soars out of the tall trees above Western Creek, and beyond it from a distance can be seen the long upland block of Mt Ironstone which holds the last of the snow, deep drifts clinging to its gullies and screes when they have disappeared from the other heights. Below Ironstone, deeply shadowed, is the great gash in the side of the Tiers where Western Creek comes tumbling down from the Plateau, through rainforest and eucalypts to the plains, its cold, clear water bringing the taste of highland rocks and lakes to the farms below. Away to the west stretches the blue line of bluffs, their cliffs and screes rising above forested ridges, shadows deepening as the sun slants across them. The line terminates in Western Bluff, known more fittingly by local people as 'Sunset Point', as it stands silhouetted against the last of the evening light.

With the increasing prosperity of the farming districts along the Tiers from the 1850s, as the country was cleared and fenced, the little villages and townships began to grow, some following the farms westward towards the Mersey, others dotted to the north and north-west where roads eventually ran through the forests to Port Sorell and the mouth of the Mersey. For a time Leith's farm on Quamby Brook was the last outpost of civilisation, the scattering of huts nearby became Westbury. Then Deloraine developed as a village at the Meander ford, where the roads divided. Other settlements followed: Western Creek, Chudleigh, Needles, Red Hills, Caveside ... each a dray journey or a day's walk from the next, each serving its own collection of farms with church, hotel, stores, smithy and a few cottages. Paling walls and shingled roofs blended into the landscape of paddock and pasture, forest and mountain. Muddy stock tracks became roads; stumps and ringbarked trunks left from the old clearings were burned or decayed into vague memories. The passing of time and shrinking of the world have favoured some of the villages; others have almost disappeared, bypassed by a more urgent age.

Deloraine dreams quietly on its tranquil reach of the Meander, its bridge spanning the river close to the old ford. The town retains many of the solid, square buildings of its growing days, converted to serve the needs of a different era. Now a modern farming centre, it has a sense of belonging to the surrounding land, even if its houses spill onto the nearby hills and a raw timberyard straggles beside the river. Beyond the English trees of the homesick settlers, the willows and pines, oaks and elms, there are hillsides of eucalypts and shapely blackwoods. The town has developed a landscape which is characteristic of the compromises and adaptations of many of the older settled regions: a blend of nineteenth century and modern buildings, a mixture of exotic and native trees, a river tamed by weirs which have spread its waters beyond its former rocky course. The more distant prospect also reflects this compromise. The farmlands are pleasant to the eye, their browns and greens defining the contours of the hills, their boundaries drawn by fence line and hawthorn hedgerow. The gray-green stringybarks with their straight trunks and asymmetry of shape are in no sense out of place, nor mere remnants of original forest. The plains accord with the blue-hazed line of the Tiers. History has altered this landscape but has treated it kindly. It has so far retained a degree of the essential harmony of mountain, plain and forest which it once possessed.

Deloraine exemplifies the small Tasmanian towns which are well adapted to their rural and partly natural landscape. There are other towns which blend with their surroundings with the same pleasant harmony. One of the most appealing is Scottsdale on the red basalt soil of the north-east. The north-eastern districts developed later than those in other rural sections of the island. Much of the better country was covered by dense forest as well as being hilly and seamed with deep gullies. James Reid Scott, after whom Scottsdale is named, was one of the earliest settlers of the inland area, having established a farm on the Ringarooma River in 1860. At this time he made several exploratory journeys across the north-east corner, identifying districts where there was fertile soil and helping to promote settlement. Much knowledge of the north-east was gained during the era of energetic prospecting for tin and gold which spanned the 1860s and 70s, and the township of Ellesmere, as it was first called, was already spreading across its forested hills by the middle of this period.

The attractive older buildings of Scottsdale were built in the 1880s and 90s, replacing paling cottages when much of the surrounding land had been cleared and a period of prosperity had begun. The big trees were ringbarked, milled or burned and the farms spread west to the foot of Blumont, eastward towards the granite ridge of Stronach and into the valley of Springfield where the Sideling track would be cut across the steep hillside above. A track through the coastal scrubs to Bridport, already well established as a village, created a sea outlet for timber and farm produce. From Scottsdale's hilltop site there is a fine prospect of farms and woodland. Blackwoods, wattles and eucalypts mingle with pines and English oaks. The landscape differs in detail from that of Deloraine, though in essence they are very similar. In place of the high scarps of the Tiers there are lower, timbered hills. Many now bear only tree-farms, while others still hold remnants of the original forests. Away to the south-west stands the high summit of Mt Barrow, deep blue in the late afternoon, framed by the nearer heights of Mt Maurice and the Sideling ridge. The town is thus set in a mosaic of greens and browns, hills and valleys, fields and forest: a landscape that will change markedly over the next decade as increasing numbers of farms are converted to monoculture plantations.

A somewhat different landscape surrounds the southern town of Huonville, the old Victoria, above the estuary of the Huon River. A township was established in 1854 at the highest navigable point on the river, though there were already settlements nearby at Franklin and Port Cygnet. In fact Port Cygnet contained some thirty houses in 1855 when Captain Butler Stoney visited it. In the early years the huge forests of the Huon Valley provided the first major industry, timber milling, soon followed by shipbuilding.

The Port Esperance blue gum forests had originally been logged by convict gangs. The high ridge country west of the Huon is relatively sheltered and has a high rainfall. Here stood some of the tallest forests of the island, immense trees whose trunks towered in straight columns for a hundred metres and more. Beneath them grew a rich understorey of man-fern, leatherwood, sassafras and other species. There was a network of skidways and tram tracks for the logs to be hauled out by bullock team or steam-powered cable. The men who worked in these forests and their families in the paling cottages both feared and loved the trees. Their work was hard, uncomfortable and dangerous, but they had developed a way of life which depended upon the forest. They were strong, resilient and highly skilled in the techniques of felling and milling, and had pride in their knowledge of the ways of forests, mills and ships, knowledge that was passed on down generations of families.[22]

As the land close to the shore was cleared and drained, the rich river soil yielded good crops, and the earliest orchards were planted. Communication with the settlements along the Huon estuary depended upon the small sailing vessels which for many years carried timber and later farm produce to Hobart, but as the settlements developed and spread a regular steamer service was maintained between Hobart and the Huon. For a long time there was virtually no land access to the scattered townships.

In 1831 Sir John Franklin had a track cut through the forests of Mt Wellington's foothills to land which was being developed on the southern bank of the Huon. This track terminated at Ironstone Creek and was long, hilly and rough, fit only for foot or horse travel, and not for the transport of heavy loads. It was widened to a cart track in 1850, but it was not until 1869 that a road was completed, using the rather impractical high-level route by way of Fern Tree and Neika on Mt Wellington. The Huon was bridged just below Victoria in 1876, the six spans of the bridge having distinctive bow-shaped supports on either side.

The great forests have gone now. Town, farmland and river blend easily on a timeless reach of water. The town itself is neat, not yet sprawling, contained by the hills as it spreads along the south bank of the river and through the valley to the north. Many buildings survive from the later years of the nineteenth century and there are the broad European trees common to all of the older towns. This is a river town. The dark waters of the Huon, stained by the peat of the south-western plains, flow silently beneath the modern bridge. On a still morning they mirror the details of houses and of the hillsides above the town. Beyond Huonville's outskirts the valley of Mountain River extends for many kilometres to the north, while the Huon itself swings down from the west, its waters gathered from the high lakes of the Arthurs, the ridges of Mt Anne and the forests of Picton and Weld. The deep river soil of the two valleys supports an extensive farming district, the fields stretching back into the hills in both directions. Above and beyond are the high ranges. Northward, blue and shadowed, stand the Wellingtons with their familiar profile of the Sleeping Beauty: Collins Bonnet, Trestle, Collins Cap, Connection ... cloud patterns reshape them and constantly change as weather systems move across from the west, now bringing mist trails out of the valleys, now patches of sunshine and deep shade. In winter the high, open summits are flecked with snow.

To the west a tangle of ridges, still majestic even without their tall forests, climbs towards the distant peaks of the Hartz Mountains which remain hidden behind the closer heights. The landscape is complex and full of movement and change. The town is a human focus in a broad natural and pastoral canvas.

Both major cities have superb settings, the potential of which has never been fully achieved. In Launceston and Hobart there are streetscapes which are formed from good architecture of both the nineteenth and twentieth centuries, and in each city there is immediately evident a wider natural vista which complements the urban, creating a sense of space and distance, as well as a reminder of a scale larger than the human.

Launceston's situation at the point where the two Esk rivers meet did not gain Governor Macquarie's approval. He favoured the conventional estuary placement at the mouth of the Tamar. Yet despite the steepness of its hills, the swamps of the northern flats and the liability of any low ground to flooding where two active tributaries join to form a long tidal river, the choice has proved a fortunate one. The city has grown in a landscape of distinctive character. It has a remarkable gift for any city in the tumbled gorge of the South Esk which breaks the hills within a few minutes' walk of the business centre, so that when winter floods are forced through its narrow dolerite walls, people in offices can glimpse the surge and tumult of the waters and hear their muffled roar.

Even in the 1820s and 1830s when the settlers' cottages clustered in the valley between Windmill Hill and Cataract Hill, Launceston was not hemmed in. The main part of the town has always occupied the flats along the North Esk where the first wharves were built, and houses gradually spread up the shallow valley southward along the Hobart and Westbury roads. There was no need to venture across the North Esk into the swampland and extensive draining works were not begun until the 1850s.

Eucalypts and casuarinas grew upon the surrounding slopes and from every rise there was a vista of distant hills and winding river. By the 1850s the town was still confined to the North Esk flat and the Wellington Street valley, with a few houses dotted about Windmill Hill and along High Street. Skinner Prout and Francis Simpkinson both painted Launceston from the Westbury Road during its early years, and show it to have been a quiet rural settlement, fields running close beside the houses and the masts of ships mingling with church spires almost in the heart of the town.

Major changes followed James Smith's discovery of the rich tin deposit at Mt Bischoff in 1871. Launceston was the main centre for mining investment as mining then, except for coal, was largely concentrated in the north-east, north and north-west of the island. Dividends from tin and gold districts such as Blue Tier, Gladstone and Mathinna in the north-east, and from gold in the Pipers River field and later from Beaconsfield in the north, all flowed through Launceston shareholders and directors. But richest of all was Bischoff and many of the fine houses of High Street and Elphin Road were built on the rewards of the 'Mountain of Tin'.

As the town grew it reached across the higher ground of High Street Hill, East Launceston and Cataract Hill to become a city of hills. After the Trevallyn bridge was built over the South Esk in 1863, the west bank of the Tamar and the heights of Trevallyn were opened to town settlement. From all these points the mountains could be seen: wooded ridges rising, tier upon tier, from the Tamar Valley towards the distant heights of Mt Barrow and Mt Arthur.

In winter the summit slopes of Ben Lomond and the rounded southern buttress of Stacks Bluff became prominent as the sun caught their snowfields to the south-east. Many residents could also gaze down the broad valley of the Tamar, where the town gradually extended across the flats of Invermay and onto the Mowbray Hill. The river gleamed in the low winter sun and townsfolk learned to predict weather changes from sky and haze along the valley and to bless the sun as mists began to part late of a winter morning.

The low-lying sheltered parts of Launceston have always been 'smoky hollow'. From that first evening in 1805 when Sergeant Dell and his men lit their campfire beside the South Esk, smoke has collected in the basin of the hills in the still afternoon air and helped thick fogs to form overnight. Once foundries and smelters, shipyards and breweries and all the other sources of smoke were thriving, supplemented by hundreds of homely chimneys, smoke layers and fogs became a constant feature of the winter landscape. Many who have first seen the town from the river on one of its more gloomy days have found it unappealing. Early on an April morning in 1878, Edward Braddon came up the Tamar as a newly arrived migrant from India, reaching the wharves of the North Esk before the fog had time to clear:

> Launceston, as we saw it that morning, had not put on a particularly smiling face to welcome us. Fog and smoke enveloped it in a grey murk, and it looked as cheerful as Lambeth on a wet Sunday. Approaching the town by the river, you see it at its worst point too - the meaner houses of the place, the few manufactory chimneys it boasts of, and the skeleton form of the gas-works are all on the river side, and there is nothing in them to please the eye.[23]

However, Braddon saw the town's setting in a different light over the next few days, praising both its attractive surroundings and the health and industry of its people. Launceston has compensations in the brilliance of its days, the late afternoon light on the slopes of Mt Barrow and Mt Arthur, and the reflections in still reaches of the rivers. The city has long been proud of its appearance. Though streets were narrow and steep, they were shaded by rows of trees which were allowed to mature. In some, such as Elphin Road, the foliage met overhead so that in summer the tiny, rocking trams travelled through a lovely tunnel of leaves. Sadly, the trees had to be removed to allow widening of the road in the age of the car. Older houses have been maintained attractively, so that the city as a whole has retained a gracious, warm character, and only on the low-lying northern flats was an air of decay allowed to develop from the early 1900s.

One of the most striking situations imaginable for a city was nature's gift to Hobart. Its harbour could shelter the fleets of the world and its mountain backdrop is legendary. For nearly two centuries painters have delighted to capture its charm, its grandeur, its freshness and its subtle, elusive light. From the water, from west and east, every angle has been recorded and still the changing moods of mountain, river, hills and shoreline have scarcely been touched upon. Like Launceston and the other older towns, Hobart has its fine sandstone Georgian buildings, its trees and parks and its streetscapes which reflect the changing styles of one hundred and seventy years.

Because the city has enveloped the riverside hills and the lower spurs of Mt Wellington, there is hardly a street which does not enjoy some aspect of the total landscape. It is a setting which, in some measure, must have affected the outlook of almost everyone who has lived in the city, and particularly those who have grown to maturity in these surroundings.

Yet in the early years of the penal settlement the very qualities of the landscape which are so highly valued now would have made the Derwent repressive and frightening. To most new arrivals it must have appeared like the end of the world, which in a sense it was. It was strange. It was unlike anything in the familiar towns and countryside from which convict and free had hailed. The great mountain looming overhead crushed the soul. Its flanks were clothed with a giant forest which seemed to have no end and which surely could never be cleared: a forest that harboured primitive, incomprehensible beings and strange animals. Even the trees were lopsided and grotesque, shedding strips of bark and dead leaves at every season. Every appearance indicated a land of opposites and absurdities. Only the process of living in this strange land, coming gradually to know and understand it, has enabled us to change our perceptions of its landscape and its meaning so that we can feel its contours as our own and so that to gaze upon its features gladdens the eye and excites the spirit. We can nurture it now that we have suffered with it.

The tiny settlement spread unsteadily and haphazardly over the years, responding to fluctuations in the island's prosperity. It first engulfed the fields and orchards that bordered the Derwent shores, then climbed into the mountain foothills. It crept into bays and over hills, crossing the river to the eastern shore and invading distant peninsulas, wooded slopes and quiet gullies where it was thought only wallabies and sheep would wander. It has taken skylines and green spaces and still it spreads, now devouring much of the surroundings which formerly enhanced its own beauty. Yet the city still has the potential to retain and benefit from one of the most attractive urban and natural landscapes in the world.

Of all the altered landscapes, it is the small towns and villages which most strongly impart a sense of belonging in their surroundings and which determine the quality of landscape experience. Wherever one moves throughout the Tasmanian countryside, they create a cumulative impression of the texture of the whole fabric. Their appeal lies in their being a part of the land without intruding upon it. They are generally of such a size that they have not spread across the fields and hills; they appear unconsciously self-contained. The small towns have not developed industrial processes to the extent that large buildings, workshops and other structures can dominate. Houses are neat and proudly kept, and even trees are permitted. The town follows the folds and contours of the land and has the appearance of organic unity and intimate growth into a context, whether this be farmland, coastline, hills or woodland.

Throughout the island the small towns link the natural and human landscapes. Beneath the Western Tiers the villages of Chudleigh and Mole Creek mark the course of the old Van Diemen's Land Company road in the sheltered green plains between the high bluffs to the south and the wooded ridge of the Gog Range. Further north-west Sprent and Ridgley characterise the townships of the undulating country, where the farms begin to meet the forests and the land is cut into steep gullies and rounded hills. Many small, attractive towns have grown along the coasts. The old bluestone buildings of Stanley nestle snugly beneath the dark cliffs of the Nut, beside the tiny fishing boat harbour. Swansea, on the east coast, looks seaward over the wide sweep of Oyster Bay to the red granite peaks of Freycinet and Schouten Island from its sheltered shore. Town and trees, sea and distant hills form a prospect which is in constant change. Dover forms part of a similar landscape, its bay framed by the shores of Port Esperance facing the hills of South Bruny. The group of villages of the Derwent Valley: Bushy Park, Glenora, Hamilton, Ellendale ... move to a gentler music. Their busiest years are behind them, their importance as local centres now diminished by the transport and farming revolutions, but their mellow character and beauty remain, their presence woven into farmlands and surrounding hills. North-east townships such as Winnaleah, Ringarooma and Branxholm are rich in past and present associations, their names now evoking images of green dairy hills, with Mt Victoria and Blue Tier clear in the distance. A century earlier the images were of the headframes and waterwheels, shafts and mullock heaps of busy mines which are now threaded into the story of the land.

These are the kinds of settlements which, scattered through the island, have lived to serve their purpose in the rural and coastal landscape.

There is nothing artificial or pretentious about them. They are simply products of their history of human activity in harmony and interaction with their natural and altered surroundings. They are fortunate to have largely escaped the tide of urban outreach. Most are far enough removed from larger centres to have avoided the close division and clutter of the hobby farm or the industrial complex which seeks cheap land. The owners of newer buildings, which in some cases are in significant numbers, often have had the sensitivity to suit their styles and immediate surroundings to those of neighbouring properties, and generally are not intrusive. The future quality of the island's altered landscape will rely heavily upon the way in which the small towns and their surroundings are perceived and managed during the new century.

7   THE MAGIC OF THE TIERS

*The climb provides time to make the
imaginative adjustment.*

THE WESTERN TIERS, those high mountain walls which guard the Plateau along its northern and eastern flanks, are not simply an adjunct to the Plateau. They are also one of the most remarkable and visible landforms on the island. A dozen or so tracks wind onto the Plateau, from the farms of the Western Creek–Mole Creek district, from the Meander and Liffey valleys and from the western edge of the midland plain. Some of these, such as the Blackwood Creek track, were formed as stock routes as early as the 1820s and 1830s, while others were cut to provide access for hunters, fishermen and trappers. The process of ascending one of these tracks and experiencing the full range of plant communities and geological structures, the change in the air and in the very feeling of the landscape, prepares one to appreciate fully the nature of the Plateau itself. It is possible to gain a clear impression of the remoteness of the high country and of its complete contrast with the lowlands through the physical effort of climbing the nine-hundred-metre barrier which separates the two worlds.

The climb provides time to make the imaginative adjustment, to accept and take an active part in the transition which involves three different landscapes, and to sense the quality of the mountains themselves, woven from forest, rock and stream.

The great beauty of the Tiers owes much to the survival of their tall eucalypt forests. From the edge of the cleared land to the Plateau itself, several different forest types are likely to dominate in turn as the ridges rise into the cooler, wetter conditions of the higher slopes and as soil types and

'... one of the most remarkable and visible landforms on the island.'
Cottage at the foot of the Western Tiers (author).

drainage patterns change. On poorly drained flats at the foot of the Tiers swamp gums may be plentiful, while a little further up the ridge the forest will be dominated by the straight, tall columns of brown-top stringybark. These in their turn give way to white-top stringybark,[24] which is more tolerant of the cooler air and grows at altitudes of up to one thousand metres. Another eucalypt which is common on the higher forested slopes is the mountain gum,[25] with its fine white trunk and spreading canopy. Finally, as the forest spreads up the gullies and across the sheltered sections of the Plateau, highland species such as snow gum, yellow gum and the sturdy cider gum[26] are best adapted to survive. The tallest trees may be at the climax of their growth and often bear the scars of wind damage in the loss of the upper part of the trunk and major limbs, or rents where other trees have smashed against them in falling. Signs of fire are usually evident in these forests, with a hollow burned in the butt of the tree or charcoal embedded in its trunk telling of a fight to survive some past blaze. As well as forming a remarkable landscape, the mountain forests offer shelter and nesting sites for a wide variety of birds and animals. On still mornings the calls of yellow-throated honeyeaters echo through the tall timber of the higher slopes. Further down the cheeky note of the gray thrush, the noisy chaffing of a flock of black cockatoos or the discordant carolling of black jays fill the gully with sound.

From relatively open dry sclerophyll forest between the farms and the foothills, some of the access tracks lead through gullies which still retain original rainforest. Higgs track climbs amongst solid old myrtles, their trunks heavily grown with mosses and lichens. Occasional high, dead eucalypts and even surviving 'widows' indicate that fire has penetrated this valley, perhaps two or three centuries ago. On the upper part of the climb are the deep green foliage and straight, slender trunks of mature sassafras, and the banks of Dale Brook support large man-ferns and a thick carpet of smaller ferns. The Western Creek track, a short distance to the east, also has an attractive rainforest belt along the stream. This track makes a more gradual ascent and as it nears the Plateau edge there are stands of King Billy and pencil pine, some dead or bearing fire scars, but most protected

'The dash and murmur of their passing carries through the forest...'
Rainforest stream, Western Tiers (author).

by the steepness of the defile. A very pleasant rainforest track follows the Little Fisher River. This track does not start from farmland, having originally linked the Plateau with the natural clearing of Dublin Plain. For most of its climb to the upland valley under the cliffs of Turanna Bluff it traverses open myrtle and sassafras forest. This band of rainforest is quite narrow, being replaced by wiry undergrowth and snow gums on the steep valley slopes above. As with the forest of Dale Brook, the giant old 'stags' standing above the canopy tell of past fire even along the floor of the valley.

The Tiers tracks share their qualities with those on many other mountains in the island where tracks climb through successive forest stages towards alpine country, such as Mt Field, Mt Wellington or the route of the old Hartz track. But they are qualities which one associates primarily with the Tiers. The forest itself creates much of the landscape value: massive, spreading myrtles and very tall *delegatensis* which rise majestically above them, the wonderful vaulting and interlacing of man-fern fronds, and the soft carpet of moss, leaves and debris. Then there is the smell of the forest, a rich mixture from sassafras, musk and other species. Added to this is the aroma of damp leaves and decaying wood in mossy trunks which have lain rotting on the ground for over a century. There are earth smells as water seeps down amongst the roots or forms rich black peat in the ferny hollows. As the track climbs, the slope becomes more rocky; these are not just the smooth rocks which have been underfoot from the start amongst tree roots and ferns. Higher up are large rocks, residuals of the ice-cap and of savage post glacial erosion which tore them from the mountainsides. The track winds amongst them and one can touch their great weathered flanks as one touches the boles of big trees, sensing the life in them. Covered thickly with moss and lichens, they often host an array of seedlings, tiny myrtles, laurel, sassafras and a drapery of ferns, so that their rough forms are softened and brought into the life of the forest. Large moss-covered boulders such as these are features of the Chasm Creek track near Meander and the Western Creek track, where the boulder-fields are never far away. In passing through the band of Permian sedimentary rock, the tracks often sidle past sheer sandstone faces and overhangs up to ten metres deep. Here water drips constantly over the opening and ferns cluster in crevices. On the Dell and Stone Hut tracks there are fine little rock shelters. When the ice-sheets and valley glaciers disappeared and the Plateau became accessible, shelters such as these would have provided good bases for Aboriginal hunting parties which pursued the wallabies into the high country. The bands of sandstone have soft, eroded surfaces which allow lichens, creepers and tree roots to gain a hold and benefit from their shelter, warmth and drainage lines. Some become miniature gardens, reflecting golds and vivid greens in the slanting valley light.

The streams are a lively, vibrant element in the magic of the Tiers, and almost every access track meets or follows one of them. The steep slopes make for a rapid descent over rocky courses, with many small waterfalls and water-cut chasms. Streams flowing off the Plateau cross very little of the peaty or tea-tree country of their western and south-western counterparts. Their waters, unstained by vegetable matter, are completely clear, running their courses over water-worn boulders, shingle-beds and broad rock ledges. The dash and murmur of their passing carries through the forest and can be heard from almost every part of the gully tracks. On the higher levels the streams wind under boulder-fields, the wash of invisible waters audible many metres above. They cascade over bare rocks towards the timber where their damp banks sustain a variety of ferns and undergrowth. As they descend, splashing noisily over small waterfalls and rapids, they may pass through pines, as does Western Creek, or high level rainforest. The typical Tiers stream hurries through myrtles, celery-top pine[27] and sassafras, and is overhung by shrubberies of laurel and waratah. Periodically there is a deep, still pool in which the rocks can be seen far down through the clear water. Smoko Creek, which flows south from Mother Cummings Peak, is a fine example: a delightful stream that twists amongst trees and boulders with tiny falls and quiet pools. Its larger neighbour, Mother Cummings Rivulet, is far more dramatic. It has cut several narrow chasms through the sandstone, one of which is spanned by a log bridge. The stream has also undercut the flanks of its gorge to form impressive 'verandahs' high above.

The Tiers have their own distinctive character, formed from forested mountainside, rock and falling water. This character is felt very strongly on tracks such as the Western Creek, Meander Falls and Little Fisher which follow their respective streams closely as they ascend, providing continual variations of the relation of water, rock and forest. The impressions of these forest streams linger in the memory long after other scenes have faded.

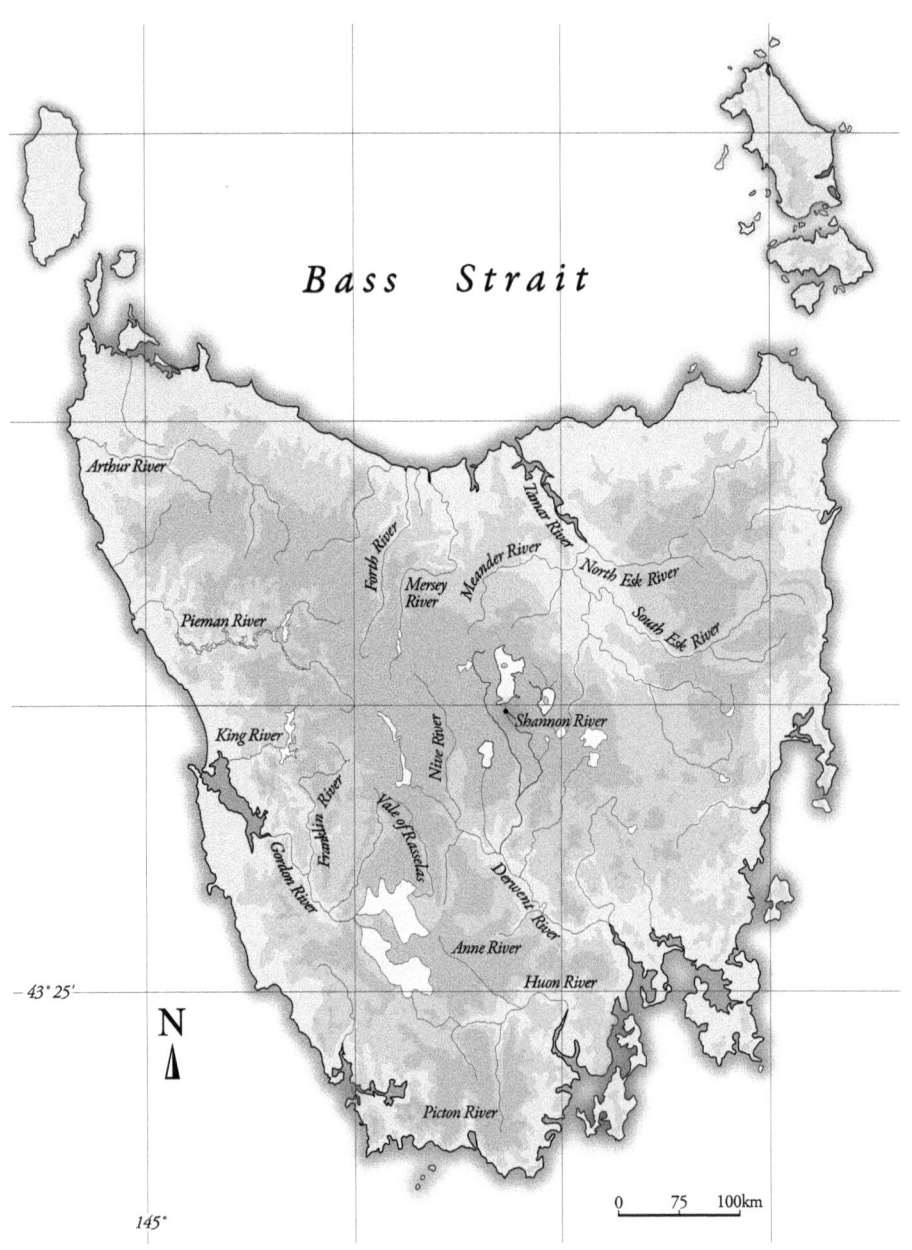

Rivers and valleys referred to in the text
(map by Louise Radloff).

8 A WORLD APART: THE CENTRAL PLATEAU

Life clings precariously to this rocky upland ...

THE HIGH COUNTRY of the Central Plateau is a completely different land from the lowlands which lie only a few kilometres below. This is the most austere and yet the most sensitive of all Tasmania's landscapes; its vegetation, climate, landforms and geological history all differ markedly from those of the lower country. More than any other part of the island, it affects those who enter it: repelling with its bleakness, fascinating with its power and subtlety. Having approached by one of the mountain tracks which climb through the gullies of the Western Tiers, or driven on a road winding from the lower levels, one is confronted by the absolute contrast that is apparent on passing the tree-line. This is a country which is dour, even hostile, and lacking the soft, colourful forms that the eye seeks through habit in any surroundings. It is a land of rock: rocks dominate in every direction. Bare slabs, boulder-fields, stark gray ridges, columns discarded, thrown down by mighty forces in the past, the rocks speak of a harsh, challenging world, a place alien to human warmth. It is later, when one is accustomed to this severity, that its beauty is perceived most clearly. For it is also a land which is capable of asserting a strong presence and of gaining the deepest affection from those who come to know it.

For much of the past million years the Tasmanian highlands have been covered by ice, and there is evidence of three major glacials during this period. The first and most intense occurred some seven hundred and fifty thousand years ago, creating an ice-cap which extended from the West Coast Range eastward across the central mountains and the Plateau. This cap covered more than six thousand square kilometres and was so thick that only the highest peaks projected above its surface. It fed glaciers which filled the valleys of the present river systems.[28] There were two more glacials during the Pleistocene epoch, the most recent climaxing only eighteen thousand years ago; the highlands have been free from the grip of its ice for a mere ten thousand years.

The Long Tarns lie on the high north-western level of the Plateau, a string of narrow lagoons cradled in a shallow valley which drains south-eastwards into Lake Butters and the Pillans system. The surrounding country bears clear evidence of the ice action that shaped it. The valley itself and the beds of the tarns were scooped out by ice moving north-west towards the Little Fisher Valley, and south-west across the Plateau, for this was the area of the ice divide at the time of the Pleistocene ice-caps. The high arc of mountains and ridges along the north-western edge of the Plateau, principally Turrana Bluff and its south-east ridge, the Walls of Jerusalem, Mt Rogoona and the Mountains of Jupiter, are the bones of the ancient divide. Ice forming north of this divide flowed down the various glacial corridors to the north; to the south of the divide the ice moved south-east and south, forming glaciers on the southern side of the Plateau. Snow deposits built up across this arc, creating a dome some three hundred to four hundred and fifty metres thick on the north-western

Plateau and spreading an ice-sheet which covered almost a thousand square kilometres of the Plateau at the height of the most recent glacial period, eighteen thousand years ago. From the divide the ice extended eastwards almost as far as Great Lake and south-east to Skittleball Plain. Beyond the edges of this sheet the lower levels of the Plateau were subjected to severe periglacial or frost action, splitting the rock slabs into extensive boulder fields. At the same time other ice-caps formed on the Cradle–Du Cane ridge and on the West Coast Range, with a smaller cap for a time covering the Oakleigh Plateau.[29]

The ice was continually moving, its main directional lines evident today in the gashes cut into the Plateau surface on a general north-west to south-east alignment. Masses of ice flowed northwards down side valleys such as the Fish, Little Fisher and Arm rivers into the major valleys of the Mersey and Forth. Ice from the Plateau, Oakleigh and Cradle ice-caps converged so that at the height of the period glaciers filled both valleys, bearing away the accumulation from several distinct caps. A body of ice over six hundred metres deep tore at the rocky sides of the Mersey Valley, carrying away huge quantities of morainal rubble and leaving a gorge which would be further eroded by turbulent melt-waters. To the south of the ice-divide the ice sheet moved south-east and other glaciers eventually carried the ice away towards Tarraleah and the Navarre Plains. In the process the deep trough of Lake St Clair, already cut in earlier glacials, was gouged more deeply by ice flowing down the Narcissus and Marion valleys, and the hollows of the large western lakes were formed. As the glacial drew to a close and the ice-sheet receded, the chain of peaks on either side of Long Tarns remained ice-bound, while the Plateau lay bare. Rock slabs were scarred by ice and by the movement of boulders dragged across them. Masses of rock were strewn across the land where the melting ice left them and in many places boulders and clay were piled into heaps and hillocks. The depressions were filled with melt-water even as the ice-front passed them.

The basic profile of the Plateau has been formed by earth movements, glacial and water action into three distinct levels or surfaces. The most elevated of these, the Higher Plateau, is the north and north-western section, close to the ice-divide, from Mt Ironstone to the Walls of Jerusalem, the open expanse of Great Lake and Lake Augusta. The Western Lakes, the Mountains of Jupiter and the Traveller Range are all on the Lower Plateau, the fall between the two levels being marked to the west by the Great Pine Tier. The third and lowest level is known as the St Clair Surface, and extends from Lake St Clair to Lake Sorell, the steep southern slopes of the Traveller Range indicating the boundary between this level and the Lower Plateau.

In the thin, gritty soils and clays left by the ice, mosses and hardy cushion plants established a foothold. Much of the ground was flat and poorly drained, especially in the depressions in which debris had accumulated. These marshy plains, still subject to severe cold, were gradually colonised by sedges and other wetland species. Before long the ground-dwellers such as creeping pine,[30] the *Richeas* and prostrate tea-tree[31] appeared among the boulder-fields, and as conditions became less severe the trees moved up into the highlands, pencil pines, cheshunt pines and snow gums becoming established wherever the peaty soils built up.

In the present warm interlude one can still sense the presence of that harsh land which had just been freed from the ice. When the wind blows hard from the south-west and snow whirls from a black sky, coating rocks and trees and rounding the sharp outlines of ridge and crag, it is not hard to imagine that time which, in the scale of plant and mountain, has very recently passed.

An interesting and beautiful approach to the Long Tarns and the Higher Plateau lies through the old ice corridor of the Little Fisher Valley. The Little Fisher is a clear, lively stream which dashes down its narrow course amongst boulders and over shingle banks, splashing and shoaling noisily, with an occasional deep pool creating a quiet haven. As the track climbs the valley close to the stream the myrtle forest rises with it, a narrow band that has survived the periodic fires which have enabled eucalypts to dominate the valley slopes. Through occasional breaks in the canopy there are glimpses of the high cliffs of Fisher and Turrana bluffs which run back towards the head of the valley. Finally the myrtles and sassafras on the stream banks give way to low eucalypt forest with a wiry understorey of *Banksia, Hakea,*[32] waratah[33] and other shrubs.

The transition from forested valley to open plateau is more gradual at the head of the Little Fisher than on many other approach routes. Below the lip of the Plateau and not far above the rainforest there is a narrow, open glen, a shelf left by the retreating ice. Close to the east stands the scarp of Turrana Bluff, sheer for three hundred metres above the screes, while to the west are the ridges of Mersey Crag. Between them this high sanctuary is peaceful and sheltered, with few signs of the harshness of the open Plateau which lies a few hundred metres above. The river, here a small headstream, wanders quietly through a succession of deep pools on one side of the valley bordered by short sedge, native grass and extensive cushion plant communities. In this secluded corner, generations of trappers once found a safe base and refuge from mountain storms. At its southern end the valley rises in gentle stages over ice-worn slabs to the Plateau, to Long Tarns and to a different world.

Everything about the Long Tarns country recalls the recent presence of ice. Ridge tops and exposed rocks have been rounded and planed; erratics up to the size of buildings and of every conceivable shape lie scattered where the ice dumped them. Hundreds of lakes and pools occupy shallow depressions among the rocks, tiny streams and runnels linking them in a complex drainage system. From the ridge north of the Tarns a wide sweep of the Higher Plateau can be seen extending south to Lake Augusta and Skittleball Hill. Westward, the skyline is dominated by the group of peaks and ridges forming the Walls of Jerusalem.

To the south-west, between Long Tarns and the Walls, lies a land of great beauty and variety. High, rounded hills are part of the old ice-divide. Amongst them are large lakes: Thor, Nutting, the Daisy Lakes and others unnamed to the north. The 'grain' of the country, scored by the flow of the ice, runs generally north-west to south-east, with the wetter hollows providing shelter for many alpine communities. As well as the larger lakes, there are countless smaller bodies of water from tarns of a few hectares to tiny pools. Further south-east, where the Plateau surface becomes more gently undulating, the frequency of the pools is even greater, so that in places there seems to be as much water surface as firm ground. On the slopes are snow gum and yellow gum, with a resilient ground cover of lower species up to two metres, such as *Scoparia*, mountain rocket[34] and cheshunt pine. However, the most remarkable trees here are the pencil pines, stands of which cover up to ten hectares, their roots intertwined amongst the rocks as they reach out for nourishment in the thin soil. Both trunks and roots have gripped the rocks in a close harmony of living and inanimate forms. Trunks of mature pines are thick and obviously of great age, while twisted and broken limbs provide evidence of the severity of conditions. A pine may suffer major damage as the weight of snow drags down a large branch and splits a long section of the trunk, but the tree is hardy and lives on, its dense wood impervious to cold and wet. There are plentiful thickets of young pine, in spite of climatic conditions which have restricted pencil pine to harsh, high altitude locations.

The smaller pine species take advantage of rocks both for shelter and stored warmth, creeping pine forms carpets and wind-pruned hedges over slabs, and cheshunt pine embraces boulders, curving its branches around the lee sides.

Pools in this region of the Plateau are perfect studies in the arrangement of rock, water and vegetation. The dark water may have around its edges a dozen or more pines; the older ones have been twisted and buffeted by the storms of centuries but the younger trees retain their graceful conical form. The roots have spread far down along the side of the pool, while some twine amongst the boulders. A few saplings stand grouped together away from the mature pines where a small soak filters down the hillside. Beneath the curve of the spreading branches the ground is

'... *the deep blue of water holding the sky*...'
The Central Plateau in winter (author).

covered deeply by a carpet of branchlets. The rocks themselves are partly hidden by the accumulation of debris and by small communities of *Richea sprengelioides, Scoparia* or *Cyathodes*.[35] Where they are clear of undergrowth their exposed sides are mottled with lichens or padded with vivid green mosses. In the clear leads near the shore of the pool bright patches of orange or yellow sphagnum moss stand out against the bright green of cushion plant or darker *Gleichenia* fern.

Pools with surroundings such as these, large and small, are scattered like gems across this untouched section of the Plateau, often only metres apart. Beyond the pines sun and shadow pick out the rocky heights of the Walls or Mersey Crag. The dark waters reflect every detail of peak, pines and sky, while some pools, perched on hillside terraces, look out across the Plateau, itself flecked with numberless lakes and tarns, towards distant mountains.

Winter alters the Plateau landscape and creates its own kingdom. A good fall builds the depth of snow up to a metre on this section of the Higher Plateau, smoothing the sharp angularity of rocks, covering boulderfields and tussocks and bringing both contrast and simplicity to the land. Snow clings in the foliage of the pines and lies thickly along the curves of their branches. Ponds freeze, as at times do the larger lakes and tarns, and seepage lines turn to hard ice-paths. A winter's day on the Higher Plateau can be frightening and is almost always exhilarating. Sky, wind and land join as one. The sky to the west assumes a dull, uniform gray, becoming darker, eventually black. Torn shreds of mist gather about the higher points and thicken rapidly. Wind has a power on the exposed ridges that at times forces one to cling to the rocks. Rain, and then sleet, come hard on the wind from the north-west, pelting viciously. When the snow arrives every object except the nearest trees and rocks disappears in a relentless whirl of wind-driven flakes which fill the air and the land so that nothing else exists. As a cold front passes, with the wind in the south-west, fleeting breaks occur between squalls: moments to be savoured. A snow-shower passes across the mountains swiftly; the sun emerges in a clear sky as the soft-edged cloud drifts away. The peaks appear, fresh-coated in new snow, remnants of cloud trailing from them. Trees shine as the sun catches ice crystals and periodically a mass falls from a branch with a small explosion of powder snow. The air is still for a while; streams can just be heard, muffled beneath the ice, while other sounds are muted. From the distance comes the plaintive call of a jay. Soon the wind rises and clouds move in, bringing the next squall.

In early spring deep drifts lie across the Plateau, particularly in the hollows and recesses of the hills where frosts harden the snow surface and the low sun fails to penetrate. There is a brilliant harmony of blue-shadowed snow banks, the intense dark green of pine against the white, the warmth of rock and the deep blue of water holding the sky.

Eastward from Long Tarns there is an altogether different landscape from that to the west. This is the burned country. Extensive fires in 1961 swept through much of the Higher Plateau between Long Tarns and Mt Ironstone and spread far to the south into the Lower Plateau. This country is immensely vulnerable to fire: the thin covering of peaty soil was in many places burned down to the rock and root systems were destroyed. The fire-prone high altitude plant communities suffered most. Dead skeletal branches of *Diselma* and other shrubs still clasp the boulders that sheltered them and once were covered by their foliage. Stands of bare pencil pine trunks cluster tragically, weathered silver and smoothed by the elements. Much of the Plateau surface in this region appears now as it did not long after the ice-sheet receded: bare except for mosses with rocks lying starkly exposed just as the ice left them.

Sufficient pockets of vegetation in this area have been spared to indicate the richness of the landscape before the fires. The attractive little pine forest beside Pencil Pine Tarn was saved by the water, though the snow gums on the hillside above were destroyed. At isolated tarns in other sheltered hollows are small groups of living trees, but all around them is bare. Further north-east, on Forty Lake Peak and towards Mt Ironstone, the snow gums have regenerated and once more provide good cover, but even if the Plateau remains free of fire for centuries to come it is unlikely that pines will again spread across those bare ridges as they did in a far colder period. The Walls of Jerusalem complex, the heartland of the Higher Plateau, has been fortunate largely to escape fires which have crossed the Plateau to the south-east near Lake Fanny and New Years Lake. The south-western slope of West Wall was burned in the 1960s, the fire killing many pines across the point now known as Mt Moriah, but the wonderful forest in Damascus Vale, the largest surviving group of pencil pines in the island, was untouched, as were small stands near Siloam and Bethesda and further north among Solomons Jewels.

The Plateau was the province of the Big River Tribe. One of their five bands, the Luggermairrernerpairrer, held the northern and western Plateau as summer hunting grounds, though for much of the year this area was too cold and wet to be tenable. Tools have been found in small scatterings at sites across this country such as the western shore of Lake Pillans, indicating widespread periodic use of the Higher Plateau. It was also crossed by other bands on their way north to visit the ochre mines of Mt Gog and Mt Housetop and the rookeries of the far north-west coast. It is also likely that the North Tribe had right of access to the Plateau both for hunting and to reach the flint quarry at Split Rock. There is no evidence of regular firing by the Aboriginal people in this part of the Plateau; the greatest damage has occurred during the period of white occupation.

Separated now by nearly two centuries from the breaking of the tribes, we can only speculate on the kind of relationship the Big River hunters created with this stern upland. Bennett's wallaby are plentiful across the area. Tasmanian pademelon are found in thickets around the rim of the Plateau and wombat and echidna are also common, so that food resources must have attracted regular visits to most parts during summer. Though shelter can be found from the sudden frontal storms which sweep in from the west at any time, prolonged cold, wet weather would have forced the hunting parties to lower levels. The open nature of much of the Plateau with its intermittent cover of pine stands and lower shrubs would have provided good conditions for stalking and for driving game, though it seems that fire was not used in this country as a hunting aid. The major features of this landscape which were so closely integrated with the lives of the hunters, the ridges, bluffs, plains and lakes, streams and boulder-fields, even individual rocks and stands of trees, would have been named and woven into the stories, songs and spiritual life of the tribe.

The windswept plains and ridges of the northern and eastern Plateau form the landscape seen most often by travellers and fishermen. To most, it represents the Central Plateau as a whole. The names themselves suggest a hard, desolate country: Wild Dog Tier, Skittleball Plain, Rats Castle, Split Rock, Barren Tier ... It is a landscape of sky and rock. Even the stretches of forest across the eastern Plateau tend to have sparse undergrowth. The soil is thin, having had little time to build through weathering and the deposition of plant debris, so that hardy trees and shrubs survive by reaching down amongst the rocks with their root systems to grasp whatever nutrients they can. Only the depressions have accumulated layers of peat and this gives a footing to sedges and tussocky grass. Just as this eastern section was most frequently visited by tribal groups and was probably the only part of the Higher Plateau occupied for much of the year by the Big River people, so it is now the only section in which there is permanent habitation, and in which fire has played a part in the patterns of growth over the centuries.

For all its severity and aloofness, the Higher Plateau is a country which appeals to the heart through its very severity, its isolation and its contrast with the ordered farmlands of the lower country. In this appeal lies its greatest danger. Life clings precariously to this rocky upland; constant human activity will change its fragile landscape irrevocably.

Apart from alteration of vegetation by fire, the evidence of human activity over the Higher Plateau has been restricted largely to the eastern section. This area has been affected by hydro-electric developments involving roads, canals and the raising of lake levels. It has also been subjected to continuous recreational use for over a century. Road access has resulted in virtually unrestricted shack construction around Great Lake, Arthurs Lake and several smaller lakes. Sheep have been pastured on the Plateau since the 1830s and grazing is still carried on south of Liawenee. West and north-west of Great Lake the effects of European land use are less evident, limited to old tracks, hut sites and fences. The route of Ritters track to the Walls of Jerusalem was marked by cairns early in the twentieth century from Lake Nameless, where it joined Higgs track from Western Creek. Stock were driven along this track regularly for summer grazing in the Walls, but there is little sign of their passing and the track is used now only by occasional walking parties. In the 1840s a cart track was cut by Humphrey Howells from Great Lake north-west to the Walls, and from there down the valley of the Fish River to Howells Plain in the Mersey Valley. Of this also no sign remains. Another track ran west from the old 'Banks' homestead near the Ouse River south of Lake Augusta to the southern end of Lake Pillans. More recent vehicle tracks, notably to Julian Lakes and Lake Pillans, to Blue Peaks, and to Lake Fanny and Lake Antimony, had more potential for damaging the Plateau surface, but these have now been closed under the World Heritage Authority Area Management Plan and should slowly revegetate. Walking tracks in the Walls of Jerusalem area are heavily used and will need constant care if they are not to cause degradation. Damage is even more apparent around Lake Nameless, particularly from horses' hooves cutting into fragile cushion and other plant communities.

Summer grazing took place also in the Ironstone–Lake Nameless area and across Balmoral Moor. In 1860, John Howells cleared a cart and stock track from the earlier track near Split Rock northwards to Balmoral Moor. Here a shepherd's hut was built, and a chock-and-log fence. The remains of both may still be found. More recent fences may also be seen in several areas.

Trapping was a far more extensive activity. From the 1880s to the 1940s trappers established their snare lines through the high country of the northern Plateau, using access tracks from the Mersey Valley and from the Mole Creek and Western Creek districts. These men usually spent several months at a time in the mountains and their hardiness and knowledge of the country were legendary. Trapping flourished at times when life was generally harder and when demanding physical toil and prolonged isolation were far more tolerable to generations of country-bred men than they would be today. It provided a reliable income in times of economic depression, particularly in the 1890s and 1930s and when both fashions and textile methods created a demand for the skins of wallaby and brush-tailed possum. Trappers worked from small huts dotted around the Plateau or the edges of the Tiers, high up in the shelter of the escarpment, though few of these now remain, the best known being the refurbished hut near the Plateau on the Walls of Jerusalem track. In the high valley below Long Tarns are the remains of a very old hut dating possibly from the 1890s, on the route from Dublin Plains to the Plateau. Its walls had been constructed from logs, the corners carefully fitted and chocked, and

'... nestling into a quiet valley at the northern foot of the
Mountains of Jupiter:'
Junction Lake (author).

the structure supported by sturdy uprights, one of them a eucalypt *in situ*. The hut was placed so that the Plateau could be reached quickly, but it was also in a sheltered location close to water and plentiful wood and on the edge of the forested valley of the Little Fisher. In the 1960s Boy Miles, one of a younger generation of trappers, began to build a similar hut a short distance away, but he died before the task could be completed.

The Higher Plateau has attracted fishermen since the stocking of the highland lakes late in the nineteenth century. Accommodation houses were built at Breona on Great Lake and by the shore of Sandy Beach Lake, both being destroyed by fire. Another fishermen's hut stood beside Lake Nameless until it succumbed to the weight of snow on its roof in the 1940s. It lay in ruins for fifty years, the neat stonework of its doorway indicating the skill of its builders, until it was replaced by a modern stone hut on the same site. The Lady Lake hut, built from timber and corrugated iron, was also much used by fishermen until it was burned in the Plateau fire of the early 1960s. It has also now been replaced.

Junction Lake lies on the Lower Plateau, the second of three levels of the Central Plateau, nestling into a quiet valley at the northern foot of the Mountains of Jupiter. In glacial times this valley was immediately below the ice-divide and lay beneath hundreds of metres of moving ice which ground its way westward down the Mersey Valley, joining similar flows from the Ossa–Du Cane ice-cap. The ice also flowed north, over-riding the plateau of Cathedral Mountain and slicing the narrow groove which holds Cloister Lagoon and Chapter Lake. From the Mountains of Jupiter the ice-sheet moved south and south-east, carving the upland valleys of lakes such as the Ling Roths, Payanna and Riengeena, smoothing the slabs along the Jupiters and the Traveller Range and removing huge quantities of morainal material to form the depression of Travellers Rest Lake. Further south the ice-sheet dropped away to the St Clair Shelf, the third level of the Plateau, where its glacier tongues jutted out to the east of the King William Range.

Being lower and more sheltered than the country of the Higher Plateau, the valley of Junction Lake is warmer and gentler than the exposed region above. On the slopes and the valley floor are areas of forest: not the tall forest of the Tiers, but broad stands of snow gum, cabbage gum[36] and cider gum which rise onto the rocky slopes of the Mountains of Jupiter. Pencil pines line the shores of the lake and extend into the nearby ridges, while some still survive beside the lakes and tarns of the fire-scarred

Traveller Range, with deep glades on lakes Payanna and Riengeena.

The Mersey is a young stream, just a few metres wide, where it flows from Lake Meston to Junction Lake. Its valley is open, with brown sedges, white tussocky grass and patches of open forest overlooked by the screes and bluffs of Mt Rogoona. In sunny alcoves near the forest edge the grass has been trimmed almost to lawns by grazing wombats and wallabies. The river enters Junction Lake through a group of ancient pencil pines which overhang the stream, creating a green, shady tunnel.

A still autumn morning by Junction Lake reveals the landscape of the Lower Plateau in its richest form. To the west, where the Mersey plunges into the forests of the Never Never, mists rise from the valley depths and drift through the trees above the outflow, slowly unveiling the rock buttresses of the Cathedral Plateau. At first there is simply the mirror of the lake, cloud reflections and the silhouettes of trees. As the sun climbs, mists begin to disperse and details appear more clearly. A high, delicate waterfall on the flank of Cathedral, Feather Fall, spreads filmy spray across the rock-face and the varied shades of the trees become apparent, the dark pines standing out from the myrtles, with distant eucalypts lighter gray. Gradually the shapes of the Du Cane peaks appear, Castle Crag most prominent beyond the Mersey Valley. To the south, high above the lake, the rounded headland of the Jupiters emerges from the mist, its gray ice-weathered slabs clear above the trees. Eventually slanting sunlight filters through the open forest beside the lake and washes a golden light across the native grass plain. These are the features of the Lower Plateau; it does not have the starkness of the higher country and gains instead a mellow quality from its taller trees, variety of vegetation, the softening influence of grasses and ferns and its tumbled hills and valleys.

The Lower Plateau extends in a wide arc embracing the forests and lakes of the Traveller Range, and to the east the ridges and valleys of the

Nive, Little and Pine rivers. Its landscape is that of a transitional region between the very high country of one thousand two hundred to one thousand four hundred metres and the milder St Clair Shelf of seven to eight hundred metres. There are gradients in altitude, temperature and climate across the area, and consequently a range of conditions to which vegetation has become acclimatised. Much of the Lower Plateau supports open forest of white-top stringybark and cider gum, though valley flats tend to be open and many of the hill slopes and high plains have been cleared. Rainforest survives in some of the damp, sheltered gullies, a fine example being the high-level myrtle forest on the shelf of the Mountains of Jupiter above Junction Lake.

The Lower Plateau and the valleys to the south were hunting grounds of the Big River Tribe, who moved north up the main rivers once winter snows had melted. White exploitation of the Central Plateau began before 1810, with kangaroo hunters venturing ever further into unexplored country in search of game. It was one of these hunters, Thomas Toombs, who first sighted Great Lake in 1815. John Beamont's expedition in 1817 was the first official investigation of the extent of the Plateau itself.[37] Governor William Sorell encouraged settlers to move into the highlands above the Shannon and Clyde rivers and by 1820 stock were roaming across the Plateau south and west of Great Lake. Over the following twenty years most of the areas on the Plateau which could support grazing had been leased, almost invariably by landholders in the western midlands and the Clyde Valley who needed well-watered summer pastures. Much of the Lower Plateau and even parts of the Higher Plateau are still grazed seasonally. As well, logging extends far into the timbered slopes such as those of the Traveller Range. With its thin soils, rocky surface and steep hillsides, the Lower Plateau is vulnerable to clearing, wildfire, soil disturbance and over-grazing:

A lake is the landscape's most beautiful and expressive feature. It is the earth's eye; looking into which the beholder measures the depth of his own nature.

H D Thoreau: *Walden*

The Central Plateau contains a high proportion of the island's natural lakes, including the largest: Great Lake, Arthurs Lake, lakes St Clair, Echo, Sorell and Crescent, the last four located on the lowest section of the Plateau, the St Clair Surface. Several of the lakes on this Surface are important for their unusual ecology as well as landscape values. Among these is Lagoon of Islands which, until recent years, contained rafts of vegetation or rhizome mats, which were built as a result of sedges taking root on floating timber, then accumulating further debris to form islands on which whole communities of plants would become established. The islands drifted about the Lagoon and would occasionally overturn and sink, so that there were always rafts to be found in every stage of development. Carbon dating of Lagoon sediments indicated that conditions had been stable for some four thousand years and that this process had been continuous over that period.[38] Changed conditions since the 1960s have caused these islands to die. The St Clair Surface also holds wetlands with their specialised communities, a feature not shared with the higher levels. Like them, though, the Surface is fire-prone and its forests are subject to occasional frost damage. In clear, still weather, which at exceptional times can last for several weeks, very cold air moves down from the higher levels and collects in hollows and on plains. In 1837 such a prolonged frost killed almost every eucalypt between the Nive River and Lake St Clair.[39] Those on the tops of rises were spared, being above the coldest layers of air. The artist Francis Simpkinson recorded the ghostly forest in his drawing of the Nive Rive at Marlborough in 1845.[40]

All of the larger lakes are attractive, their appeal lying in the perspective of distant shores and hills and in the colours and tones of the water surface, particularly in still conditions or on days of varied cloud patterns. Each is surrounded by forest and some lie beneath steep ridge-lines. While each lake has its own distinctive qualities, together they form an outstanding group. It is not the lakes alone, however, which give the St Clair Surface a unique landscape character. The marked drop from the Lower Plateau, bounded in the west by the Traveller Range, carries fine eucalypt forest. On the Surface the timber is generally lower and more open, the hills and ridges rocky. Areas of forest are separated by plains of yellow and brown button grass and by marshes, while further east are extensive white-grass openings. Beyond are the mountains. From the open country near the Nive there are glimpses of the Wentworth Hills, Mt Hobhouse and Wylds Craig blue in the distance to the south, while further west, beyond the Clarence River, the sharp outlines of higher peaks command the skyline: Rufus, Hugel and the square mass of Olympus. To the south-west the three finely proportioned peaks of Mt King William I gradually become more prominent. It is a country with a quiet beauty, though some travellers find it unexciting and drab. This approach from the east makes the first sight of Lake St Clair all the more surprising and memorable.

St Clair fills a long, narrow valley amongst the highest mountains in the island, its length providing a strong sense of scale and distance. The lake is dominated to the west by Mt Olympus. Seen from the south, the square profile of the dolerite platform of the mountain, rising above dark, forested slopes, is the major focus of the landscape. Below, the lake and the wooded flanks of the Traveller Range curve away into the northern valleys, to the peaks and rock walls of the Du Cane Range. From the northern end of St Clair, Olympus is even more dominant, its forests, buttresses and columns rising steeply from the lake shore. W C Piguenit was fascinated by St Clair. Although he twice ventured up the lake by boat and sketched Mt Ida from Echo Point, he preferred the south-eastern shore and the prospect of Olympus looming over the lake, the water leading the eye toward the distant Du Canes. From the Frankland Beaches and from the Derwent Basin the artist made drawings in 1873 and 1887, some of which he used later to create his acclaimed St Clair paintings. Piguenit felt a romantic brooding quality about the lake and in all of his works except for one 1873 painting the mountains are shrouded in drifting mists, their forms reflected darkly in the water. Piguenit's responses have been shared by many visitors to the lake over the years. One of these was a companion in C P Sprent's party of 1887, James B Walker, who saw it on an afternoon of westerly squalls:

> ... reached the rise on the lake shore in a blinding snow shower. The lake, or rather the mountains round it, were covered with flying clouds and mist, and perhaps this added grandeur to the effect, as the snow showers passed over and great peak after peak loomed through the gloom, forming a splendid vista of mountains seen through a gap between two wooded hills that rise steeply from opposite shores near the south end of the lake. We all agreed that we had seen nothing so fine in Tasmania ...[41]

Francis Simpkinson, who visited St Clair with Skinner Prout in 1845, was also deeply moved by its beauty, making eleven sketches of it from different points. He was attracted to the patterns of detail, such as the bleached dead tree trunks reaching into the water and the intricate jointing of dolerite columns on the mountain faces. His treatment of the landscape is meticulous in its fidelity to form and texture. Rather than brooding mountains, Simpkinson saw the complex interplay of light and shadow within the great arc of sky and mountain extending into the distance.

The St Clair Surface, like the Lower Plateau, was affected by human action both in the time of the tribal Aborigines and after white occupation. In the mid-1830s the frontier of settlement was considered to be 'Shorefield', a comfortable inn eleven kilometres beyond Ouse Bridge. However, the plains to the west were rapidly being occupied even then. In 1842 the Victoria Valley probation station was established and convict gangs worked on building the road to Marlborough on the Nive, with out-stations at Seven Mile Creek and eventually at Marlborough itself. In 1842 W J T Clark, described by Calder as 'the great millionaire', took up the Bronte estate on the black soil of the Nive, which had been selected originally by Lieutenant Arthur Davies. Clark's sheep and stock had already been pastured as far west as the King William Plains and Mt Arrowsmith. From this time there was constant occupation of the Marlborough–St Clair country by stockkeepers and shepherds. A police post was maintained at Marlborough, though it was seldom manned, and the 'township' consisted of a two-storey brick building and the remains of the old convict quarters. By 1850 Governor Denison had ensured that a solid bridge was in place across the Nive.

Gradually settlement spread west along the St Clair Surface. Clark had built a stock station beside the Derwent near Mt Charles, not far from the present Derwent Bridge settlement by 1860, when Tully's prospectors were glad of its shelter, and by the time Sprent's party walked along the Linda Track in 1887 Robert Orr lived in his neat log hut near the Travellers Rest River. The old track crossed this stream before going on to the Derwent and this was a popular camping place, so the name was appropriate. At this time the land beside the Clarence was being farmed and travellers on the Linda Track were able to purchase supplies here, including bread and milk. There had always been some fire management of open country in this area by Big River hunting parties, but with European settlement the pattern changed. Settlers believed that firing the plains along the Surface regularly would increase their stock-carrying capacity and this resulted in the frequent and extensive wildfires reported by those using the Linda Track. Even today, when such justification has been discounted, the Nive–Arrowsmith strip is one of the most fire-affected areas of the state.

The Central Plateau is a valuable and vulnerable part of the tapestry of the island's landscape. It has no close counterpart elsewhere and is likely to play an increasingly important role in Tasmania's future as a landscape resource. The fragile nature of all three levels requires that careful management be maintained.

9   VALLEYS WILD AND GENTLE

The valley is now in a tranquil stage of its evolution.

THE VALLEYS OF TASMANIA are relatively short. Because the mountains and plateaus rise sharply, the rivers have cut deeply into their slopes, descending rapidly to the lower country, often through deep, dramatic gorges. Once on the gentler slopes and flats below, the streams broaden and wind their way towards the coast through a very different landscape. Above the mountain rivers and their tributaries stand some of the island's tallest forests. Between them, the valleys of the Derwent, Huon, Tamar–South Esk and Mersey, contain much of Tasmania's most fertile soils and contribute substantially to the total agricultural yield as well as providing some of the most attractive rural landscapes.

The Derwent River between Ouse and Granton is never far from high hills. Below New Norfolk it is hemmed in so steeply by the Wellington Range and the ridges of Mt Dromedary that its course becomes a narrow pass through the mountain chain. The slopes rise sharply on either side allowing little room for cultivation, leaving small settlements such as Dromedary, Collinsvale and Molesworth set back in the higher recesses of the hills. Upstream, however, the valley is wide and undulating, its flats lined with poplars and the dark green squares of hop-fields. The river twists among smooth grassy ridges which have descended from distant heights. At times falling over a rock bar, or shoaling down a series of rapids and then slowing in a long, tranquil reach, its waters create scenes of constant change and movement.

Much of the Derwent Valley was open country before the coming of white settlers. There was extensive native grassland stretching up the river to High Plains and the higher country of the Ouse, Clyde and Dee rivers. The timber itself was often free of undergrowth, cleared periodically by burning, for this was the heartland of the Big River Tribe and at least three groups hunted over the central Derwent: the Braylwunyer near Ouse, the Pangerninghe further downstream about the Clyde, and the Leenowwenne in the hills and flats above New Norfolk. It is still possible, in the grassy vales and open woodlands that remain, to visualise the valley as it was then; its beauty still transcends the clutter of roads, fences, sheds and power lines. The Derwent has been dammed in the central section of its course to form the long ribbon of Meadowbank Lake, an attractive storage in the pastureland below Hamilton. Elsewhere the mid-section of the river has been little affected by humans. The major visual change of the riverside has come with the removal of the big eucalypts which formerly stood along its banks, their branches reaching out across the water. Gone too are the native shrubs which once provided a margin along its course, to be replaced by blackberry, gorse and willow. But the hills above retain low trees, and the small settlements such as Bushy Park, where the Tyenna joins the Derwent, have created a pleasant pastoral landscape. Here the changes to the land have often complemented the natural setting, with stone buildings, hop-fields and oast-houses, exotic and native trees and rich green river flats. The nearby hills give a sense of intimate enclosure.

Francis Guillemard Simpkinson De Wesselow (1819–1906),
Near New Norfolk, Van Diemens Land October 14th '48,
pencil, watercolour and chinese white highlights, 26 x 37.7,
Presented to the Royal Society of Tasmania by the artist, 1900
AG2132 (TMAG)

From high points above Gretna one can see across the lower valley to the Wellington Range, a view of great depth and colour, with the blue peaks often snow-capped, over arched by changing patterns of cloud. Simpkinson found the wide vistas of the mid Derwent Valley in the 1840s some of the most pleasant rural aspects of the colony. He recorded in his paintings details of the land which few others stopped to examine, such as the colourful sandstone bluffs and weathered formations near New Norfolk where the Derwent has carved away the hillsides. He also loved the view of the peaks of the Wellingtons from the township. From further up the valley he captured the still reaches of the river below Joseph Spode's home 'Shooter's Hill', and other prospects of river and mountains from 'Ivanhoe' north of Plenty and 'Kinvara' near Macquarie Plains. Over the years most of the trees of the early paintings have disappeared from the pasture-land, so that the valley hills are now bare, their thin grasses drying quickly to brown by early summer. One of the oldest farming districts of the island, the Derwent Valley retains much natural beauty in the distant forms of the land, the contour and colour of pasture and those stately trees that remain.

The valley of the South Esk shares many of the features of the Derwent Valley. Often parched and brown through the dry months, no grassland could be more lush and rich than the river pastures near Avoca in the time of spring growth. Here also a backdrop is created for the valley and its placid river by the steep wooded foothills of the Ben Lomond massif. From many points even low in the valley the great buttresses of Stacks Bluff can be seen, high and blue in the light haze, above the fields and ranks of forested hills.

In the Esk Valley the sense of the human past is strong. It was a natural boundary between the hunting grounds of the Ben Lomond and North Midland tribes, with the Oyster Bay people also coming inland at times along the South Esk as far as the foot of St Paul's Dome. The hunters made full use of the open country which supported good populations of wombat, wallaby, emu, echidna and probably Forester kangaroo. John Glover has left impressions both of the nature of the Esk Valley and of the lives of the Ben Lomond Tribe who lived and hunted around the base of the mountain, though the tribes had vanished before Glover settled on the Nile. His 1834 painting of the crags of Stacks Bluff from the Talbot property conveys the dominance and complexity of the mountain. Other scenes of hunting and corroborees around Mills Plains and near his home on the Nile recapture the activities of Aborigines along the river and amongst the open woodlands, and perhaps express his own sense of their lingering presence in the landscape a few short years after their removal.[42] The Esk Valley has always been a natural movement corridor for people. Before white settlement it enabled the inland Stony Creek and Ben Lomond bands to travel seasonally to the coast or to Moulting Lagoon, and the Oyster Bay groups to cross to Norfolk Plains hunting areas or to visit the ochre mines of the north-west.

Following white settlement, the naturally open woodland of the valley was occupied for grazing by the mid-1820s, as very little improvement was required apart from the simple slab and bark huts of the stockkeepers. By the 1830s the villages along the valley, Avoca, Fingal and St Marys, had begun to form: at first a police post, then a store and cottages, followed by court-house, church, hotel, blacksmith, barracks ... Solid, prosperous homes were built on the pastoral leases, good stone being readily available. By 1840 the high platform of Stacks Bluff overlooked a well-settled rural landscape. This blending of mountain, valley and forested hills held just as strong an appeal for the colony's artists as did the Derwent Valley. Apart from Glover, Piguenit sketched the dominant 'butts' of Ben Lomond from the farmlands below, and Simpkinson painted the mountain and valley from Fingal and from Break o'Day Plains. After one hundred and sixty years the valley is still bordered by the wide sweep of tree-clad ridges lifting from the fields towards the dolerite bluffs and it retains the complex patterns of colour and tone, and the clarity of light, that the artists valued so highly.

Once it has freed itself from the foothills of Ben Lomond, the South Esk winds through the northern midlands, through country settled before the 1820s and cleared of much of its timber since that time. In place of white gums, wattles and various shrub and understorey species, the river's banks are now lined in many places with large areas of gorse, willows and other introduced plants. Tree-cover in the surrounding country has been reduced to a thin scatter of stunted eucalypts and small patches of scrubby bushland. An occasional tall, spreading gum still suggests the majestic sight which the timber along the river must have presented when the valley was settled.

The North and South Esk unite at Launceston to form the Tamar, flowing north to the sea through one of the most beautiful valleys in Australia, a drowned remnant of the much larger system which, during the glacial periods flowed out across the Bassian Plain, draining melt-waters from the Plateau and Ben Lomond. The valley is now in a tranquil stage of its evolution. Farmlands shape the rounded contours of its sides and above them wooded hills form the skylines, rising to Mt Arthur in the east and the Asbestos and Dazzler ranges in the west. In the earliest decades of white settlement, the sheltered, alluvial soils served as the first granary, yielding crops as soon as the ground was cleared. Over the period since, much of it has been farmed intensively, with orchards and more recently, vinyards, lining the hillsides along the middle reaches.

Since the first whaleboats from Paterson's settlement explored its forested recesses, the Tamar Valley has delighted the eye, characterising for Tasmanians many of the foremost landscape qualities of the island. It seemed always to be green and lush, even in the driest summers, and the most casual traveller felt something of the tranquillity and prosperity of the little farms which dotted the slopes. In his travels through Tasmania in 1853, Captain Stoney journeyed by boat along the whole length of the Tamar, finding the valley to have few equals in the island. By that time some of the hillsides had been cleared and cultivated, but there were still many places which carried original forest, the journey thus providing continual contrasts:

> Along the river side all the way are handsome places, or fine romantic hills, which, as the course of the river leads from one defile to another, opens some pretty spot to view. Here a neat village is seen slumbering in a tranquil valley; there some handsome mansion appears; anon, you are lost in the woody highlands overtopping the narrowing stream; again an estuary opens to view, and the wild scenery enchants the eye, till at length the open sea spreads itself before you.[43]

The settled lands of the Huon are less extensive than those of the Derwent or Tamar: much of the river's course lies through the mountains, plains and forests of the west and south; steep, high rainfall country that resisted the axe and the plough, though not the chain-saw. It is the estuary of the Huon that provides its widest valley landscapes, the well-watered hill farms of the little settlements between Franklin and Esperance with their tilted pastures, tall trees and well-kept farmhouses, many dating from the 1880s and earlier. The Cygnet side of the Huon is similar: hill country, originally heavily forested. The shore was intensively cultivated, the forest gradually cleared to spread the farms up the gullies and onto the higher ground.

The Huon has always been a valley of small farms, traditionally orchards, dairying and mixed holdings. Most visitors respond to the sheer beauty of the country on either side of the estuary. A young man who arrived from Lancashire in 1913 seeking work and a start in a new country, typified this response both to the land and its way of life. 'The country was very beautiful and the Huon Valley, backed up by the great mountains, is a sight not easily forgotten.'

He went on to describe the property of a versatile small orchardist at Woodstock, from whom he obtained work and friendship:

> ... my landlord and foreman, is a past master of the job altogether. He milks one cow, kills a sheep when meat is wanted, learnt me how to pick the fruit and make a case, showed me a bit of tree-felling and hardwood chopping, is going to take me out with his double barrelled gun and also show me how to shear a sheep, does all the pruning and grafting and has already lent me one or two books on the subject ... I don't think it costs much to live out here, as they live pretty much on what they grow ... I think this spot approaches my ideal and I will try to get a home together here if possible.[44]

The young man succeeded and established a flourishing farm nearby at Wattle Grove.

Similar accounts may be written about the other rich and attractive valleys of the island: the Mersey's middle reaches in the Kimberly district, the lower Forth and the lovely green hillsides of Gunns Plains where the Leven breaks from its dramatic gorge. It is the valleys which have traditionally been the mainstay of orcharding, dairying, hop-growing and close cropping. They have their own particular landscape character, a blend of the rich visual impact of the patterns of intense cultivation, of trees that are valued, of neat unpretentious houses and farm buildings. As the young migrant saw, the forests and high hills have a presence that accords well with the human landscape.

The upper valleys and tributary streams of the larger rivers, except for those of the west, are part of an entirely different landscape from that of their more sedate lower reaches. Above the grassy flats, the farms, the open hillsides and back runs, lies a far wilder face of the rivers. This is a landscape dominated by precipitous mountain ridges and by high peaks. Here the rivers flow through rain-swept button grass plains and valley floors covered with dense tangles of tea-tree, *Bauera* and cutting-grass. They have cut their way from the high ranges in narrow, rocky gorges which never cease to echo with the rush and surge of their waters. Above them stand the tall native forests of the island: one of the greatest temperate forests remaining in the world.

The headstreams of the Huon exemplify these river forms. The Huon drains a huge area of the south and south-east, an area that is mountainous and wet. Several of its tributaries are substantial rivers in their own right and have greater volumes of catchment waters than do well-known streams in drier regions. The main course of the Huon was once longer, rising in the rainforest and wet sclerophyll ridges on the southern slopes of Mt Wedge and winding across the flat stretches of button grass and tea-tree plains from the foot of Mt Anne to the ancient moraines of the Arthur Range. The Huon Plains, as they were then known, ran west to Lake Pedder, and south of Mt Solitary to the spurs of the Franklands. Since the flooding of the valleys in the 1970s this wide basin has drained westward into the Serpentine and Gordon rivers; the mountains rise now from a featureless expanse of water. The course of the Huon across the plains was marked by lines of tall eucalypts and tea-tree thickets, as it is still where it swings south into the Arthur Plains. It was this distant line of trees across the Huon

'... the mists would clear across Pedder to reveal the
great curved line of gray-green peaks...'
Lake Pedder (author).

Plains that revealed the course of the Huon River to Wedge and Calder as they stood on the slopes above Lake Pedder in 1835. This was the southernmost probe of the campaign by Surveyor-General George Frankland to map the sources of the three major river systems: Derwent, Gordon and Huon. Prior to its flooding, the broad sweep of valley extended from the foot of Mt Anne north-west beyond Lake Pedder, along the course of the Serpentine, its brown and gold button grass leads running far up the spurs of the Frankland and Wilmot ranges as it swung towards the distant gorges of the Gordon.

On a still morning the mists would clear across Pedder to reveal the great curved line of gray-green peaks fading into blue where the form of Mt Sprent stood sharp against the western sky. During the course of the day there were constant changes of light and texture as the sun's angle altered and cloud moved across from the west. The broad beach of summer, delicately sculptured by wave harmonics, possessed a luminous quality; its quartz sands, pale in the high sun, assumed a faint red flush in the slanting light of late afternoon. The sand contrasted sharply in any light with the dark, peat-stained waters of the lake. Pedder's surface could be a brilliant deep blue, fading to gray or near black under cloud cover. In the shallows close to the shore, and in Maria Creek, the water was golden brown. High above, always changing, ever subtle in its tones, stood the Frankland Range, its skyline reflected in every detail by the dark water: Frankland Peak, Secheron Peak, The Throne, The Citadel, The Lion and the other peaks ranged in line westward. Beside the lake, on the spurs of the range or on the plains, there was a strong sense of space, a product of the immense sweep of this landscape and of the way in which the eye was led towards increasingly distant features. It was not a landscape of detail but of forms: the shapes of peak, ridge and spur, of the lake itself, of plains and ranges fading into the distance. The beach on a still, moonlit night was an enchanted place, which at times kept visiting parties walking its sands until the early hours of the morning.

Lakes Pedder and Maria and the streams from the northern slopes of the Franklands drained into the Serpentine and thence into the Gordon. A very low watershed, noted by Wedge, separated this catchment from that of the Huon until the construction of the impoundment. The Huon still gathers the northern run-off from the Western Arthur Range, rocky creeks dropping at intervals through steep defiles from the high lakes of the range, each crossing the plain in a thin band of trees, *Bauera* and tea-tree scrub.

Open button grass and tea-tree country extends south-east from the Arthur Plains, where the Cracroft collects the waters of the Eastern Arthurs in the valleys below Mt Hopetoun and Mt Bobs. This is country which bears little trace of human presence away from the dams and the roads. Aboriginal people did not occupy or traverse it in postglacial times. The earliest track through the south-west to Port Davey was cut in 1836 through the valley of the Huon, past the foot of Mt Picton and along the Arthur Plains. Alexander McKay and his convict gang were entrusted with this project without the direct field supervision of a surveyor, a rare situation for the time, and a measure of the respect which the ex-convict McKay had earned for his bush skills and leadership. Although piners had worked on the Huon and the Picton since the 1830s, few of the individual mountains or rivers were named or charted, even when J R Scott's party walked along McKay's track to Port Davey in 1873. It was not until T B Moore's first journey south of the Arthur Range eight years later that a detailed sketch map was produced and individual features were named.

A major source of the Huon, the Anne River, cuts deeply through the ranges south of the Mt Anne complex. It rises beneath the high cliffs of the Eliza Plateau, in the wooded bowl of Lake Judd, and penetrates the maze of spurs running from Schnells Ridge as it flows towards the Huon through a series of deep gorges and fine, timbered valleys.

These are the headstreams that run from the heartland of the southwest, from white-flecked peaks, from button grass ridges and plains, from narrow gorges and high moorland lakes. In many of the south-western valleys there is dense vegetation: rainforest, wet sclerophyll, tangled masses of *Bauera* and tea-tree scrub. But the big forests lie to the east and south.

Two major tributary rivers, the Picton and the Weld, and a number of lesser though substantial streams such as the Russell and the Arve, drain the forested slopes of the south-eastern ranges. The mountain forests of this region form a significant landscape in their own right, a landscape which is steadily changing but which the island can ill afford to lose. The Picton Valley stretches south from its junction with the Huon to within ten kilometres of the south coast, its furthest catchment high on the ridges of Pindars Peak, nearly fifty kilometres from the Huon. On its journey north the Picton gathers its waters from a great array of high mountains. From the La Perouse–Mt Bisdee chain in the far south the river flows past the timbered basin of the Roberts River and beneath the ridges of Mt Bobs, Adamsons Peak and the Hartz Mountains, and eventually joins the Huon north-east of Mt Picton. From the uplands and slopes of all these mountains and from the ranges which link them the Picton gains the waters of thousands of streams that cascade down through the forests with a constant flow in what is a very high rainfall area. On many of the heights, such as the Hartz, Bisdee and Picton, there are vantage points overlooking the long valley. One of the finest is the saddle below Pindars Peak which provides a view of its whole length and of the mountains that stand upon its rim. Often partly hidden by clinging mists or smudged with a passing rain squall, the beauty of its forest-clad depths is heightened by the patterns of ridge and gully and by the variety of shades which denote different forest species.

In the valley itself is a mosaic of high eucalypt forest, rainforest and old burns clothed with regrowth and the dense tangle of scrubs that thrive after fire. The shafts of giant swamp gums rise straight and dominant for a hundred metres, their canopy small in proportion to the pillar of the trunk. Even the old fire-killed stags are majestic in death. Beneath, on wetter slopes, understorey species grow to fifteen metres. The forest floor is littered with the debris of ancient, mossy trunks, jagged stumps and wind-torn branches. This forest rises high on the sides of the mountains and ridges, gradually diminishing in stature until cold and wet allow lower, hardy vegetation to replace it. Here, in the cooler air, King Billy pines thrive, their dark foliage and mossy limbs reducing the light. Often only the dead, silver remains of the pines are seen, scattered across an upland ridge or valley, marking the course of an old burn. On sections of the valley floor and in gullies cut deeply into the hillsides, myrtles are dominant, rising above banks of horizontal[45] and laurel,[46] sassafras and magnificent cloisters of giant man-ferns along the streams. In the stream-beds themselves, the rocks and banks are thickly padded with mosses which, in the fleeting rays of sun that manage to penetrate the canopy, glow with brilliant greens and gold. Gray and green lichens clothe the layers of fallen timber and slim spars of horizontal and laurel, and grow far up into the limbs of myrtle and sassafras, creating small gardens and ferneries high in the forks and along level branches. Throughout the forest there is the rich, pervasive smell of damp earth, wet leaves and rotting wood which, once one has known it, returns to haunt the memory.

The Weld River also has a deep, direct course, flowing south-east from the slopes of Mt Mueller, where it rises close to the headstreams of the Huon. As well as draining the wide circle of hills north of Mt Anne, a large arm, the Snake River, takes the waters of a basin enclosed by the Anne complex, the Gallagher Plateau and Mt Weld. These wet, sheltered valleys nurture the great forests of the south-east, as do the valleys of the Styx, Arve and Russell, and the many streams that tumble down the gullies of the Hartz Mountains, Snowy Range and Adamsons Peak.

The forest of the south-eastern valleys is largely old growth and very tall forest, much of it, after several centuries free of fire, close to the climax of its growth. As such, it forms a unique and spectacular landscape. An extent of mature temperate forest of this richness and area has a value as part of the total island landscape that is far in excess of any economic value it may have as a material resource. To replace it over time with either plantation or regrowth forest would diminish not just this landscape, but the quality of the island as a whole. No other mountain valleys contain the area and variety of forest found in the Huon catchment. At the time of white settlement it stretched almost unbroken from the Arthur Plains to the coast, covering valley, ridge and mountain spur with its canopy, leaving only alpine moorland and small plains of button grasss. Such an area of forest allowed abundant interaction and diversification within species, and maintained conditions for the development of a rich and complex range of life-forms. Over the past two centuries this great forest has been steadily eroded, by the coastal timber settlements, by piners working up the Huon and Picton, and more recently by the timber companies with their mechanised clear-felling and harvesting of large areas.

The upper Derwent does not have the same broad expanse of timbered country in its catchment, though on each of its major sources there are significant forests. Much of the Derwent's flow comes from the lake country of the Central Plateau by way of the rivers east of Lake St Clair such as the Nive, Shannon and Ouse and a host of smaller streams. Even in this country, on the southern fall of the Lower Plateau, there is fine eucalypt forest, particularly that growing close to the Travellers Rest River and Clarence Lagoon. The tallest trees are further south, however, in the Tarraleah Forest, where the Derwent cuts through the ridges east of Mt Hobhouse in a narrow, dramatic gorge which blocked Frankland's exploring parties in 1835. A most vivid account of the Derwent gorge was written by the leader of the first party to penetrate this country, the young surveyor John Darke. Darke had been sent by Surveyor-General George Frankland in March 1833 to gain a general impression of the upper Derwent, and was travelling from Marlborough on the Nive towards Wylds Craig. With his two convict bushmen, Cunningham and Goodwin, he had succeeded in crossing the steep defile of the Nive, when unexpectedly the party began descending into another steep gorge:

> We descended with extreme difficulty, the hills being in some places perfect walls. We were obliged to hand our dogs down several precipices from one to the other, to the manifest danger of all parties. Goodwin had a narrow escape from a large stone which rolled almost upon him from above, breaking his gun to pieces on its way.

At the foot of the gorge, the Derwent was difficult to ford. 'Cunningham, who attempted to cross, was nearly carried down …'[47]

Darke was almost certainly the first man, white or Aboriginal, to traverse the Tarraleah Forest, between the Nive and the Derwent, a forest which extends high onto the slopes of Wylds Craig. It was completely primitive, bearing no trace of previous human passage, and lying well away from fire-cleared tribal hunting grounds or movement corridors. To Darke, relatively inexperienced in travelling the wilder recesses of the island, it was a barrier of almost unlimited extent, whose huge trees had stood for centuries:

> We passed through a thick scrub with great difficulty for about four miles. We were frequently obliged to crawl on our hands and knees owing to the many fallen trees, and the ground was a rich mould (almost mud) appearing formed by the decay of vegetation for an immense period of time. Fire, I suppose, from the moisture of the ground and the appearance of the trees, has never visited it. The forest is composed of immense Stringy bark, Myrtle and (other) gum trees with Light wood, sassafras and Fern trees forming the brush wood.[48]

This forest originally stretched virtually unbroken southward around the slopes and spurs of Wylds Craig, into the Florentine Valley, along the Gordon and Tiger ranges, and rose high onto the western fall of the Mt Field Plateau. It covered the Florentine Divide and joined the forests of

'... *much of the upper Forth Valley retains its original landscape quality.*'
White gums, Forth Valley (author).

the Tyenna and Styx rivers. Some of the tallest trees in the island grew in these valleys, though now only remnants of the original forest remain.

The northern rivers, though smaller streams than the Huon or Derwent, also flow through deep, timbered valleys of unsurpassed beauty. The Mersey River leaves the Plateau below Junction Lake, dropping through the magnificent open myrtle forest of the Never Never, to a grassy plain beneath the cliffs of Cathedral Mountain. Here it swings north, plunging in a series of high waterfalls around the very foot of the mountain in a steep, forest-filled gorge, before emerging to wind slowly across the native grass flats of The Paddocks. The river retains a narrow border of myrtles which arch completely across the stream, as well as tall, straight wattles, sassafras and eucalypts. These plains are enclosed in a complete circle of mountains in a superb valley landscape. The dark myrtles are offset by the white and gold of native grasses and by the intense green of the moss-covered banks. Above the plain on every side the slopes rise steeply for up to eight hundred metres, with forest to the screes and buttresses.

On the grassy valley flats of the upper Mersey, Aborigines hunted wallaby summer by summer over thousands of years after the ice cleared from the highlands, their stone tools still lying in the rock shelters where the hunters made their fires. In the turbulent years after white settlement the secluded Paddocks became known to a few roving spirits. It was possibly information from Matthew Brady that led Bothwell grazier H M Howells in the 1840s to make a cart track from the southern end of Great Lake westward across the Plateau. After crossing rocky, exposed country, the track was taken through the Walls of Jerusalem and down into the forest of the Fish River to the opening on the Mersey still known as Howells Plain. Here for some years stood a hut with a flourishing garden, and stock were driven annually over the Plateau to the Mersey for summer pasturing.[49]

In the later years of the nineteenth century trappers from the north re-discovered the Paddocks and built their huts on a grassy rise, setting their snare lines far into the surrounding mountains. Surveyors plotted an optimistic railway up the valley and through the Pelion Plains bound for the west coast, but like the surveyed lines, the railway remained a concept on a map. The Lee family brought their stock from Mole Creek for summer grazing, ringbarking and felling the big gums to enlarge the grassland, ditching and draining the plain. Paddy Hartnett cut his horse-track from the Paddocks up through the forest to a paling hut close to Kia-ora Falls and on to his large Du Cane hut nestling under Castle Crag. Other plains in the upper Mersey Valley were also used by trappers and stockers, Fields' old hut on Howells Plain surviving for over seventy years until it was finally inundated by the waters of the HEC Lake Rowallen. But the forests that clothed the mountainsides remained beyond the reach of loggers until the 1960s, when a road was built along the valley floor and the two HEC lakes were created. This road provided access to the forests and the trees began to go, even on the steep valley slopes, which were cable-logged.

The valley of the upper Forth is as steep as that of the Mersey, though it is generally narrower and its course is more direct as it runs north towards the sea. A band of myrtle and associated species borders the river, but elsewhere the valley is clothed with high eucalypt forest. From points overlooking the valley near Lemonthyme the crowns of Pelion West and its neighbouring peaks stand blue and clear, but the upper section is so precipitous and narrow that any glimpse of the surrounding country is blocked by its walls until the final zigzag section of the old Pelion Mines track is reached, when the majestic pinnacles of Mt Oakleigh appear, poised in the sky far above the canopy. Lacking the plains of the upper Mersey and its imagined potential for railways, the valley was left to the prospectors and trappers of the 1890s to open. Patons Road was cleared along the flats close to the river for thirty-five kilometres from the Lorinna farms in order to access the thin deposits of coal and copper in the Pelion–Barn Bluff region. From Patons Road a steep, nerve-testing zigzag track was benched up a knife-edge spur beside Commonwealth Creek in 1900 to serve the Barn Bluff Copper Mine near Lake McRae. A few selectors cleared land as far south as Gisbournes Hut in the early 1900s, but the quiet of this remote and beautiful fastness was little disturbed before the 1970s, when a brief revival of wolfram mining led to the rebuilding of Patons Road to the mine, a road that began deteriorating into a foot track soon after mining ceased. Logging took place on the sides and floor of the valley some distance above Gisbournes and the stately white gums which graced the river flats nearby have long since been felled. At present much of the upper Forth Valley retains its original landscape quality.

The rivers of the west differ significantly from those in other parts of the island, just as the climate, topography and vegetation differ. The mountainous nature of the western country ensures that the rivers are confined for most of their length in deep valleys that fall steeply from the highlands. The high rainfall of the west produces strong flows and creates conditions for dense forest growth in the valleys. In the south-west the land is generally lower; there the river valleys are long and broad, and many have extensive, peaty button grass plains through which rivers such as the Giblin, Olga and Davey wind without the headlong rush of the mountain streams further north. Those valleys draining the ranges of the far south and along the south coast, however, are wetter, have a lower fire frequency, and are better drained; thus they are clothed with very dense, moss-covered rainforest. The New River is a fine example: its valley runs for nearly twenty- five kilometres from Lake Geeves to the New River Lagoon with hardly a break in its forest canopy.

The valleys of the western rivers vary from one another, but in different ways from their counterparts in other regions of the island. There has been virtually no agriculture in the west, the soils and topography being largely unsuited to domestication. The coastal plain is also quite narrow, with steep hills and rocky gullies running down to the coast in many places. The main changes brought about by human agency since white settlement have been through mining, timber harvesting and hydro-electric water storage. Mining began in the 1880s and has resulted in the destruction of landscape quality in the King and Queen valleys, and mine tailings and residues have affected the banks of the Pieman. Timber was the earliest industry of the west, beginning with the piners of Port Davey and the lower Gordon in the 1820s. However, large-scale harvesting of forests did not commence until the 1960s and has chiefly affected the middle and upper reaches of the Arthur River. Hydro-electric storage lakes have been formed on the Pieman and its tributaries and on the upper Gordon and Serpentine. Apart from these changes and the effects of greatly increased fire frequency since the 1880s, many of the western valleys have remained substantially as they were prior to white settlement.

It is along the western rivers and their tributaries that the most rich and prolific rainforest is to be found. For many visitors the characteristic landscapes of the west coast are based upon still reaches of the Gordon and Pieman, with ancient myrtles far out over the black water and mist wreathing the heavily forested slopes of the valley. Boardwalks and information displays beside these rivers now enable cruise passengers to enter sections of mature rainforest, to see its beauty for themselves and to learn something of the plant communities within its cool recesses.

But the Gordon of these lower reaches is a different river from the torrent which has chopped through the ranges in its middle course or which flows beneath giant stringybarks at the edge of the Vale of Rasselas.

Like the Franklin and the Pieman, the Gordon creates a set of different landscapes. Its source, Lake Richmond, nestles into the side of the King William Range close to the high mass of King William II. Its early course lies through dense eucalypt forest and a few small button grass openings. It breaks from the forest south of the King Williams, near Darke's Teneriffe Marshes, running south through the Vale of Rasselas where the Great Western Railway was to have made its way to the mining fields of the west coast. The Aboriginal name of the valley has not been recorded. Named by Wedge, probably at the suggestion of Frankland, the Vale of Rasselas recalled in its remote, peaceful location the 'happy valley' of Samuel Johnson's romance, an apt association for such an attractive natural valley. The thirty-kilometre plain of yellow and brown button grass is nowhere more than five kilometres wide, and is broken by stands of eucalypts and patterned by streams with their lines of trees. The Vale is surrounded by mountains. In the north rises the shapely blue peak of Wylds Craig, dropping into the timbered Gordon and Tiger ranges which flank the Vale to the east. The cliffs of Field West may be seen above and beyond these lower hills. Southwards on a clear day the sharp crest of Mt Anne stands out above a tangle of hills. Along the western side lie the Denisons, with two high points and a series of sharp, open ridges sheltering a cluster of lakes. Mt Wright and The Thumbs rise abruptly from the button grass of the Vale at its southern end, the craggy peak of the latter suggesting a man's extended thumb. Far to the north, the profile of the King William Range floats above the valley haze.

The Vale has always been a natural pass through the mountains. The Aborigines certainly knew of it and were seen there by Goodwin and Connelly during their escape from Macquarie Harbour in March 1828. Whether they ventured as far west in pre-settlement times is open to question, but access was not difficult from the King William Plains. Darke visited it twice in 1833 and Frankland's party under Wedge used the Vale to move through to Lake Pedder by way of The Thumbs and Wedge Plains in 1835. The Dawson Road, cut through the hills from Dunrobin Bridge to the Florentine in 1846, was intended to open the Vale and the extensive button grass plains further west for grazing. Flocks were pastured in the Vale in the later decades of the nineteenth century, but the sour, tussocky flats did not yield to English grasses as had been predicted, despite stocking and regular burning. As well as the Great Western Railway survey, at least two other railway surveys were undertaken through the Vale: those of James Moore in 1907 and E D B Innes in 1909. A town reserve was declared at Huntley, near the Great Bend of the Gordon River, and huts were built at the river crossing on the survey track, above the present flying fox. The osmiridium strike by the Stacey brothers on the nearby Adam River in 1925 brought considerable activity to the locality. The Vale and the surrounding valleys were closely prospected, and when the Adamsfield diggings sprang to life a pack-track was cut from Fitzgerald, later upgraded to a cart track, with a depot at the Florentine River crossing, a few kilometres below the Vale. It was three men from the diggings, Ernie Bond, Paddy Hartnett and Bill Powell, who built a cottage they named 'Gordon Vale' on a piece of fertile ground north-east of Mt Wright. Their plan to farm the Vale, like other visions of taming the button grass country of the south-west, soon faded and Bond remained alone on the property in a self-imposed exile until 1952.

The Gordon flows quietly through the Vale, in summer shallow enough to ford in many places. After rain, the catchment drains quickly and the dark water can rise several metres in a day, swirling over partly-sunken logs and spreading across low ground beyond the banks. In past ages the river's bed lay on rock strata which overlaid its present surroundings; deflected west by a range long since eroded away, it cut down through the hard quartzes and schists of the ancient pre-Cambrian surface to form the narrow gorges which take the river through several parallel mountain ranges on its way to Macquarie Harbour. The drama of its course is exciting. The sudden sweeping turn of the Great Bend takes the Gordon from the open Vale into a shattered defile two hundred metres deep beside The Thumbs. To the west the process is repeated, the river crossing broad valleys and slicing through the intervening ranges. The most impressive of these gorges are the Splits, little known or photographed before the 1970s. Recalling the first of these, the late Olegas Truchanas described the Gordon as seemingly entering a tunnel as he approached it in his kayak. So narrow was the cleft that even from a short distance upstream no sky was visible at the top. The river surged in a torrent through a gap a few metres wide. He was forced to portage the kayak over steep, scrub-covered ranges of over four hundred metres to avoid these cauldrons.

Like the Gordon, the Pieman flows westward from the high central mountains of the island. Its major tributaries, the Mackintosh and Murchison, have carved steep valleys far back into the high country. These rivers flow swiftly, carrying huge volumes of water into the Pieman. The valleys, and the array of mountains above them, have formed a major barrier between the western region of the island and the more sheltered central and eastern parts. Westerly weather systems break upon the exposed slopes of the mountains, sending every creek cascading down towards the valley floor, the sound of rushing water filling the air. These conditions have also helped to create the dense forests of the western valleys. The characteristic landscapes are those of tree-clad ridges dropping steeply, tall eucalypts on the higher slopes, the dark green canopy of rainforest on the valley floor and covering the lower hills. Even the shorter streams rising in the lower ranges, such as the Donaldson, Heazlewood and Huskisson, have substantial flows. They also have cut deeply into the hills over the course of time, and their catchments are heavily timbered. Before dams and forest harvesting changed many of the valleys, the western rivers were wild in every sense. Until recent years, much of the country through which they flow was trackless and had known no human intrusion apart from prospecting and the driving of an occasional exploratory adit. Although their forests do not extend in the same expansive sweeps as those of the south-eastern valleys, the western rivers often reveal both a more dramatic landscape and one which is more varied over a short distance from high country to coastal plain. Here also, the sheltered depths, high rainfall and significant extent of the forests have together nurtured a wonderful diversity of plant species.

Tasmania's deep valleys, particularly those of the southern and western rivers, have been the island's reservoirs of life. As the successive glacial periods gripped the higher country and ice enveloped the mountains and plateaus, the forests were confined to the deeper valleys where they provided habitats and micro-climates for a wide range of other plant and animal communities including, in the Pleistocene period, man. When the twelve-thousand year winter was over the glaciers retreated, the forests reached out from the depths and reclaimed the higher ground. At first they clothed the open, windswept savannahs; gradually, with cold-adapted species in the vanguard such as pencil and cheshunt pines, creeping pine and the *Richeas*, they re-occupied the highest levels.

The formative processes of the past have created a landscape of intense beauty, richness and variety. This is evident in the qualities of mountains and highlands, valleys and forests, coastlines and streams throughout the island. Beauty, harmony and aptness are also evident in much of the human environment of farmlands, towns, buildings and streetscapes developed over two centuries of white settlement. The landscape values of Tasmania remain high, with judicious development often complementing natural features.

Section III

KINSHIP AND MANAGEMENT

10   ABORIGINES AND THEIR LAND

*Knowledge is never allowed to fade, for in it lies the
safety and future of the tribe.*

THE LANDSCAPE which the earliest white settlers found in Tasmania was one that had already been shaped by thousands of years of human occupation. For at least thirty-five thousand years the Aboriginal people have occupied the long south-eastern peninsula of the continent. When the seas rose at the end of the last Pleistocene glacial, between twelve thousand and ten and a half thousand years ago, one group was left on the island. Nature had made them exiles, but this was an exceptional group of people, belonging to a very resilient and adaptable race.

Australian Aborigines have maintained the longest continuous culture of any society in the whole period of known human prehistory, reaching back beyond the time when they entered the continent in the north and north-west some fifty thousand years BP. Throughout this period they sustained a strong and evolving social fabric and developed their arts, religion and technology in response to the country of their tribal kinships. The group that remained on this island also set a remarkable record, in becoming the people who have endured the longest period of complete isolation from all other human contact. Small populations were also stranded on King and Flinders islands. On Flinders they survived for nearly four thousand years before vanishing for reasons not yet apparent, though possibly numbers fell below the critical level of about five hundred. Not only did the Tasmanians survive, but they adapted to substantial changes in climate and vegetation and to life on an island which has finite resources, indicating a continuing harmony with the land and flexibility as a social group. During the ten thousand years in which they were isolated, the Tasmanians established an equilibrium in their treatment of the land which averted its long-term degradation while enabling them to live well in the coldest region of Australia.

Knowledge of the Tasmanian Aborigines and their relationship with the land is limited. Even in 1803–4 when settlements were established on the Derwent and Tamar, there had already been considerable contact between coastal Aborigines and white people. Very few settlers' reports were able to convey an authentic account of tribal life as it had been before contacts began. Many reports were based upon hearsay and popular beliefs of the time, perhaps the most obvious visual example being Glover's depictions of corroborees in the mid-1830s, well after the surviving Aborigines had been taken to Flinders Island. During the two brief decades in which white settlers and Aborigines co-existed in relative peace and the tribal structure was still intact, few attempts were made to record in detail the way of life, beliefs, languages and traditions of this unique people. The settlers were preoccupied with the practical concerns of developing farms, towns and industries. Most were not equipped with the skills necessary to observe and record the facets of Aboriginal life, and the cultural structure and climate of the early settlements reduced the likelihood of such interest or studies. Some compiled lists of words and names; a few made sketches and described what they saw of Aboriginal life. The explorers of the 1830s observed burned areas of land and the remains of huts, but little else was recorded. By far the most detailed descriptions come from the diaries of G A Robinson, who spent several years in the company of Aboriginal people, learning sufficient of their languages to communicate, and noted their customs. Robinson was to some extent a sympathetic observer, though he was limited by his poor education, mind-set and quirks of character. He saw some of the tribes in their own lands, but by the time he began his work of 'conciliation' all the tribes had been drastically affected by the bitter conflict and by pressures of white pastoral expansion, sealing and other activities.

Other evidence of the relationship of Aborigines with the land comes from a number of different sources. Members of the Tasmanian Aboriginal community have not only gathered historical records, but have also retained traditional knowledge and stories passed down through successive generations from their forebears. The writings of early European voyagers are of particular interest, as they encountered the Aborigines in the decades before white settlement and before sealers, whalers and others had made significant contact. They were therefore able to see the Tasmanians in their normal patterns of life, and in some cases to relate to them in terms of mutual respect and acceptance. Of some ten expeditions which visited the south-east of the island between 1772 and 1802, two in particular, those of Bruni d'Entrecasteaux (1792 and 1793) and Nicholas Baudin (1802), stayed for a relatively long period and left observations of substantial value. Over the past twenty years there has been extensive archaeological work on living and hunting sites throughout the island. This has involved examination of middens and hut locations, rock shelters and caves, yielding knowledge of life in recent (Holocene) times as well as in the more distant past. Excavations of deposits in caves and shelters occupied during the Pleistocene glacial extending back to thirty-five thousand years BP have provided details of numbers and movements, and of the food and technology of those early hunters. It is also possible to infer some characteristics of the way in which the Tasmanians regarded their land by referring to other Aboriginal people of south-eastern Australia, as well as to evidence from the land itself, evidence that is often present in the observations of white settlers and explorers, and still exists in the contemporary landscape.

Conditions of life for most of the Aborigines' long period of occupation were very different from those of the past few thousand years. If any people needed to understand their surroundings completely, and to adapt effectively to them, it was the inhabitants of the peninsula. The last Pleistocene glacial peaked at about eighteen thousand BP, and the region was affected by extremely cold conditions for over twelve thousand years, a period in which ice-caps spread across high plateaus and glaciers filled the higher valleys. People lived on the peninsula during the whole of this period, and then coped with a new set of conditions as the land became warmer and more densely forested from eleven thousand years BP onward. During most of this time there would have been some contact with other tribes in the south-east of the continent to whom those on the Tasmanian peninsula were related. Whole groups of people would have moved into and out of the peninsula. It was in the final stage of occupation, the last eight thousand five hundred years after sea levels rose, that many changes took place in the technology of the mainland tribes, changes that could not be shared with the Tasmanians.

During the final Pleistocene glacial the Tasmanian region was far more open than it is at present, with large areas of sub-alpine savannah, and it was this openness, so desirable for driving game such as wallaby and emu, that attracted the Aboriginal hunters. With sea levels lower throughout the period, receding to between one hundred and thirty and one hundred and fifty metres below the present level at the height of the glacial, much of the continental shelf was exposed, creating a far broader coastal plain around the higher land mass. This plain was probably covered by tussocky grassland, low scrub and open forest, affording scope for rapid movement. Lagoons and marshy flats were habitats for birds and fish, both welcome items in the diet, as well as eggs and edible water plants. These people had no aversion to scale-fish, and their stone tide-traps would have been very effective in the shallow inlets.[1] The coastal rock shelters and other Pleistocene living sites which could reveal much more about their lives are now hidden beneath the sea.

Inland, conditions were more severe. Below the snow-covered highlands and the glacier tongues, the forests were far down in the deeper valleys, leaving a broad area of lower range and valley country open and accessible across the southern third of the Tasmanian peninsula and through the eastern highlands. The open eucalypt forest, grasslands, heaths and pockets of low alpine scrub attracted game and the hunters followed. In the valleys there were caves and shelters that provided warm, dry living sites through the bitter winters, and at higher levels overhangs which served as periodic refuges for hunting parties. It is the remains in these caves and shelters across southern and central Tasmania which are now providing a more detailed view of the way in which during the last glacial the Aborigines adapted to their harsh environment. The caves of the Maxwell, Franklin, Cracroft and Florentine valleys are a timeless link between the people who first claimed and learned to live with this land thirty-five thousand years ago and their descendants at the present time.

From twelve thousand BP conditions began to change: the long winter slowly relaxed its grip on the land. Sea levels began to rise, and the glaciers to retreat from the valleys. By ten thousand five hundred BP the forests were migrating up the slopes, with eucalypts steadily re-colonising the open grasslands of the ranges, a process which was aided by fire and the dry climate which succeeded the glacial. This was followed by a moister, warmer period between eight thousand and three thousand six hundred BP. By three thousand BP the southern and western mountains had regained their dense cover of myrtle, *Banksia*, cutting-grass and the various other species which render human and animal movement difficult. Repeated firing had also promoted the leeching of nutrients from many western areas, allowing button grass and heath to extend across them. The coastal plain dwindled to a thin strip as the sea invaded the remainder of the continental shelf and flooded across old hunting grounds to establish the present shoreline. No longer was it possible to move rapidly up the eastern side of the peninsula, across the Bassian Rise, and into the south-eastern part of the continent. Those who remained faced living on a greatly reduced area of land.

Much of the old inland hunting land had to be abandoned. The tribes could not live in the forested hills between the south coast and the Arthur Range, nor in the tangled ranges and rainforests drained by the Gordon and its tributaries. The old refuge caves such as Wareen, Kutikina, Bluff, Wargata Mina and Ballawinne which had served so well in the hard times had long been deserted. The west coast ranges also offered nothing for the hunters. Not only was the vegetation too thick in the west and south, but the game itself was quite scarce there. Even the open country consisted largely of button grass plains or wiry heathland. Wallaby, emu and wombat preferred sheltered native grass, and were far more abundant in the open lowlands or around the edges of the plateaus. Forest was still important as a source of food: brush-tailed and ring-tailed possum, quoll and the smaller animals such as pademelon and bettong were to be found under its sheltered canopy and amongst the fallen debris, but it had to be relatively open and accessible.

Conditions were far milder on the island than they had been on the ice-capped peninsula, so that later generations of Tasmanian people did not need to be as flexible, alert and opportunistic as their forebears. The climate would continue to be harsher than that of any other part of Australia, so that fire and shelter were still vital elements of life, even if the Tasmanians could eventually discard the sewn animal skin capes of the cold times.[2] Caves and shelters around the Holocene coastline were exploited, such as those at Rocky Cape and Sisters Creek. A major benefit of the milder climate lay in the Central Plateau's becoming free of ice and the lessening severity of conditions in the higher country. As vegetation spread up the valleys of the melt-streams and across the Plateau, this became a new summer hunting ground. The horizontal Permian rock band which underlies much of Tasmania's high country was particularly useful, as this band provided dry, comfortable rock shelters for hunting parties adjacent to a wide area of the Plateau.

With the loss of much of the coastal plains and southern mountains, the Tasmanians were forced to create new hunting grounds. One of the most widespread adaptations of the Holocene was the increased use of fire in management of the land. The denser forests of the island were not visited; in regions such as the southern forests and the Florentine, progress through the dense undergrowth was difficult and hunting was impossible, even if game had been plentiful. Open forest, grassland and heath were ideal, and these occurred in many places. Such open areas could be sustained and extended by the use of fire, while dry sclerophyll forest could be opened through periodic burning of undergrowth. In the midlands, parts of the north-west and north-east, the Norfolk Plains, the broad valleys such as the Derwent and South Esk, and along the east and west coasts there were quite extensive areas of native grasses and heaths, often with scattered eucalypt, wattles or other trees. These open lands required regular grooming, and over several thousand years the Aboriginal people refined their use of fire as a tool, employing it with fine skill and judgement. Periodic burning encouraged regrowth of eucalypts and other fire-adapted species, but the increased animal populations that were attracted to these areas restricted the number of seedlings which survived; this process kept the forest open and undergrowth low and sparse, facilitating movement by hunting parties. Fire was used to drive game towards the hunters' spears as well as to clear the ground. A graphic account of a hunt of this kind near Hells Gates, Macquarie Harbour, was given by James Kelly in his description of the whaleboat journey of 1815.[3] Importantly, burning was also used in areas of grassland in order to attract game to the tender new shoots which appeared after winter.

The employment of fire in tribal hunting lands appears to have been constant during summer months. All of the early sea expeditions that visited the coasts during mid to late summer, beginning with Tasman in 1642, observed some fires, and in unusually dry seasons these were widespread. Extensive burning was reported by Tasman, Marion du Fresne (1772) and Furneaux (1773), the last two arriving in late summer when the country was at its driest. This also applied to Baudin, who noted many fires in January 1802, though there was no sign of them when he returned in March.[4] The hills and plains of the coastal belt, particularly the south-east, appear to have been burned regularly; it is likely that fires in forested or remote inland regions were far less frequent than they are today.

The grasslands and open woodlands which had been fire-managed were occupied by the flocks of the early waves of white settlers in a process that accelerated after 1820. The frequently used hunting grounds around Risdon Cove and along the eastern shore of the Derwent, the southern midlands and the lower Derwent Valley were taken up first, and as settlement extended similar areas were found in each region, until by the early 1830s most clear land was being grazed. The Aboriginal owners were forced away from their lands by the sheer numbers and superior force of the whites. Some of the plains kept open by the Aborigines began to grow over again when they were no longer subjected to burning. This was especially noticeable in high rainfall areas such as the Surrey Hills and Middlesex Plains. After the failure of the Van Diemen's Land Company sheep and stock venture in the Surrey Hills, this scattering of grassed plains and belts of forest was used by Fields for running their cattle, though with little success. Despite this, undergrowth grew back in the 'brown forest' which Hellyer had found quite open in 1827, and scrub began to invade some of the attractive white-grass openings on which he had found Aboriginal huts. By the 1950s relatively little open country was visible from Hellyer's first lookout, St Valentines Peak.[5]

Burning was not confined to traditionally open areas which were groomed regularly by successive generations. Formerly timbered or button grass country was also fired in order to extend existing hunting grounds or to open new areas. When the tribes were under pressure from white settlement and bounty-seekers in the late 1820s, they were forced to move into country further west than they had formerly penetrated, which had hitherto been avoided as being too cold and wet and lacking native grass, and where game was not plentiful. They began firing the button grass in these regions in an attempt to create hunting fields beyond the reach of whites. Hellyer found in October 1828 that the valley of the Sophia River ('Cranbourne Chase') had been recently burned, and Sharland noted that the same had happened in the Loddon Valley below Frenchmans Cap, in March 1832. Sharland also saw huts along the upper Franklin, where a track had been burned through pockets of scrub. Gould even found old burns and the remains of a hut in the open country around Lake Ewart in February 1860. None of these areas was likely to have been frequented prior to white settlement.

When the shoreline stabilised, the Tasmanians found themselves on an island which would, with their own modifications, sustain a small population indefinitely. The situation did not call for fundamental changes to the way in which they had lived for thousands of years. Although the usable land area had shrunk in the course of four thousand years, these were people whose knowledge of that land extended over a period of twent-five thousand years, and they found little difficulty in adapting as their world changed almost imperceptibly around them. Over this long period they had accumulated an intimate knowledge of food sources, the animals, birds, fish and plants which inhabited each region. As well, they had an understanding of the patterns of the land: patterns that changed very slowly with the coming of the gentler climate, and determined when a particular food was abundant in a certain location or when a place had to be avoided. Any major threat would have come not from the lack of food or severity of climate, but from a failure to manage these resources or to adhere to their own traditional disciplines. The Aboriginal people could not allow any locality or resource to be over-exploited and degraded, and the whole pattern of their life evolved to prevent this.

There is no firm evidence of the total number of Aboriginal Tasmanians at the time of white settlement, but this is generally considered to have been between three thousand and six thousand, and had probably been stable at this level for a considerable time. It was a number that the island could readily support. The two key elements in their use of resources were the thinly scattered distribution of the population and the constant movement of groups or bands, both within their tribal territories and across those of other tribes. There were nine tribes of language groups, of varying sizes in different parts of the island; a tribe was composed of several bands, each having its own section of the tribal territory. Within a band there was a further sub-grouping of extended families or hearth groups, each of about ten people.[6]

Most tribes' territory included a section of coastline, where the most readily obtainable food sources existed, though some bands had individual sections which lay inland. There were two exceptions: the Big River Tribe, taking its name from the Ouse, occupied the central highlands, Derwent Valley and part of the southern midlands, and the Ben Lomond Tribe's territory spread around the Ben Lomond massif, including the South Esk Valley, North Esk and Nile. Both had seasonal access to the north and east coasts by negotiation with surrounding tribes. Movement was basic to tribal life. Apart from visits to ochre mines and tool quarries, there were seasonal events which drew bands from considerable distances. Notable amongst these were the mutton-bird harvest at the rookeries of the far north-west and north-east, the swan gathering on Moulting Lagoon on Oyster Bay, and duck and emu egg collecting at several localities. Territorial access rights were reciprocal: in return for visits of the Big River Tribe to the east coast, the Oyster Bay people could hunt on the high Plateau country in summer. Tribes whose territory was largely coastal also moved constantly. Their main food consisted of abalone, warrener, molluscs and crayfish, all readily obtainable by the women. So expert were the Aboriginal women in the water that they could quietly infiltrate a group of seals basking on offshore rocks, or haul themselves down to a depth of twenty metres or more using strands of kelp in pursuit of crayfish. Important components of the diet were penguin, mutton-bird and seal, all of which provided oil essential for the retention of body heat. To obtain these creatures it was necessary to travel periodically, often for long distances when it came to visiting seal colonies and rookeries. While the sea provided a major part of the diet, wherever the band was located it was still possible to climb for brush- and ring-tailed possum and to hunt wallaby, emu, echidna and other animals as did the inland tribes. Thus all of the coastal plains and heaths were likely to be burned from time to time either during the hunt or to attract game to the new growth. Bands living away from the coast depended largely upon animals; they moved through areas where wombat, possum, emu and wallaby were abundant, and where tracking and hunting were not difficult. In all areas there were seasonal sources such as birds' eggs, fruit, berries, roots, tubers and fungi such as native bread.[7]

Strategies for obtaining favoured foods were still developing at the time of white settlement. Over the past three thousand years the offshore islands had become more attractive as sources of seals, mutton-birds and sea-birds' eggs. Women were able to swim to some of the closer ones, such as The Doughboys off Cape Grim, but most islands were out of reach of swimmers. Thus the canoe was developed as a means of reaching them. These craft were made from three tightly bound bundles of reeds or bark held together with a net of vine or with cutting-grass rope, and tied tightly at bow and stern.[8] Usually four people were able to travel in one of these canoes, which were about four and a half metres long and almost a metre wide. The canoes were said to become waterlogged after a few hours, but some were evidently made of more durable material. In craft such as these, regular visits were made to Hunter, Bruny, Maria and Schouten islands, and more daringly across twelve kilometres of open sea to Maatsuyker. Mutton-bird rookeries and sea-bird nesting sites on some of the other south-western islands would also have been accessible by canoe, including De Witt, Breaksea, Ile du Golfe, Trumpeter and Flat Witch.

In obtaining food and managing food sources, travel was essential. On average, a band would probably remain in one place for no more than a few days before moving on in a trek of two or three hours to the next site where there was water and access to food. Some locations would support a group for substantially longer. The major exception to this general pattern of movement occurred on the west coast, where conditions often made travel, and even living, very unpleasant, with prolonged periods of cold wind and heavy rain. The North-west and South-west tribes met this situation with characteristic adaptability and resilience: they built 'villages' of sturdy and commodious beehive huts in key locations along the coast and used these on their journeys to shelter during bad weather.

The pattern maintained over thousands of years of small bands moving constantly along the coasts and through the open countryside had major implications for the land and the landscape. The overall number of people on the island, and the number in any particular region, remained at a level for which the available resources were more than adequate. The distribution of the population and its social structures were such that nowhere was there a concentration beyond the capacity of the land to sustain them. In the mild south-east, where the density was greatest, the nature of coast, islands and open country enabled many bands to live well with relatively little effort. Constant movement ensured that no single location became over-used or degraded, and the wide variety of foods which were utilised meant that no single item or animal population was over-taxed. At the same time, the systematic use of fire maintained a substantial area of plain and open woodland in most coastal and many inland regions, establishing a pattern which enabled the vegetation to adapt over a long period and retain natural stability. The great inland forests and fragile alpine country of the island remained untouched.

The relatively simple technology of the Tasmanian tribes was quite adequate for a people living in a resource-rich and isolated environment, without creating significant disturbance to soil or vegetation. There were no hafted tools: no axe which could fell a tree, though notches could be chipped in the trunk to facilitate climbing after possum. Stone tools apparently became smaller and more efficient towards the end of the period of isolation. Reeds and kelp enabled the Aborigines to make strong, effective baskets and containers to carry tools and other possessions while travelling, and tightly wound sheets of bark made a slow-burning torch to carry fire. It is difficult to accept their reported inability to light fire; there is no reliable evidence of any method of creating it, but it is also unlikely that fires or torches could have been kept alight by isolated groups travelling in wintry conditions, or on the small clay hearths in canoes on long voyages such as that to Maatsuyker Island. Without hafted axes or similar cutting tools, Aboriginal track-making was achieved through the use of fire. A route which led through scrub or high undergrowth was simply burned out so that it became a series of openings. A frequently used track would have been worn into a pad over time, as it is today, but without the pressure and cutting edges of boots such a pad would take longer to impress in grassland or on the forest floor.

Well-used tracks were established in many places, some of these existing for centuries in the vicinity of ochre mines, quarries, rookeries and other frequently visited sites. One of these tracks ran along the valley of the Blythe River, connecting the Surrey Hills with the ochre mine at Mt Housetop and with the coast near Emu Bay. Others can be traced still by the series of clearings, particularly those reported in the journals of exploring parties. Wedge made use of these clearings on his journey from the Balfour area to Circular Head in May 1828. A major route crossed the Middlesex Plains, linking the Mole Creek country with the Surrey Hills, a path followed by the Van Diemen's Land Company stock road. It is possible that this track also provided a link with the Plateau by way of the upper Mersey and February Plains, a route that would give the Big River people access to the far north-west. Robinson and his guides used many of these tracks in their years of travel about the island in the early 1830s. The South-east and Port Davey tribes had some difficulty in keeping a route open across the forested ranges and wind-packed scrubs of the south coast between the Recherche district and Cox Bight; it is little wonder that Robinson's party complained bitterly about this weary journey.

Like the tracks, Aboriginal shelters made little impression upon the landscape. They were simple, but were generally not quite as crude and ineffective as has often been reported. For bands in the south-east, east and north-east who lived in comparatively mild conditions, an elaborate

*The Middlesex Plains:
the plains were kept free of undergrowth by regular burning by
the Noeteela people of the North Tribe (author).*

shelter was not necessary. Baudin's men described the simple arrangement of bark and branches propped up as a wind-break for a hearth group as the most primitive of structures and as evidence of the backwardness of the Tasmanians themselves. However, for bands who would spend only a week or so in summer in one place, such shelters or bivouacs were quite adequate. Bligh found a more elaborate shelter at Adventure Bay, a well-built half-dome covered with bark strips, demonstrating that the same people were able to erect more sturdy structures.[9] Hellyer described similar huts during his first crossing of the Surrey Hills in March 1827.[10] Large sections of bark had been carefully cut from the trunks of eucalypts to roof these huts, and the inside of one had been marked with the curved emblem or 'moon' shape of the common body cicatrice.[11] Like the nearby 'painter's hut' which contained drawings of animals, this may have revealed the influence of whites; the Aborigines were quick to recognise and adopt European ways which suited their lives. The most elaborate huts were those of the two west coast tribes. These were not only required to shelter groups of people from prolonged wet conditions, but they were also permanent structures that parties could use as stages on their journeys along the coast. Robinson reported seeing 'villages' consisting of several of these huts in his west coast travels. The most detailed description of a west coast hut comes from Jorgen Jorgenson's journal of the west coast expedition of Van Diemen's Land Company personnel under Clement Lorymer in March 1827. North of Temma the party came across:

> ... a very compact native hut far different (as are all the huts in this quarter) from those seen to the Eastward. It was a complete piece of Gothic Architecture in the shape of a dome, and presenting all the first rudiments of that Science. It was made to contain 12 to 14 people with ease. The entrance was small and not above 2 feet

high. The wood used for the principal supports had been steamed and bent by fire. The huts as well as Baskets and other things produced by the western natives evince great ingenuity, and the nature of the country compels them to build compact dwellings to shelter them against the bleak winds.[12]

Substantial huts such as these were often surrounded by a low, circular earth bank, a number of which may still be found along the west coast.

The Tasmanians had a varied, simple but entirely adequate technology which enabled them to live with the land and to modify the land to their needs. Their shelter was sufficient for their comfort; their weapons and tools were suited to the foods they sought. They travelled light, carrying only a few essentials, made tracks where they were needed, and moved when and where their needs would be most readily met. Of the material and practical aspects of the Aborigines' lives a great deal is now known. Of the spiritual bonds which tied them to the land and which transcended all else, we know almost nothing.

Of all the aspects of Aboriginal life, that which was least open to the understanding of whites was the Aborigines' view of the world and the depth and complexity of their spiritual lives. Yet this was fundamental to understanding every other element of their lives, in particular their relationship with the land, and without it knowledge of their activities and technology, however detailed, remains superficial. There were many reasons for the settlers' ignorance. Beliefs form an area of life that is accessible only through a sound grasp of the different levels of language. Vocabulary was learned by both societies rather than the elements of syntax, resulting in the development of a 'pidgin' language which had application only to practical situations. It is doubtful whether any white person gained sufficient command of a dialect to understand more than simple stories.

More importantly, in the crucial early years while the tribal fabric remained intact, and the elders survived with their store of intricate ritual and encoded belief, no white would have won the confidence and acceptance of the Aborigines to be accorded this kind of knowledge, even if any of the white community had the interest to seek it. Such matters would not be open even to all members of a tribe. Later, Robinson learned some of the traditional stories and recorded a few of the Aborigines' ideas of the spiritual world, but his own concern was to turn their minds away from their old beliefs and to bring them to Christianity; he had little interest in, or sympathy for, Aboriginal mythology. He used his Aboriginal people's knowledge of the land, of tracks, places and tribal boundaries, but he had no curiosity concerning the way in which they and their forebears related to the land itself.

For ten thousand years the Tasmanians had been isolated from the other Aboriginal people of south-eastern Australia. But for thirty thousand years before this they had belonged to the stream of Aboriginal culture. Groups would have moved freely along the flat coastal shelf and across the Bassian Plain into Gippsland, the Port Phillip and Westernport districts and the mild country further inland. For some, visits south into the Tasmanian peninsula may even have been seasonal. The occupants of the peninsula would have shared languages, kinship ties and trade with the other south-eastern tribes. Later, in their isolation, much that was common to the culture of the south-east would have been maintained by the Tasmanians for many generations. Their tools were those of the south-east, except that over the long time-span of separation the range became simpler, smaller and more limited. Language changed, as would be expected, evolving in the form of regional dialects. There is insufficient linguistic evidence to link the Tasmanian languages with those of south-eastern Australia. Additionally, the Pama–Nyungan language group probably spread across the south of the continent some four thousand years BP, long after the isolation of Tasmania. There has also been little genetic research to establish the kinship of the Tasmanians with mainland peoples.

One of the great strengths of Australian Aboriginal culture is its conservatism: its ability to retain essential codes and traditions over many generations. Over thousands of years the myths and rituals are handed on, enabling each generation to define its place in the physical world in the context of the powerful underlying and pervading world of the spirit. No Aborigine can consider that his life is fulfilled unless he has passed his knowledge to the next generation, and this imperative is the basis of all initiatory rites. Knowledge is never allowed to fade, for in it lies the safety and future of the tribe. In the same way the codes of the social fabric are passed on: the lines of blood kinship, the ownership of specific places, the birds and animals which are owned by, or taboo to, particular bloodlines, the strict rules governing marriage. Equally strong are the sacred matters of country and of spirit which are revealed to initiates, to certain elders, or to those guardians charged with preserving and communicating this special knowledge of place. This conservative strength would originally have been part of the Tasmanian culture in isolation, just as it was a part of every other Aboriginal group. Little by little, however, even the strongest culture would have lost some of its force in the complete absence of contact with the mainstream.

There is some evidence of these continuing traditions in Tasmania. The social structures and disciplines were those of the Aboriginal people as a whole, particularly those relating to marriage. It was vital for the survival of a small, isolated group that genetic integrity be preserved. Consequently, the marriage-kinship lines of the tribes and bands were observed over ten thousand years. The Tasmanians continued the traditional burial practice of cremation, followed by the breaking up of remains, which were placed in a shallow pit. This tradition goes back at least twenty-five thousand years to Lake Mungo, and was widespread throughout Australia. The common use of ochre provides further evidence of a continuing link with earlier rituals. Hunting methods, and particularly firestick farming, were very similar in their application, given regional variations in conditions, to those of mainland tribes. The cultural record of the Tasmanians in the form of painting and petroglyphs is not extensive when compared with the extraordinary richness of rock art throughout continental Australia. Much of the earlier work is undoubtedly in former coastal sites drowned by the rising seas. There are hand stencils, ochre and finger lines of the cave-dwellers of the Pleistocene glacial, but more important in their way are the more recent petroglyphs at sites such as Sundown Point, Greens Creek and Mt Cameron West, for in these may lie evidence of continuing cultural features in the lines, circles and arrangements of dots, suggesting to some researchers the oldest Australian rock art, the Panaramitee. This tradition takes its name from a location in the south-east of South Australia; its methods and motifs can be found over a wide area at sites as far away as the Cape York Peninsula. Panaramitee petroglyphs have been created over a period of forty thousand years and are still being incised on rock-faces in parts of Central Australia in what is probably the longest continuing form of cultural record of any race of people. The main Tasmanian sites, such as Mt Cameron West, date from well into the time of the Tasmanians' isolation and as well as indicating clearly the maintaining of a tradition from the period before isolation, they also provide some insight into the spiritual life of the Tasmanians.

No Aboriginal art is purely decorative. Every painting or engraved subject has a specific function in relation to spiritual power, ownership, kinship, the resources or boundaries of the country or the spiritual and ancestral beings associated with a place. The petroglyphs attest to the continuation and communication of this spiritual life into the relatively recent past. Rock art was not apparently a part of Aboriginal life in Tasmania at the time of white settlement, but other forms of art played an important role in ceremony and in everyday life. The most common form of visual art was the constant use of the line, 'moon' and circle motifs both as cicatrices on various parts of the body as powerful protective agents, and on the interiors of huts and grave coverings. Songs and dancing were other forms of art through which the spiritual life of the people found expression. Observers such as Robinson have described the Tasmanians' love of dancing around the evening fires, especially during their exile on Flinders Island, where strong efforts were made to ban these 'pagan' rituals. Robinson and others were permitted to view the dancing, but there were no witnesses or reports of the corroborees for which clearings were made, such as that described by Baudin's men, which was hidden amongst the trees on Bruny Island. This had been carefully prepared, with 'chambers' screened by bushes off to the sides.[13] It resembled the bora-ring of many of the mainland tribes, and suggests the continuation of key ceremonies such as initiation.

The Tasmanians had a strong oral tradition, with stories and traditions being passed down the generations. Many of these are preserved today amongst the Aboriginal people. Plomley refers to a creation story of the South-east Tribe in which ancestral beings named Moihernee and Droemerdeena made the land and all things in it.[14] Stories often concerned the familiar animals and birds that they saw about them, and a number of these stories have been collected and published under the title *Taraba*.[15] These relate to the Tasmanian devil, wattle bird, platypus and other creatures, and embody at least two levels of meaning. They are a remnant of the rich store of myth which would have existed before the breaking of the tribes. Once the island would have been criss-crossed by a network of myths relating to places, origins and the nature of the land. James Cowan summarised the central place of myth in the relationship between people and the land:

> Where the process of myth fulfils its most potent symbolic ordering of belief is in the area of landscape. Aborigines ... are deeply attached to their land. Alone among traditional peoples they have made the land into a variegated icon capable of embodying all that they believe. Landscape is mythologised so completely that there is hardly any countryside not accounted for in myth and story.[16]

The core of Aboriginal existence lay in the spiritual relationship between people and the land. Of all the beliefs and traditions which were most likely to survive the long period of isolation, the ones that would have endured most strongly were those defining this essential kinship with their surroundings. There can be no evidence now of its specific nature; no hint of this would be revealed to the white invader, even if he were sufficiently perceptive and open to comprehend. But its quality can be inferred from the world-view of tribal Aborigines in south-eastern Australia, its strength and endurance from its importance in Aboriginal life throughout the continent, and from the continuation of so much else common to this life.

To the Aborigine, the landscape had three dimensions: physical, social and spiritual. The three were inseparable and indivisible. He saw the land clearly, in immense detail, with its openings and forest, hills, streams and shelter. He knew the animals that lived in it, their habits, their tracks, their seasonal movements, their value as food and the methods of securing them. He was aware of the seasons in which hunting was allowed for particular game, and of the plants and other food that might be gathered in their own time.

Every person knew the complex codes that applied to the land in his or her own territory: the totemic rights and obligations, which families of the band had rights or ownership over specific parts of it, the other members' rights of access to these parts, the neighbouring bands who were allowed to forage and hunt at particular times, and the more distant bands of tribes who were permitted to cross this land for accepted purposes. The country of a man's or woman's own band was crossed by numerous kinship lines. Sections of it were the special preserve of his or her family; its members and those whom they married had rights to it that others did not share, except by exchange of obligation. To be born at a place conferred rights to it; to be related through blood or marriage, even of distant kin, also carried rights to land in their preserve which might lie many days' journey away in the territory of another band of the tribe. This complex map of kinship and rights was basic to one's knowledge of the land. It defined the individual's place both in relation to the people with whom he or she came into contact and to every feature of the land itself. It also opened to members of a hearth group or band a wide variety of resources to which they could gain access through the network of kinship and reciprocal rights.

An Aborigine's totem also drew him or her close to the land. Every person identified from birth with a particular totem, usually an animal, which was one of those belonging to the band or tribe. This totem became a lifelong identity, and one to which that person would eventually return. It was another aspect of self. It linked one with the eternal spirits of the Dreaming, when the totem was created, and with the land itself in a timeless relationship. Cowan wrote of the Aborigine's totemic identity:

> ... it grounds him in a spiritual as well as a physical locality - a locality that he identifies as being his 'country'. This implies custodial responsibilities towards his totem area which must be exercised at

prescribed ritual moments. Knowing his country's songs, knowing how it was created during the Dreaming, knowing the symbols of the body paintings associated with his totem - these are all part of his totemic identity.[17]

The land was further invested with a life of its own; a life which embraced the people who lived upon it. Over a thousand generations the Aboriginal people had become woven, flesh and blood, into the fibres of this island. Each locality of a band's territory had its particular significance within the spiritual framework: the land belonging to a band in the tribal territory was both a physical and a spiritual resource. Its people knew who had created it, and could point to the enduring evidence of its creation. A prominent rock or stand of trees or a stream along which they hunted each possessed its spiritual or ancestral being who provided the bounty of the hunt. There were places which only people of a certain family or their kin might approach; others where only men, or only women were permitted. A few places were dangerous to the spirit: no one went there. Always there were sites accessible solely by the initiated or by designated ones among the older men who cared for these places and carried out the rituals necessary for the health of the land and its people.

The land as the Aborigines knew it, then, was a domain of the spirit. Every feature had its place in the complex fabric of myth and creation legend built up over thousands of years. Every object had its role and was identified by name and by association: each stream bank where the women dug with their sharpened sticks, each crossing of a river, each plain where men hunted, each patch of forest where there were possum, each grassy hillside where wombats tunnelled, each overhang that made a dry, secure shelter. Every place had its spiritual link with the people who lived and hunted close to it.

The health and well-being of land and people were identical, not consequential. It was part of the blood bond of the tribe and the band to maintain the health of their land, just as a family would maintain one of their own kin who was in need. Only when it was properly cared for in practice and in spirit could the ancestral beings help to provide the fruits of that land. It was important, therefore, to keep a hunting area clean and clear by firing every few years so that the undergrowth did not grow too thickly for the hunters. The grass of the river flat had to be cared for, so that the spirit of the place would bring wombat and pademelon to feed on the young growth. A band which 'owned' a mutton-bird rookery would restrict access to others for a season so that its numbers could be maintained at a healthy level. Such a view of the land is constant and fundamental to Aboriginal life, and is too strong to fade even in ten thousand years of separation.

The Tasmanian Aborigines' tribal structure and way of life may have survived for longer and adapted in many ways had white settlement remained on the small scale of the first two decades, even with the toll of European diseases. Their resilience and ability to adopt whatever they saw as contributing to their lives, such as the white man's dog, would have facilitated this. Inevitably, massive change would have come about in the longer term as it did in mainland Australia. With the huge influx of sheep in the 1820s, however, when selectors pushed their flocks across the midland plain, along the Derwent and Esk valleys and into almost every grassed opening in the island to which they could gain access, the tribes lost far more than their traditional hunting lands and the food resources that had been so rich and reliable. They also lost with this land the spiritual forces which had sustained them in their long journey through time.

SECTION IV

TWO CENTURIES OF PROGRESS

11   ASPECTS OF EUROPEAN SETTLEMENT

Even its clear light, the shapes of its hills and sharp
contrasts of plain and forest began to lose some
of their strangeness.

THE FIRST SETTLERS in Van Diemen's Land came to a strange and alien place. It was a mountainous island, so mountainous and rugged that much of it was obviously worthless. As well, it was largely covered by such tall, dense forests that it would take immense effort to make it productive. Even the trees of these forests were not the kind which the newcomers could readily accept: they did not spread graceful branches and offer kindly shade, but instead were huge and untidy, their limbs growing randomly, narrow tilted leaves allowing sunlight to penetrate, trunks shedding masses of bark. Beneath them progress was hindered by rough, resilient undergrowth that tore at clothing. A forest landscape was jarring to English eyes and English senses; there had been no true, primitive forest in Britain, unaffected by human activity, since Roman times. The crowns of the eucalypts rose unevenly with here and there a gaunt white 'stag' splitting the canopy, or a ragged gap where some giant had fallen. These endless forests nurtured a strange, primitive people and an equally mysterious collection of animals and birds, the like of which few had ever encountered. The most hopeful prospects in this gray-blue landscape were offered by the grassy, tree-dotted openings resembling, as was often observed, the run-down estate of some old nobleman in the southern counties. The story of this landscape over two centuries of settlement centres largely upon these dominant forests and the settlers' attitudes to them. Within half that time the landscape would be changed almost beyond recognition.

A forested, mountainous landscape it might be, but like any other colony it had to be rendered habitable and productive. Some day, perhaps, the gentler parts of it might even be tamed to resemble the English countryside. Its usefulness was beyond question. The French appeared to have a close interest in it, as indicated by the presence of their two major expeditions under d'Entrecasteaux and Baudin. Any permanent French settlement would pose a potential threat to British trade routes to the Far East, as well as to existing colonies and future interests in the Pacific. The island was an ideal location for a penal settlement, isolated away at the other end of the earth, where unlimited numbers of convicts from the crowded hulks might work out their salvation in the forests. And those very forests might well provide sturdy spars and timbers for British ships in a developing frontier of the Empire.

The colonists came in order to use the island and whatever it could produce. They settled it without recognising any prior claim by its Aboriginal inhabitants, and assumed without question their right to occupy every part of it and to change it however they saw fit. The Aborigines were at once subject to British law, and similarly the land itself was viewed as one in which the application of traditional methods and perceptions would result in a colony which was subdued and brought to resemble the model of

Britain herself. The assumed right to use, to change and to re-order was at the heart of the settlers' relationship with the land, and it applied to people of every station in the society from Governor to convict, landowner to stockkeeper. To the settler, the right to use land in any way he pleased was simply a natural assumption, not even consciously considered. The right to dispose of land has always been a basic tenet of belief in western society; God had given mankind the use of the land to make it productive and to shape it for man's purposes. This authority was naturally vested in the Crown, giving it the power to possess a country which did not apparently belong to a civilised people, and to use it for the benefit of those who settled it: it was theirs to do with as they chose.

The majority of those who formed the early settlements saw little beauty and little worthy of preserving in the Tasmanian landscape. A few were, like Prinsep, influenced by the Romantic painters and poets, and could see in their surroundings some of the Romantic qualities that they admired: the prospect of mountains, long sea inlets and picturesque headlands. Most, however, retained the strong eighteenth century vision of a landscape upon which human order had been imposed and in which industry thrived. A land without a recognisable order was a challenge to the mind and senses. The colonists yearned for an open countryside with fields and hedgerows, gently flowing, willow-lined streams and pleasant woodlands. Forests of giant eucalypts cowed the spirit. This society would begin to take its place spiritually in the island after two centuries, but even then many would still feel their forebears' sense of alienation.

For nearly twenty years the new arrivals had little impact upon the landscape apart from establishing and extending the two major settlements on the Derwent and Tamar. During this time the bridgeheads were being consolidated. A cart track crossed the midland plain from south to north linking the two small townships; expeditions ventured inland as far as the

Central Plateau and the coasts were explored. Land was taken up across some of the clear country, the former hunting-grounds of the midlands and the large valleys, where outposts were set up which would eventually become towns and villages. But the great expanse of forest beyond was not yet challenged.

The major expansion began in the early 1820s with the success of wool shipments to Britain, which led in turn to the arrival of increasing numbers of sheep. In the next two decades the selectors pushed west up the tributaries of the Derwent, east along the South Esk, up the plain of the east coast and into the north-east, and beside the middle reaches of the Meander and Mersey. In the period to 1820 about seventy thousand acres had been allocated by the Crown to selectors in the form of grants, most of this being within easy access of Hobart and Launceston. By 1833 a further two million acres had been granted.[1] The Aboriginal survivors were removed to Flinders Island, allowing the flocks to be pastured without hindrance on all grassed land in the island. This occupation steadily changed the landscape. Over a few years, timber on the runs was pushed back as more of the flats and hillsides were taken up. The thud of axes, the rasp of cross-cut saws and the smoke of clearing fires were the inevitable accompaniments to pioneering life. At the same time the coarse native grasses were burned and ploughed, to be replaced by English pasture until the settled districts began to bear some resemblance to the green country which the new Tasmanians had left behind. Many of the settlers felt drawn to their land, even in the very early years. The hard, unremitting toil involved in taming the stubborn native ground and making it into agricultural land, the seasonal rituals of sowing and harvesting, of caring for flocks and living on the land itself, gave them a deep attachment to it. Even its clear light, the shapes of its hills and sharp contrasts of plain and forest began to lose some of their strangeness.

Once they had moved from the rough bark huts which had been the first structures on the selections, and had settled into more permanent homes, people longed for reminders of the places they had left. The families in paling and shingle cottages planted useful fruit trees with perhaps a holly or a few pines as a shelter from the wind. Their more prosperous neighbours who had broader acres and a handsome sandstone home sought to change their surroundings, so that they could look out upon homely, familiar English trees and an English garden. A formal carriageway was lined with elms, oaks or pines which would eventually

'... *people longed for reminders of the places they had left:*'
Redlands, Plenty, an island of English trees (author).

arch across it, shielding it from the warm southern sun and providing a deeply shaded approach to the house. Around the house itself were more English trees and shrubs, lawns, borders and flower-beds, divided by gravel paths and terraces. Louisa Meredith described in loving detail the garden of 'Cambria', one of the pioneer estates of the east coast, as it appeared on her arrival in 1840:

> The noble veranda into which the French windows of the front rooms open, with its pillars wreathed about with roses and jasmine, and its lower trellises hidden in luxuriant geraniums, became the especial abiding-place of my idleness ...
>
> A large garden and orchard, well stored with the flowers and fruits cultivated in England, were not among the least of the charms 'Cambria' possessed in my eyes ...[2]

The garden was an island, a protective sanctuary where eye and spirit could rest, away from the sharp forms and penetrating light of the surrounding country.

Once the grasslands and open forest of the eastern half of the island had been taken up, the only way to acquire land was by embarking upon the laborious task of clearing the forest. The districts that grew the giant trees of the north-west, north-east and south-east were some of the most fertile in the island, the red soils of the first two formed by the breaking down of the basalt sheet. The great forests which the early settlers had despaired of ever clearing were now found to grow upon the most promising agricultural land. So by the 1840s there began a relentless drive to push back the palisades of trees, a drive which, in its many forms, has continued into the present time. Along the north-west coast tiny settlements sprang up at the river mouths away from the lands already occupied by the Van Diemen's Land Company. The Don, Leven, Duck, Blythe and a dozen other little inlets and estuaries became beachheads in the war to win land from the forests. The timber itself was valuable, though only a fraction was saved, and during the 1840s and 1850s it formed one of the island's foremost exports, as huge quantities of palings, shingles and other timber were shipped from the north-west aboard tiny schooners and ketches to build much of early Melbourne. When the Victorian goldfields exploded into life in the 1850s the demand for timber was insatiable; many a strong young sawyer earned far better money cutting and splitting in the north-west forests than his companions who sailed off to make their fortunes on the diggings of Ballarat or Castlemaine.

As the forests began to fall back, the first crops went into the ground beneath the ashes of the burned undergrowth. To many, the task of winning a place from the forests seemed overwhelming; the tiny clearings grew with constant work from dawn to dark, day after day for months, even years. The perseverance and courage of the pioneering generation on the edge of the forests were legendary, often rewarded with little more than subsistence, at least for a long time. In many cases it was the second and third generations of families who benefited from their efforts.

Fire was one of the most effective weapons used by the land-clearers against the forests. To remove the dense undergrowth and understorey species with axe, saw and scrub-hook without the aid of fire cost enormous time and effort. Commonly the first step in clearing areas which were not first cut over by the timber millers was to ringbark all of the larger trees. The smaller species were then quickly lopped and the undergrowth fired. The unburned debris was piled into heaps for burning later when it had dried, or was allowed to rot. The fire left an ash bed which was turned into the soil before sowing. This method ensured that the first crop was in the ground within months of a selector's moving onto his block. Often these scrub fires went far beyond the land that they were intended to clear, devastating miles of surrounding forest, a consequence not seen as detrimental by men struggling to carve a place for settlement in the endless masses of trees. A contemporary writer described, for the benefit of intending immigrants, the process of clearing a selector's land; he did not attempt to disguise the difficulties:

> It is heavy clearing in the aggregate of sections - what is locally known as 'scrub'; but the term is not appropriate, and is apt to mislead a stranger. Scrub includes tree ferns 15ft high; a variety of the smaller timber species known as musk, dogwood, sassafras, teatree, & c, with butts 6in diameter, and

'... the demand for timber was insatiable ...'
Timber tram, Don Valley, c1870 (author's collection).

20ft to 30ft high; underneath is often a labyrinth of small deadwood of this kind in all stages of decay. Over this growth of scrub tower the gum species (Eucalypti) reaching a height of 200ft to 300ft, trunks 3ft to 6ft diameter, with bare stems 60ft to 100ft up, and comparatively little expanse of branch ... The heavy timber in clearing operations is rung; the scrub is felled in the spring, left where it falls for the summer months, and burned in the autumn, without previous handling. The 'burn off' is the event on which the prospects of the settler hinges for success as regards a good beginning, the timber left after a fire sometimes entailing a large amount of labour to pile into heaps when the autumn rains set in ... the ashes make a good seed bed for grasses without other preparation.[3]

Once they had become established, the early farming districts which had been won from the forests in this way were marked by large numbers of huge ringbarked eucalypts towering like white spires across the hillsides or lying like fallen giants in all directions. Many of the settlements of the north-west and north-east carried these reminders of pioneering days until well into the twentieth century. The dead trees posed a danger in every wind as limbs and sections of trunks crashed into fields or even fell across barns and other structures. Edward Braddon purchased a small, run-down property on the hillside above the village of Forth with a sweeping view of the coast, but the task of clearing the logs and standing trees challenged even his lively spirit:

Hard work is before us to clear those paddocks of the logs that now lie here and there upon them, and in the gaunt white trees that are still standing there is ample labour for the future. Standing at one of our gates and looking across the slope that rises from it southwards, I counted over a hundred of those weird gums that stand around and about our house, and all of these must come down upon our fields in the course of years. One giant of about 350 feet, looks as if it would "drop in upon us" in our cottage home some day. What a house-warming it would give us! We are not worse off than other people here-away in this respect. The white gum trunks are to be seen by the hundred on every farm and every hill and vale of Forth. The country around us looks like a depot for Titan telegraph-posts; but I find one gets used to their presence on the scene, and does not, after a time, look upon them as such terrible eyesores. The landscapes to be seen everywhere along the NW coast are exquisitely beautiful in spite of the vertical white lines that streak them.[4]

As was the case in many other parts of Australia, land-clearing resulted in overkill and the needless destruction of thousands of trees in each district which would not only have served as valuable timber eventually, but would also have provided shelter, shade and retention of ground water. Too often this young society saw the native trees as an enemy obstructing the onward march of progress and settlement, fit only to be vanquished with fire and saw. Braddon himself was aware of the destructive nature of this widespread clearance:

> By clearing gradually [the settler] would avoid one error into which settlers have fallen - the error of ringing trees without sufficient consideration of the advisability of killing them off. In many instances the trees upon the hills about the Forth, that have been ringed, would have been better left alone. The land upon which they stand will never grow any crop but grass, and the grass would have benefited by the slight shelter of the green trees, and the moisture retained by the living tree roots, more than enough to

compensate for the drain of the trees upon the land for sustenance. This wholesale ringing of trees upon the hills must affect the water-supply, and unquestionably it detracts from the beauty of the scenery.[5]

For sixty years between the 1830s and 1890s the clearing of forests proceeded steadily, and during this period the Tasmanian landscape underwent greater change than in any time before the present. It was cleared for crop-land, for good pasture and back runs. Some of the land which was cleared was on steep hillsides or on ill-drained flats, or was composed of soils so poor that the land was useless and was allowed to overgrow with bracken and blackberry. Indiscriminate burning also continued throughout this period, with large forest fires regularly threatening outlying farms and townships. There was little effort to control either the destruction of forest by fire or the clearing of land. No agency oversaw the protection of streams or river headwaters, nor was any regulation placed upon the harvesting of timber until almost the end of the century. It was not until the mid-1880s, with the appointment of a Conservator of Forests, that a significant move was made to regulate or restrict the destruction of forest. George Perrin's second annual report contained a comprehensive and clear-sighted set of recommendations for establishing the management of forests on a rational basis.[6] Perrin drew attention to the damage that was being caused by the removal of forest, particularly in the headwaters of the island's rivers:

> Destroy the timber in the same ratio in the next five or six decades as has been done in the past 50 or 60 years, and I venture to assert that the then condition of the rivers will considerably astonish persons who have seen them in their prime, when the rich soil which, in the course of a few years, may be or had been producing grand crops, will be precipitated into the rivers and form the mud-banks ...

He was especially severe on the treatment of the headwaters of the Tamar, Mersey and Leven:

> Continue the deforestation process a few years more along the banks of the Mersey, and cut down the timber on its headwaters, and plenty of employment will be found for half a dozen of Messrs Kennedy & Sons' steam dredgers in future years.

Very little action resulted from the Conservator's report, even though Edward Braddon was Minister for Lands and Works, and knew from his own experience of the waste of valuable forest. Perrin himself had to spend most of his time in the field, often on arduous journeys along bush tracks and visiting remote timber mills and mining leases. So poorly resourced was he that he even lost the use of his one small room in the Lands Office, "'jumped' by the Mining Department", and his documents, correspondence and professional library deteriorated in a musty cupboard. It is not surprising that he accepted almost immediately the position of Conservator of Forests for the Colony of Victoria.

For the next decade, despite Perrin's warnings, the destruction of forests continued unabated. Added to the wasteful clearing and casual firing of forests in the farming regions of the island, the major mining districts of the west coast, which had been developing rapidly through the 1880s, contributed to the destruction process by the complete stripping of timber from mining leases and burning of vegetation on a massive scale. The year 1896 proved particularly bad for fires throughout the state. To a great extent the outlook of the earliest settlers still prevailed in people's attitudes to the forests. Subconsciously, Tasmanians had never regarded them as being expendable; the forests seemed so vast and so intractable that no effort should be spared in reducing them and bringing all of the arable land into production. Many people still found forest trees uncomfortable, even threatening. They stood as a living affront to a society which had for so many generations in other lands accepted fields and small woods and open countryside as being the proper order of a civilised country. Even the substantial benefits which properly managed forests could generate were largely ignored, despite the very early development of a timber-milling and export industry. In districts where milling had taken place there was no system in hand to foster regeneration or to harvest in rotation, and many areas of milled forest, particularly in the south-east, had become badly degraded.

By 1898 it was obvious to some that a desperate situation existed. If the remaining forests were to retain any value for the Crown, a rational system of protection, regulation and plantation establishment would have to be introduced. Surveyor-General Edward Counsel, an experienced bushman and capable administrator, reported to Braddon on the current state of the forests.[7] He pointed out that:

> ... extensive forests growing right out to the shipping ports ... have been 'worked out' for miles and miles inland without ... advantage to the Treasury.

He also drew attention to the '... considerable demolition of timber ... by reason of the extra prevalence of spreading fires.' His major concern, though, lay with the practices prevalent in the west coast mining districts, with which he was personally familiar. There, he reported:

> ... there is a wholesale and reckless destruction of the forest growth, young and old, by bush fires in all directions during many months of the year, whilst there is no constituted authority at the present time to prevent the lighting of such fires ...

Counsel recommended the proclamation of forest reserves, the introduction of a royalty system, protection of regrowth, and 'stringent measures' to eliminate the lighting of bushfires. He also suggested that a further report be obtained from a 'specialist in Forestry' in another colony, almost certainly with George Perrin in mind. Braddon, by now Premier, wasted no time in securing Perrin's services from the Government of Victoria.

It had been eleven years since Perrin made his first report. On his return to Tasmania he saw at once that the situation of the island's forests had deteriorated in the very ways he had predicted:

> The condition of Tasmanian forests is infinitely worse today than it was at the day of my Report in 1886-7. Another decade of waste, of private monopoly, of fierce bush fires, of neglect by the Government ... must ultimately result in disaster ... Indeed, lack of that supervision I then advocated has already led ... (through) waste, vandalism and the preventable ravages of fires, to the destruction of so much valuable timber ... No further time should be lost in taking steps to save from reckless destruction the valuable forests of Tasmania.[8]

In his report, submitted in May 1898, George Perrin pulled no punches. He divided the island into eight regions and summarised the situation in each one. He began by looking at the Huon district, the southern forests, which had been and continue to be, the heartland of the timber industry. The picture was depressing:

> Where formerly stood magnificent blue gums in the 'beds' at Geeveston, Port Esperance, Lady's Bay and Hastings are but the remnants of fine forests wrecked and decimated by indiscriminate felling and lack of proper care.

No attempt at reproduction has been made or care taken to control the bush fires which every two or three years have destroyed the young trees as they sprang up, and hence ruin and desolation mark the sites of forests which have supplied immense quantities of splendid timber.

In point of fact, the Huon district is practically worked out. Year by year it is found necessary to extend the tramways further and further inland from the mills, and very shortly the whole of the accessible timber which is found on a strip of land running back from the coast for from 5 to 12 miles will be stripped to the dividing range.

In the north-west and north-east the situation was little better. About the headstreams of the Forth:

> ... as in the Huon, the ring-barker and saw-miller have worked havoc, and fine forests, which should have been permanently reserved by the State, are in the hands of the selectors.

George Perrin's harshest censure, however, was directed at the wholesale destruction of forest on the west coast mining fields. In the Pieman Valley, where Huon and King William pine formerly were plentiful, 'As all along the West Coast, the miners have made sad havoc among the trees.' Of the area from Heemskirk through to Mt Lyell he concluded:

> All through, however, indiscriminate felling and fierce bush fires have already destroyed large quantities of the useful timber I saw in this district ten years ago, and have completely changed the face of the country.

The miners let nothing stand in their way when either prospecting or clearing a claim, and Perrin's comments on the mining community slated this narrow pursuit of their own interests at the cost of the country:

> The presence of the miner on the West Coast has, of course, resulted in the usual gross carelessness and sometimes malicious vandalism ... Miners, as a rule, are bumptious individuals with reference to their supposed 'rights', but when, under cover of 'miners' rights', the holders by wantonly and wastefully destroying living forests occasion great national loss, the State ought to step in ... In order to clear prospecting claims it is quite an ordinary custom for the prospector to set fire to the timber and let the flames spread at will over as much of the surrounding country as they can reach.
>
> This is ignorantly regarded as a creditable and serviceable exploit in 'clearing the country' ...

Perrin's criticism is borne out by the records of exploring and prospecting parties which routinely fired the country. On his gold-seeking expedition early in 1859, W A Tully lit fires that burned out the Collingwood Valley and spread into the Raglan Range and the ridges near Pyramid Mountain and Rocky Hill; he and his men were almost trapped by their own fires. When C P Sprent first entered the Pieman Valley in March 1876, he 'had the satisfaction of seeing a grand fire sweeping everything before it.'[9] In the following year Sprent burned Dempster Plains. Even some of those who responded to the beauty of the western country, such as the artist W C Piguenit and his friend Colonel Legge, were not above lighting an occasional fire. Having enjoyed a splendid day on the summit of Mt Olympus early in 1887, they lit the button grass of the Cuvier Valley on their return, and:

... a huge fire sprung up at night and burned all the following day, so the next pedestrians who ascend Olympus will have better walking than we had.[10]

It was simply the custom of the time.

Perrin's report, like Counsel's, was accompanied by strong, clear recommendations for establishing government control of the island's forests, including a royalty system, gazetting of state reserves, protection against fire, and the training of forest officers. From this time, forestry began to be established on a professional basis and the timber industry regulated, both to the immense benefit of the state, though land clearance and timber harvesting would continue to be matters of major concern.

By the end of the first century of settlement, the effects of land clearance, widespread burning, and stripping for mining had changed the landscape over a very large part of the island. It was fire that continued to be the foremost agent of change, and as access to more remote regions became easier more forest, heathland, alpine country and coastal woodland were subjected to frequent burning. With an increasing population, every summer became a bushfire period unless conditions were unusually wet. Ironically, 1898, the very year of George Perrin's report, was a year of severe fires. But only exceptionally bad years were noted in the records, summers when fires were either very widespread or menaced populated districts. 1914, 1915, 1927, 1934, 1951, 1959, 1961, 1967 ... the destructive fire years were faithfully recorded, though the intervening years also saw fire in some parts of the island. Attitudes to fire in scrub or forest country have been casual, even in quite recent times, and 'burning off' has been a common and widely accepted practice in all rural areas. The Solicitor-General's report on the 1967 fires made the comment that:

The practice had grown up over the years of permitting fires in bush and scrub country to 'burn free' so long as they were not menacing lives or property. ... it was not considered economic or necessary to combat such fires.[11]

It is often argued that wildfires are a natural and necessary part of the process of renewal and regeneration in the forest cycle, providing canopy space and an ash-bed which enable eucalypt seedlings to survive and eventually replace trees which have reached the climax of their growth, ensuring that a forest does not degrade. This is true of situations in which controlled burning is carried out in appropriate conditions and at carefully determined intervals. Wildfires are rarely started by natural agents. Lightning strikes do cause fires, but usually in Tasmania electrical storms are accompanied by significant rain, which quenches any fire before hot spots develop. Bushfires are properly called wildfires: they are 'wild' in every sense. Some are lit accidentally or result from misjudgement, usually as 'escapes' from camp-fires, burning off or regeneration burns. By far the greatest proportion are lit deliberately and maliciously to destroy bushland or to provide a spectacle, or in the mistaken belief that fire somehow 'does the country good'.

Hardy, fire-adapted species such as eucalypts, tea-tree and button grass can tolerate and even benefit from fire. The damage occurs when such fires are so hot that tall forest trees are destroyed; most eucalypt forest now has its quota of gaunt white 'stags' standing well above the present canopy, indicating the height and grandeur of the former forest. The removal of undergrowth and understorey species can leave the ground unprotected, and on steep slopes this often leads to damaging erosion. The resultant soil disturbance can also, when relatively close to farmland, roads or human habitation, assist invasion by exotic species such as blackberry, thistle, ragwort and gorse. A succession of fires will destroy regrowth and can badly degrade former forest. In Tasmania, a fire does not have to spread far before it destroys plants and communities which are not fire-adapted. Thus King William and Huon pine have been wiped out in many western valleys, King William and pencil pine in the mountains. Once a fire penetrates the higher country its consequences are particularly devastating, as it destroys species which have virtually no tolerance, burning through the root systems and even stripping the layer of peat and soil that covers the rocks. The worst examples are seen on the peaks of the West Coast Range close to Queenstown, but areas of the Plateau have suffered the same fate. Fire that extends into rainforest often leads to the replacement of rainforest species by eucalypts and other colonisers. Rainforest can regenerate, but only if it is remote from eucalypt seeding and usually in regions which have high rainfall throughout the year.

The recognition of some areas of high landscape or ecological value by including them in national parks, reserves, World Heritage or conservation areas has provided a degree of protection from fire. Over the past fifty years, fires have occurred even in many of these, damaging sensitive locations such as The Labyrinth, Mt Olympus, Mt Rufus, Frenchmans Cap, several parts of the Central Plateau, Port Davey, Freycinet Peninsula, the Denison Range and Rocky Cape. Fires are frequent along the Lyell Highway. Methods of prevention and control, in particular those introduced since 1967, have resulted in some lessening of wildfire frequency. It is also possible that public perceptions of fire and of the natural environment are gradually changing and that there is less of a tendency to set alight to forest. There are, however, sufficient people who wish to create the spectacle of fire, or who have some antagonism to the preservation of native vegetation, to provide sources of fire whenever conditions are hot, dry and windy. Apart from clearing for agriculture, settlement and forest harvesting, fire has been by far the greatest agent of change acting upon the Tasmanian landscape since white settlement. Over the two centuries it has had a considerable effect in every region. If even the present frequency and distribution of wildfire are sustained into the twenty-first century, the future of the remaining forest landscape, especially of old-growth eucalypt forest, rainforest and highland shrublands, will be exceedingly bleak.

Other changes to forest landscape have come at an increasing pace in the second half of the twentieth century through developments in the timber industry itself. As an island containing large tracts of forest, Tasmania has had a rich timber resource, first exploited by convict gangs on Mt Wellington, the Tasman Peninsula and the Huon estuary. Huon pine was exported in the early years of the colony, soon followed by hardwood, and from the 1840s there was a lively trade in palings and other building timber to Victoria. The amount of timber harvested has always been surplus to the island's needs, so that a potential for export has always existed. The fine hardwoods of the great climax eucalypt forests found a ready market, at first in the other colonies, and later in Europe and North America. Once the industry had begun to be regulated in the early years of the twentieth century it was supported by a reserves system and protection of regrowth forests. By 1965–66 nearly six hundred and sixty-eight million super feet of hardwoods were being harvested annually from the various forest areas throughout the state. Most of this timber was destined for use in building, either in Tasmania or at its export destinations. A relatively small quantity was converted to pulp for paper-making to supply the three mills existing or nearing completion at that time: ANM at Boyer, APPM at Burnie and Wesley Vale, and APM at Geeveston.

When it operated under strict control this system represented a rational and moderate use of forest resources. Logging was largely selective, so that a forest retained its integrity, its original species mix and diversity of plant and animal species. The landscape suffered a low level of intrusion, and forest areas were sufficiently large to allow full species movement and diversity. Much of the timber was used in various forms of downstream processing, and that not used locally formed a high quality export. It was shortly after the mid-1960s that the export of pulpwood was initiated, an aspect of the industry that was to grow rapidly over the last three decades of the century and which was to impact significantly upon the forest landscape of the island. The former selective harvesting could have been contained within relatively small areas of forest, and progressively moved out of old-growth native forest to be based largely upon plantation timber. The change to a high-volume woodchip-based industry created a demand for very large areas of forest, and led to the use of more efficient harvesting methods. When it was introduced, harvesting for woodchips was presented purely as a method of 'utilising' the low-grade timber and debris hitherto left behind after securing saw-logs. As the Forestry Commissioners expressed it in 1964:

> The increased demand for pulpwood has led to the utilisation of trees and timber that would otherwise have been wasted.[12]

With increasing demand for woodchips from overseas markets, extensive concessions were granted to major companies, often to the detriment of small, selective timber mills. Forest which was to be harvested was surveyed into sections, or coupes, and each was clear-felled. The saw-logs and veneer logs were sent to be milled, some of the minor species went to specialist mills and craft workers, the remainder was taken for chipping. At the end of harvesting the coupe was burned and seeded, the original forest range of species often being replaced with a commercially desirable monoculture. Specialised chip-loading facilities were constructed at ports such as Triabunna, Longreach and Burnie, where mountains of chips were stockpiled. Huge bulk-carriers called at these ports to take loads of woodchips to destinations in various Asian countries. By the 1990s purchasing countries such as Japan, which had access to vast quantities of timber from the poorly regulated forests of developing countries, gained a strong economic hold over world marketing and were able to force the harvesting companies to produce larger volumes of woodchips from ever better quality timber at progressively lower prices. Tasmania had become dependent upon large-volume woodchip exports, and had little choice but to yield to 'market pressures'.

Harvesting became a highly mechanised process. Access roads were built rapidly with the aid of heavy earth-moving machines, and networks of these roads spread deep into the forests of the timber districts. The Hampshire and Surrey Hills became a large tree-farm, stretching for many kilometres across the country. Felling and haulage were undertaken more efficiently than had been the case in the past. In the late 1950s the extraction of timber had been revolutionised by the advent of the chain-saw, the increased availability of the bulldozer and of versatile motor transport, all of which enabled small, skilled teams to fell and remove quantities of timber which even a large workforce could not have obtained in the 1930s. Improvements continued to be made to equipment and techniques, with the development of machines for harvesting, stripping and loading logs. Cable-logging made it possible to remove timber from very steep slopes which previously had been inaccessible. As well as the physical and ecological effects of removing forest from these slopes, this form of logging created a considerable visual impact, the bare hillsides being even more intrusive upon the landscape than other clear-felled coupes. By 1994–95 pulpwood production from native forest alone had reached one point eight million tonnes annually. The levels of production of both millable timber and pulpwood will be sustained for at least twenty years by virtue of the Regional Forest Agreement between the state and Commonwealth governments. This Agreement has been designed to preserve fully the harvesting levels of the forest industries, considered vital to governments which still see the state's economic future as dependent upon continuing exploitation of natural resources. At the same time the Agreement attempts to address in part the growing concern of scientists and ecologists at the long-term effects of such large-scale harvesting of native forests.

Forest harvesting of this magnitude has brought about substantial changes to the island's landscape. These changes have not been restricted to remoter areas or those deep within forested valleys and mountain ranges. State forests close to settlements, farmlands and roads have been clear-felled, and woodchipping contracts have proved attractive to owners of forest on private land, as these present both an immediate financial return and an effective method of land clearance. Thus many of the attractive stands and pockets of remaining bushland disappeared from farming districts during the 1980s and 1990s. Clear-felling and seeding have not generally resulted in the eventual restoration of the original forest. Naturally, there cannot be an age-mix of trees. The towering climax eucalypts which were once a feature of forest landscapes are becoming increasingly rare, restricted to a small number of parks and reserves; much remaining old-growth forest lies outside permanent reserves. Some of the areas cleared were originally covered either by pure rainforest or by mixed forest, with rainforest species providing the understorey in wet sclerophyll forest. These will most likely become eucalypt forest in time, particularly if rotation rates of eighty to one hundred years are maintained. Extensive areas are being re-sown as plantations. Pine plantations have been established in Tasmania since the 1930s and provide a valuable source of softwoods; although an exotic feature in the landscape, the pines take some pressure away from native forests. By the 1990s new plantations tended to be composed of eucalypts, which contribute little to landscape values, being monocultures of uniform age planted in rows as tree-farms. Forest that has been designated for future saw-log harvesting has also been affected by the process of thinning, in which smaller trees and saplings are cleared to allow the remaining trees accelerated growth. The harvesting of substantial areas of native forest has the potential to create other problems in the future. The extensive networks of roads, many of which are open to the public, inevitably increase the probability of accidental and deliberate wildfires in locations where these will be difficult to control and which lie close to sensitive wilderness areas. They also increase the possibility of the spread of pathogens such as *Phytophthora cinnamomi* to vulnerable native species. There is no means at present of assessing the long-term effects of large-scale clearance and replacement of the island's native forests on water flow and retention, on climate and on biodiversity. All of these have implications for the landscape.

The rate of clearance of native forest in Tasmania still exceeds replanting. According to the report of the Bureau of Rural Sciences released in April 1999 after a three-year study using satellite imagery, the major causes of clearance in the period 1990–1995 were forestry operations (27,270 ha) and plantation establishment (8,270 ha) rather than farming activities (4,000 ha). The total area of land cleared each year is currently averaging close to 10,000 ha. Relative to Tasmania's small area, this places its rate of clearance ahead of all other states at 0.295%.

As early as the 1970s some foresters were aware of increasing concern on the part of a public becoming steadily better informed about forest issues, and more likely to express that concern through representative bodies. This concern was focussed not only upon ecological matters such as biodiversity, soil disturbance, drainage and stream degradation, but also upon such wider questions as the declining amount of native forest, the long-term effects of the loss of forest on water and climate, and the loss of visual amenity in the landscape. The initial response to these concerns was to introduce strategies to minimise the visual impact of clear-felling, regeneration burns, roading and quarrying. A speaker at an industry symposium in 1972 described the 'emotional reactions' of people to harvesting methods and suggested that a cosmetic response was appropriate, 'Much can and must be done to minimise the aesthetic shock of harvesting...'[13]

Amongst the methods advocated were the avoidance of clear-felling near tourist roads, provision of 'screening strips' alongside roads in harvesting areas, and planting for regeneration in 'sensitive' places. The answer to community concern at that time was to hide or diminish visual effects. These methods were expanded throughout the 1980s and 1990s as public reaction to the large-scale clearance of native forest intensified. Disquiet was expressed not only through the conservation movement but also by many people with no particular conservation commitment, by means of letters to the press, comments on talk-back radio and through a variety of other avenues. Amongst these voices were those of visitors whose impressions were vital to Tasmania's tourism industry. While governments showed little inclination to address the cause of community concern or to review the policy of forest clearance, professional foresters responded to changing attitudes by employing an even wider range of strategies to divert attention from clear-felling and other operations. A manual produced in 1990 offered an extraordinary classification of landscape values in the island and set out detailed procedures for 'landscaping' areas of clear-felling so that they would be less noticeable from likely viewpoints.[14]

Hopefully, at the beginning of the new century, the state will develop a more far-sighted and sensitive approach not only to expressions of concern but also to the issues which have rightly generated this concern, and will recognise the close dependence of the community on the ecological future and the landscape values of native forests which, in very wide and important ways, belong to the community.

Ultimately, it will not be professional foresters and others working in the industry, nor a government department, nor even the multinational resource companies, that will be responsible for the cumulative effects of large-scale forest harvesting on the island's landscape quality. These will depend upon the long-term direction of the state's economy and on the way of life of its people. Forests are not inexhaustible, nor are they growing simply to be farmed and harvested. Their value to the community far exceeds their economic worth, and this value must eventually be added to the economic equation.

The mining industry has left the island with less widespread though more concentrated degradation, in spite of having played a major role in its economic development. Mining of coal began at Saltwater River in 1834, and coal has been extracted from various sites ever since, the major mines being located in the South Esk Valley. The mining of metal ores, however, has been of far greater economic importance, and of more significance in its effects upon the landscape. Although gold was discovered at Lefroy, east of the Tamar, as early as 1849, substantial fields were not developed until the 1870s, at places such as Mangana, Waterhouse and Beaconsfield. The Tasmania Mine opened at Beaconsfield in 1878. Tin was also mined at many alluvial sites throughout the north-east from the 1870s, including productive fields at Gladstone, Derby and Weldborough. Alluvial mining has continued on several fields into recent years and quite extensive scars remain near the foot of Mt Cameron, along the Ringarooma River and at various other sites. These may yet be rehabilitated.

The west coast fields were the largest and the most important for the state. Mt Bischoff, the 'Mountain of Tin', discovered by James 'Philosopher' Smith in 1871, was worked profitably for over seventy years. Its success provided the impetus for intensive prospecting on the west coast, and over the next three decades fields mushroomed at Heemskirk, Zeehan, the King River and Mt Lyell.

The miners of old had little concern for the effects of their labours upon their immediate surroundings, or upon the environment generally. There were difficulties enough to contend with, in the struggle to live in lonely camps in harsh and remote country, and to win ore from the cramped, wet shafts of the western mines. They believed they were serving their country through their efforts; the notion of protecting the bleak, scrubby region in which they worked would have been quite inconceivable to them. It is only in the last few decades that the industry has become sensitive to its ecological and aesthetic impacts, and that legal obligations have been put in place to ensure high standards of environmental integrity and landscape rehabilitation. During the major period of mining on the western fields the mining companies' priorities lay in obtaining their ore by the most direct and practicable means, concentrating or smelting it wherever this was most convenient, and returning the best possible dividends to their shareholders. A seared, scarred landscape was a sign of extensive workings, and if not of profitable mines, at least of energetic managers who were sparing no effort to develop the mines.

At the birthplace of western mining, Mt Bischoff, the mountain still bears deep scars in the eroded faces and gullies where the rich cassiterite was sluiced. The dense scrub of the region is slowly reclaiming the bare gravels, but this process is slow and the slopes continue to erode. The exposed yellow sides of the mountain stand out when viewed from thirty kilometres to the east. Further south, above the town of Rosebery, the summit of Mt Read has been scored by exploration tracks as companies probed the highly mineralised rocks. Many of these tracks are on steep slopes, and the heavy western rainfall causes severe gullying. A program of rehabilitation has now been instigated. The route of the Hercules haulage, disused since the late 1980s, remains unvegetated, as does the site of Williamsford township in the valley near the foot of the haulage. A planting program following closure would have ensured that some of the original native species returned and competed with exotic plants which are inevitable relics of town sites. Hopefully, the Hercules Mine open cut high on the mountainside will eventually be rehabilitated, a major undertaking in itself. For large mines, Rosebery and Renison Bell have created relatively little intrusion upon the landscape. In the past, the banks of the Pieman River almost to its mouth were thickly silted by mine tailings, but effective tailings dams at Rosebery now retain this material. The surroundings of Zeehan, once covered variously by eucalypt forest, tea-tree, rainforest and button grass, is still a scrubby, depressing light-industrial site fifty years after the last mine ceased operation. Churned-over flats, old tailings dumps and evidence of more recent prospecting activity are obvious in all directions. The devastating wildfire of 1985 which burned out an extensive section of the northern west coast brought a further setback to the recovery of the town's surroundings. The nearby site of Dundas has been more fortunate, having had a far shorter life as a town. Forest has reclaimed most of the old workings, leaving a grassy clearing and a few pine trees as evidence of where the town stood. In a number of localities such as the Tyndall Range, vehicle tracks have been left to disfigure the landscape, their courses deeply scoured by water. These are most noticeable in the open country south of Macquarie Harbour, where many hundreds of kilometres of tracks twist through the hills, their exposed white gravel starkly evident from a great distance. No rehabilitation has been attempted, even of the airstrip.

The earliest prospectors and miners who worked the alluvial gold of the Linda Valley marvelled at its beauty. From the first wooden huts the lightly timbered slopes rose steeply towards the summit of Mt Owen. On the upper part of the mountain there were King William and cheshunt pines, and the dark green of alpine vegetation offset the delicate pink of the summit rocks. Miners would sit outside their huts on a fine evening enjoying the sight of the late sun upon the mountain. Nearby, the Queen Valley was filled with ancient rainforest so dense that Gould's party took nearly four days to cut a rough track across it to Howard's Plain in 1862. The Mount Lyell Copper Mine began life in 1892, with its first workings at the Iron Blow at the head of the Linda Valley, and its smelter in the Queen Valley. By 1897 the smelter was in full operation, and from this time the sulphur-laden fumes, carried by the prevailing westerly winds, began to kill the vegetation on the flanks of Mt Lyell and Mt Owen. Summer often brings long periods of fine weather, even on the west coast, and it was not long before fires raced through the dry, dead trees and undergrowth, burning the peaty soil down to the rocks. The heavy rains of the western winters sent masses of water cascading down the bare slopes, and without vegetation to moderate the flow or roots to hold the surface together, the water gouged deep gullies and eroded the slopes, so that plants had little hope of regaining a hold even when smelting methods changed. Over a century the Queenstown community has become attached to the bare, tortured hillsides, and resists attempts to revegetate them, though visitors are shocked at the sight of the denuded landscape and the area has become an emblem of the consequences of destructive mining methods of the past. Even here, however, there are some hopeful signs for the future. New methods of treating mine tailings by recent mine operators have resulted in an improvement to the Queen River, once an industrial sewer and one of the most heavily polluted streams in Australia. Wattles are spreading across the lower flats and gullies where a little soil has accumulated, and even on the hillsides there are occasional hardy specimens of the *Juncus* rush and other colonisers. Still the erosion continues. Perhaps one day, revegetation may be encouraged and assisted, so that these hills, which have provided such riches, may be given back their natural cover, and their beauty may be seen once more.

A legacy of settlement, land clearance, fire and soil disturbance has been the introduction of many species of exotic plants, some of which have become significant features of landscape wherever post-Aboriginal activity has taken place. The colonists brought their carts, ploughs and other implements, which invariably carried seeds. Horses, stock and birds ensured that these spread rapidly. Even now, cars, trucks, bulldozers and other machinery are active agents in distributing these plants. Close to towns, garden refuse is commonly dumped in bushland, and in even quite remote areas off-road vehicles spread seeds and pathogens. Some exotics were deliberately introduced from the earliest times by individuals and by 'acclimatisation' societies dedicated to adding familiar European features to an alien land. Obvious in many landscapes are willow, which lines and clogs streams in settled districts, and blackberry, an opportunistic invader of damp gullies and hillsides. Worst of all, perhaps, is gorse, a most difficult plant to eradicate, which has colonised whole paddocks and established itself along stream banks, roads and railways throughout the island, its bright orange blossoms following timber tracks deep into west coast forests. It was planted originally by pioneer east coast settlers to form hedges around their paddocks, together with hawthorn. Briar, hawthorn, cotoneaster, pampas, thistle, dock ... the list is a long one, with most of the invaders proving well adapted to Tasmanian conditions. It is now common to find dandelion, thistle and ragwort in the high, fragile regions of the Central Plateau.

Tasmania has always struggled to maintain its economic viability. Its area, particularly its limited extent of arable land, its small population and its isolation from mainland and overseas markets have all combined to reduce its ability to compete with the larger and more populous states. This is in spite of the value of its per capita production exceeding those of its competitors, due largely to the strength of its mining and farming sectors. It has attracted only a small number of major industries, most of these dependent upon natural resources such as timber and minerals. Consequently there has been little intrusion upon the island's rural landscape by industrial complexes. The few cases in which industries have been sited in such a way that landscape values have been affected stand out simply because they are exceptional: the former Tioxide and Electrona plants and the Port Latta pelletising operation are amongst the foremost of these. The island suffered badly in the depressions of the 1870s, 1890s and 1930s due in part to its degree of reliance upon agriculture and its small industrial base. The depression of 1932–1939 was especially devastating, and its effects profoundly influenced contemporary and future political leaders. Albert Ogilvie, Premier from 1934 to 1939, and Robert Cosgrove who succeeded him in 1939, were determined to make Tasmania less vulnerable in times of recession, to create a broader and more stable economic and employment base, and in particular to build its industrial sector as a more certain source of employment. They were convinced that the state's future prosperity and stability lay in attracting large industries, the major incentive being the development of the state's potential for generating hydro-electricity, which would be made available at a competitive price to large users of power.

The Hydro-Electric Department had been formed in 1914, private generating stations having been built at Duck Reach near Launceston in 1895, Zeehan in 1904 and Lake Margaret in 1913. The first major operation of the new Department followed the acquisition in 1914 of the property and undertakings of Complex Ores Ltd, when the level of Great Lake was raised by the construction of a dam across its outflow at Miena. This was the first of several changes to the lake's level over five decades. When Waddamana power station began operating in May 1916, the state's process of hydro-industrialisation had commenced, though the Commission was not created until 1930. The alteration of existing lakes, the creation of new ones, the changing of stream courses and the construction of roads, canals, transmission lines and other infrastructure would bring a new force to bear upon the Tasmanian landscape over the following eighty years. Some of its proposals, notably the Lake Pedder and Franklin River schemes, would lead to widespread dissention within the community as attitudes and values changed.

Next to agricultural clearance, forest harvesting, fire and settlement, hydro-electric development has been one of the major agents of change, as well as creating an economic benefit. But it is a benefit that has come at a cost, quite apart from the long-term financial burden which the state has had to carry. Hydro-electricity is derived from a renewable energy source, and is one of the cleanest and most reliable forms of energy. It has enabled the state to attract essential industries, particularly those which are heavy power users, providing both employment and economic growth. The era of hydro construction itself created employment for a considerable workforce and gathered together communities which became a distinctive part of Tasmania's social history. The complex and extensive storage and generating system which these communities built ranks as one of the state's greatest achievements. Apart from the power it generates, the dams, roads and even settlements have served as valuable amenities, providing a wide range of recreational activities. Tourism in particular has benefited from the building of well-engineered roads to some of the island's most attractive scenic areas, and from access to the country's finest fishing. The new hydro lakes themselves are generally attractive and have been provided with appropriate picnic grounds, ramps, lookouts and other facilities.

Hydro construction has brought many benefits, but as is the case with most agents of change there have also been inherent losses and compromises. Like the forest road networks, Hydro roads provide access to regions which were previously difficult to reach. Some of these are even more fragile and vulnerable than those accessible by forestry roads, particularly in the central highlands and the south-west, and the risk of wildfire and of introduced pathogens in these places has increased considerably. The planned closure of the Mt McCall HEC road, which leads into the heart of the World Heritage Area, was blocked by Ministerial overruling of the World Heritage Area administration. The 1999 World Heritage Area Management Plan indicates that along this road there is now evidence that it has become 'extensively infected' by the dieback disease *Phytophthora cinnamomi*. There are additional pressures upon the land resulting simply from large numbers of vehicles and people entering these regions. The inevitable infrastructure and services detract from landscape values, though efforts have been made to minimise their impact. Transmission towers have been painted so that they blend with their surroundings, and some rehabilitation has taken place in gravel pits and road cuttings. Realistically, there are no measures that can hide thousands of kilometres of road, buildings, dams and other structures, or that can restore a compromised view-field.

The storages themselves intrude upon or blend with their surroundings in varying degrees, and estimates of their effects must remain to some extent subjective. Many of the smaller storages are unobtrusive, winding through narrow valleys along the courses of the upper Derwent, Forth, Mersey, Pieman and a few of their tributaries. They are generally overlooked by wooded slopes or pasture, are quite attractive and do not cover land which was ecologically significant or which formed part of an important landscape, though some of the island's mountain history lies beneath them. Meadowbank, Repulse, Catagunya, Cethana, Barrington ... each has its own particular quality, seen in conditions which complement dark waters and clear reflections. They are pleasant man-made storages, and offer no pretence to be otherwise. A few afford even greater scenic appeal; Parangana is quite dramatic, with the scarps of the Mersey Valley poised above and the blue gorge of Devils Gullet cutting the mountains to the east. Rowallen would also be attractive in its valley setting if the timber had been cleared before it was flooded. This lake covered the grassy clearing of Howells Plain, a lovely opening beside the Mersey, dominated by the cliffs and columns of Clumner Bluff, with steep, forested slopes on either side. The old hut had stood on the plain for ninety years, and generations of trappers and stockmen had lived there or stayed on their way to the mountains. In the remote upland valley between Mt Murchison and the Tyndall Range the small Lake Plimsoll was created as part of the Henty-Anthony scheme. Its access road forms an alternative to the Murchison Highway south of Tullah, climbing around the base of Murchison and winding through the button grass ridges towards the Tyndall Range. The valley was hidden and little known, but the developments have taken the peace and remoteness, the unique character, from one of the most attractive corners of the West Coast Range. How is such a loss to be measured?

A number of storages have been formed by altering existing lakes, with some inevitable loss of landscape values. The level of Great Lake has been raised on three occasions since 1914, with consequent changes to the shoreline and adjacent vegetation. Reynolds Neck was originally a narrow passage in the lake but has now widened substantially. With the raising of the level of Lake St Clair in 1952 the fine Frankland Beaches at the southern end of the lake were covered. It was from here that George Frankland described this wonderful mountain fastness when he led the first party to its shore in February 1835. In summer the beaches extended along much of the western side of the lake. On the Central Plateau several lakes have been changed, notably Augusta, Mackenzie and Sandy Lake. All were enlarged, the last two being merged to form a single body of water. Sandy Lake was almost unique in possessing a beach, as its name suggests, a rare remnant of the sandstone cap which was eroded from the Plateau. Beside its northern shore were the remains of an accommodation house, beloved of fishing parties who climbed the Mole Creek and Parsons tracks on horseback in the period 1903–1920. Below the outflow of Lake Mackenzie were the attractive Parsons Falls, where the Fisher River plunged down a rocky ravine towards the Devils Gullet. The water now flows through a concrete flume and the falls are usually dry.

The creation of the largest water storages has led many in the community to question the values of development involving major landscape change in areas of high scenic and natural quality, even when that development is justified for all kinds of good, practical reasons. Lake King William, which occupies the plains south of Lake St Clair, was filled in 1952, on completion of the Clark Dam at Butlers Gorge in the previous year. By the end of 1966 both the dam and the lake had been enlarged. The storage stretches along the eastern flank of the King William Range, and has an area greater than that of Lake St Clair; it has substantially altered the view-field from the surrounding mountains. Two larger storages are located in the south-west, having been created as part of the Gordon Power Scheme, Stage I, completed in 1972. The Gordon River, the major river of the south-west, was impounded to form Lake Gordon, the water backing up along the course of the river and covering hundreds of square kilometres of plains and tributary valleys to the north. To create the second storage, dams were constructed on the Serpentine, the Huon and close to Lake Edgar, causing the inundation of the Serpentine Valley and Huon Plains. In the process, the unique Lake Pedder was drowned, the name being conferred subsequently on the larger impoundment. Creation of this storage led to widespread opposition both in Tasmania and in other states. Although opponents of the scheme did not succeed in preventing the flooding of Lake Pedder, public awareness became focussed upon Stage II of the Gordon Scheme, which proposed the damming of the Franklin River.

The two large artificial lakes lie across the heart of the south-west, a region of incomparable landscape value. Although the lakes are not unattractive in themselves they and their roading and other infrastructure form a dominant visual human alteration in a formerly remote and unaffected wilderness. They have attracted further activity in the form of boats, camps and road traffic. Such a development confronts the community's attitudes to the land and affects, often profoundly, the different levels of interaction of people with their natural surroundings. The south-west had a particular importance, not simply for its natural beauty, but because it was the last substantial area which did not bear the marks of human intrusion.

The rural landscape of Tasmania changed little during the first half of the twentieth century. In the 1930s and 1940s there were still significant numbers of small holdings, most of which were mixed farms. Through the depression years of the 1930s small farms could maintain families, even if they could bring in little income or reduce debt. Following the Second World War, many changes took place across the rural land, noticeable even to the passing observer. There was a steady decrease in the farm labour force. Work was now readily available in the towns, and many people found the situation of a steady, regulated factory or commercial job preferable to farm labour or continuing the struggle to maintain a small holding. Many small farms were merged into larger properties under pressure of economic forces: the bigger farm was a leaner operation and gave a better return. Wages of employees rose, while family members were now less inclined to remain and help to run the farm when the city offered independence and variety. Vehicles and machinery became more readily available to farmers from the 1950s; numbers of conventional tractors grew from six thousand two hundred and seventy-two in 1956 to ten thousand five hundred and fifty-six ten years later. These changes were accompanied by what was virtually a 'grass revolution' in the 1950s, a move from cropping to grassland. The crops which required intensive labour both in growing and harvesting, such as small fruits, suffered the greatest decline. Sheep and stock numbers increased steadily, demanding fewer hands to look after them and bringing good returns through high wool and beef prices; numbers more than doubled between 1920 and 1965.

Despite these developments in the nature of farming itself, there was little overall change in the area of land being farmed in the state through the middle years of the century. From the early 1930s until 1972 this remained constant at about forty per cent of the island's land. However, from 1972 there was a steady diminution in this area, even though some bushland was still being cleared. By the mid-1990s the proportion of agricultural land had fallen to approximately twenty-seven per cent.[15] Several reasons for this fall are apparent. Some property which had formerly been marginal farming land was allowed to support regrowth timber or was converted to plantation forest. Many farms both in rural districts and close to towns were sub-divided into hobby-farms and no longer classified as commercial properties. Hobby-farms could be established on relatively poor land that would not normally be worth cultivating or using as pasture, as the new owners did not depend solely upon them and were often content to run a very small number of stock or to encourage the return of native vegetation. Added to these factors were two others which had a bearing on changing landscape patterns: the rapid spread of urban settlement and the phenomenon of the rural-residential block.

The last two developments originated in changes which affected people's lives in the first three postwar decades. Firstly, home ownership came within reach of increasing numbers of people, a trend that was fostered by rising levels of prosperity, and which was also an outcome of the desire for material stability and security in a society which had weathered the dismal, anxious years of the 1930s depression. The goal of almost every family was to have a home of their own, a home which was different from that of their parents: a new brick house with an enclosed garden for the children, and space to call their own. The banks and other institutions made sure that finance was accessible for housing loans to make the dream come true. It was cheaper and pleasanter to turn away from the confines of the older inner suburban streets where they themselves had grown up, and to move out to the newly developed sub-divisions with other young families. Secondly, people became mobile: car ownership was becoming almost universal. With continuing prosperity, hire-purchase and rising numbers of double-income families, multiple car ownership was common by the 1970s. Families could live where they wished, no longer bound to tram and bus routes.

The cities and towns spread, and in three decades the landscape which surrounded them changed dramatically. Hobart's suburbs took up what had hitherto been farming land along the river to the north as far as Granton, then stepped across the Derwent to the open hills and pasture of Bridgewater. On the eastern shore the suburbs filled the quiet inlets along the river, marched eastward across the hills to Cambridge, south to Carlton and South Arm, and north to Risdon. They climbed into the mountain foothills and straggled beyond Strickland Avenue and Fern Tree, and followed the southern shore beyond Kingston. In the process, little townships that had been quite distant from the city in the 1940s were absorbed. New suburbs were created overnight, and even new cities such as Glenorchy and Clarence were formed to marshal the spreading suburbs. Sleepy hamlets like Sorell and Kingston, Rokeby and Brighton suddenly became bustling centres, each surrounded by growing networks of streets. The same process was taking place as Launceston pushed its suburbs through the hills and along the Tamar, and it was repeated to a lesser extent in the newly declared cities of Burnie and Devonport and in the larger provincial towns. The 'urban sprawl' was not a uniquely Tasmanian phenomenon; it was common throughout the major population centres of Australia and in much of the western world. But in Tasmania its effects were even more apparent as proportionally more of the countryside was swallowed by the tide of suburbs and ribbon development, and the visual impact upon the landscape was considerable.

After the mid-1960s the countryside was seen increasingly as providing a desirable atmosphere for living, away from paling fences, Hills Hoists and the rows of suburban rooflines. Thirty minutes' drive into the country there were farms whose owners were retiring from the land or were finding their small holdings uneconomical. They soon realised that land sub-divided would bring a far greater return than a farm sold as a whole. By the mid-1970s when the surge of life-awareness burst upon middle Australia, the idea of a house set among the fields or along a quiet stretch of coast appealed to an awakening yearning for a less stressful way of life, in a place where there was space, privacy, a view of hills or sea, and a sense of being part of a rural or natural landscape. Old farmhouses were bought up and painstakingly restored, albeit with modern comforts and stylish timberwork. Developers very soon realised the value of land at a distance and put increasing pressure on farmers to sub-divide. Local government saw its immediate interests served by acceding to rural-residential applications, where the developer installed the services, boosting the rate-bases of sparsely populated municipalities. Those who moved into the countryside or along the coast usually possessed the capital to build an elaborate house in brick and tile with outbuildings, a stable perhaps, double garage to house the four wheel drive, a leafy approach road... So the houses moved across the open land through the 1970s, 80s and 90s, beside the rivers and estuaries, onto the hillsides, into the mountain foothills and along the wooded shores. Land was quite cheap at first, and the rates were low. An hour's drive from town was a small price to pay; after all, in Melbourne or Sydney an hour was nothing. By the 1990s each city was surrounded not by open farmland or timbered hills, but by many hundreds of houses of all shapes and sizes dotted across the fields, peeping from the trees, squatting on skylines and highly visible hillsides, transforming the rural landscape into a broad sub-divisional belt.

The spread of houses into the countryside involved not only those who worked in the towns and cities and simply wished to live beyond the suburbs. With a more general desire for the rural or coastal experience, the humble seaside cottage went through something of a metamorphosis and gained renewed appeal. Beach and coastal areas became prime real estate, even in districts quite remote from the cities; large blocks were fenced off around almost every accessible piece of channel or waterway which afforded a water frontage or a broad view of attractive countryside, and roofs appeared among the trees. Access drives led off country roads to open up considerable stretches of 'desirable' foreshore not only within range of the towns but, by the 1990s, in almost every part of the eastern half of the island where local councils would approve 'development' and landholders were willing to sell. Headlands with fine views, or quiet beaches, were advertised in the national press as prizes for the discerning purchaser–and the houses spread. This situation was not restricted to the coasts; the rural valleys and hillsides also had their quota of distinctive residences scattered across the quiet farmlands and into the timbered heights. In an island with limited open land, the effect of such a migration is cumulative and substantial.

The shack by the sea, or by one of the highland lakes, is not a recent feature in Tasmania. Seaside cottages were quite common in some locations from the late nineteenth century onwards, and numbers increased in the 1920s in places such as Bruny Island and the Channel district. Soon after a cart track was formed to Great Lake, camps and rough huts appeared, followed later by huts at Arthurs Lake and other Plateau lakes. Fishing parties made the long journey by cart and on horseback over the rough road from Bothwell, undeterred by discomfort. However, the advent of the family car and of better roads hastened the spread of shacks in several parts of the island, both in the highlands and along the coasts. Small settlements developed, particularly along the north and north-west coasts close to the beaches and river mouths, on the west coast at the Arthur River, Pieman Heads, Trial Harbour and Granville Harbour, and as far south as Southport. On the Central Plateau, shacks proliferated along the western shore of Great Lake, eventually occupying almost all of the land adjacent to the shore except the exposed open heathland in the central section. Buildings ranged in style from the basic tin sheds and converted railway carriages of earlier days to solid houses that resembled their suburban counterparts. Transportable ex-HEC houses were popular, as were the 'fibro' cement sheet constructions, vertical board and corrugated iron. Suburbanised front gardens were not unknown, complete with a variety of exotic garden plants.

The shack-building era has had a significant impact upon various landscapes. In the coastal settlements there has been encroachment upon heathlands, old dune formations, foreshore and coastal woodlands, many of which were ecologically vulnerable. The visual impact has been even greater, the shacks usually presenting an incongruous intrusion into an attractive section of coast or estuary. Beside Great Lake the ribbon development of shacks and houses has created a discordant element in what is otherwise one of the most pleasant highland landscapes along a tourist road, where an open forest of snow gums reaches down from the rocky hills to the lake shore. The shack-builders of the highlands and coastal settlements are not, of course, responsible for the loss of landscape values in either of these situations as, apart from a few formal reserves, there has never been any clear guideline or requirement at state level stipulating where structures may or may not be built, or ensuring that buildings conform to high visual standards. They were not required to be sited and landscaped in appropriate ways so that they did not intrude upon, and detract from, their surroundings.

By the closing years of the second century of white settlement, much of the island's landscape had been drastically altered. Substantial areas of the original forest had been cleared for agricultural land and for timber, with large-scale harvesting of timber continuing. Fire has affected much that remains and poses a constant danger. The farmlands which contributed so much to the pleasant quality of the settled regions have themselves suffered substantial intrusion from sub-division, suburban and town development, and the rapid spread of monoculture plantations. Vulnerable highland country is under threat from fire, forest clearance, buildings and roads, while the accessible coastline has severe development pressures upon it. Such a brief period of occupation by a relatively small population, most of this time prior to the advent of motor vehicle, bulldozer and chain-saw, has wrought such widespread changes that the future of the island's landscape must be viewed with profound misgivings. Loss of landscape values has far-reaching implications for those who make their lives here, both now and in the century to come, and for the state's economic future.

SECTION V

POWER OF A MYTH: THE PRACTICAL TRADITION

12   BUILDERS AND CRAFTSMEN

*With these skills came a pride in his own self-reliance,
and a belief that no matter how isolated or how far from help,
he could rely on his own hands to meet any demand.*

FROM THE FIRST DAY that white people stepped ashore in Van Diemen's Land they changed and adapted the island to the requirements of a European society. For two centuries Tasmanians have wrought upon the island's landscape, adapting and modifying it in a multitude of ways. The very process of accomplishing this task engendered in the colonial society a large and varied body of skills that could be applied to any undertaking upon the land. In addition, the process developed in this, as in other Australian colonies, a strongly practical view of the land. Theirs was a culture that placed the greatest value upon the physical and intellectual abilities which brought about change. Today this culture persists at the core of Tasmanian society, and it continues to influence our attitudes to the land.

    Practical abilities were paramount in a developing colony. Every step in establishing the settlements, from the earliest encampments to the towns and farms, required the application of these abilities, and those who possessed them prospered. All of the material fabric of a modern society had to be created in a short time, and extended as further land was settled and developed, so that this outpost could flourish as a model of its British parent. To enable this to be accomplished a large labour force was provided in the form of convict gangs and assigned convict labourers. The new colonists learned to use axe and saw, adze, auger and chisel upon hardwood that was far tougher than anything that sawyers and carpenters had ever encountered. They discovered that for the construction of buildings

'A number of fine architects ... left a legacy to the state in their solid handsome buildings ...'
View of Launceston, c1900 (John Watt Beattie). AOT.

and ships the forests of their island offered some of the finest timbers in the world.

Almost every task required some adaptation to the conditions of the raw new country, and the exercise of ingenuity and self-reliance. Away from the main settlements, a settler was forced back on his own resources in establishing his place on the land. His assigned servants were usually not skilled in any trade which was applicable to his situation, and neither were the family members who accompanied him. Even on the way to his selection, the assigned men often worked in front of the loaded drays to clear a path with axe and mattock. The first bark hut was put together in a few days to provide temporary shelter while a site was chosen for a cottage and the timber prepared for building. This had to be close enough to a stream for a barrel of water to be hauled to the house on a sled. The men of the party cut saplings for the frame and split slabs or palings, leaving them to dry and season for a few months while initial clearing was taking place. When the time came, a four-room cottage could be built in a matter of a month by two men. On the cleared land, horse and bullock were the only sources of power until traction engines began to appear in the 1880s. The ploughman guided his single-furrow plough, with tedious weeks of back-breaking toil needed to break the ground, taking three days with one bullock to plough half a hectare. When the ringbarked trees finally toppled across the paddocks their trunks were burned and the stumps laboriously grubbed out. A deep hole was dug around the stump, its roots cut, and the stump itself pulled clear by bullocks, to be burned later when it dried out. Smaller logs were dragged to the side of a paddock and chocked one above the other to make dog-leg fences, replaced eventually by the universal split-timber post and rail. Barns, stock shelters, household furniture, outdoor ovens and a hundred other necessities the settler learned over the course of a few years to contrive, to build or to repair. With these skills came a pride in his own self-reliance, and a belief that no matter how isolated or how far from help, he could rely on his own hands to meet any demand. This air of confidence permeated the early colony; it was the answer of people thrust into a strange and often threatening environment, and it was to persist through successive generations.

Those early, confident years created other traditions. A number of fine architects such as James Blackburn, John Lee-Archer and Henry Hunter, as well as scores of convict masons, most of them nameless in the records, left a legacy to the state in their solid handsome buildings and in the many other structures which made up the built environment of the island. Warm, figured sandstone was readily available throughout the midlands and south-east, and the early builders made full use of it. Their eyes and hands were in sympathy both with the stone and the surroundings of their buildings, so that even the most utilitarian parapets and culverts, barns and commissariat stores stand easily upon the land. Where stone was not available, kilns and ovens were soon constructed, and convict brickmakers turned out tens of thousands of soft, red bricks. Robin Boyd wrote of the old buildings that:

> The rugged stone walls, the crumbly bricks, the clear cedar and the few other ingredients are all intrinsically beautiful materials used honourably and sympathetically ...[1]

Hobart is fortunate to possess numbers of these early freestone buildings, still expressing elegance and proportion in their lines, even though they are surrounded often by mixed styles of later years. There are several churches, quite apart from the stately St Davids, which have a fine simplicity of line, in particular St Josephs and Holy Trinity. Augustus Prinsep described the growing town as he saw it in January 1830. After twenty-seven years it was emerging from its first stage as a collection of hastily built wooden huts, to become the handsome capital of a colony:

> ... with a peaceful harbour, a fine metropolis, with towns, streets, shops, and pretty shopkeepers, like some of the larger towns of Devonshire or Sussex ... nothing can be less uniform than the houses, which present every shape and size, from the primitive wooden shed, with its outside counter, to the smart London haberdasher's shop, with its glass windows and stone facings, and 'Swan' in gold letters, over the door ... rows are even starting up here and there; and two-storied houses, though still a novelty, are becoming less uncommon. This is the case with the principal streets - the Macquarrie and Elizabeth; the former containing most of the public buildings and the houses of official persons, and the latter the best shops ...

> In 1819 the Gaol-house was the only brick building; and even five years ago there were few others, wood being so exceedingly plentiful. Since that time, however, an admirable material for building has been brought into use, - a dark-coloured freestone, which is gradually replacing the wooden tenements, and not only looks handsomer, but is actually cheaper than brick. The houses are uniformly roofed with wooden shingles, which have exactly the appearance of large slates.[2]

Public buildings such as the old Lands Building in Davey Street and the Barracks dominating the heights above the town, have a confidence and firmness of form in their masonry which reflects the values of the young British colony. These, and the freestone buildings of the New Wharf— Salamanca—are products of a society founded on the work of men's hands and the skills of sound tradesmen. The convict workmen were often harshly and unjustly treated, but from harshness, injustice and deprivation came lasting monuments to their understanding of stone and their ability to handle their tools carefully and capably. The solid stone mansions of prosperous shipowners, merchants and officials once on the edge of the town, but now surrounded by narrow, inner suburban lanes, preserve the same high skills. Their owners were practical men who had made their way by their wits, their ability to grasp opportunities and their willingness to work for clear, material goals. The houses they built have a value for the city far beyond anything their builders or owners could have imagined.

The builders' and designers' craft can be seen in a wide range of structures other than buildings. Two of the most notable of these, the Bridgewater causeway and the Hobart (Mt Wellington) water supply facility between North-West Bay River and Ridgway, perform their functions today, supplemented by later extensions, just as sturdily as they did when they were completed. Later generations complemented the work of the earlier builders and masons: Tasmania is fortunate in having one of the richest collections of nineteenth century buildings of all the states. The late Georgian and Victorian Gothic mansions attract notice, but scattered through the cities, towns and countryside are hundreds of other attractive inns, homes, barns, stables and cottages which demonstrate a continuing tradition of craftsmanship and design.

The fine, durable timbers of the island were attractive both to builders and craftsmen. The light, close-grained Huon pine was discovered in the early years of settlement, and by 1820 a pining industry had been established based on Port Davey and Macquarie Harbour. Pine was soon found to be splendid timber for building small vessels, while the tough, resilient eucalypt hardwoods of the Huon estuary were equally valued in the construction of larger ships. At many small inlets around the island's coasts the building of sailing vessels became one of the earliest industries, while in the south, the 'blue gum clippers' were built on slipways within sight of the great forests from which their timbers had been hauled. It is not recorded how many ships were built in Tasmania over the course of the nineteenth and early twentieth centuries, the major period of shipbuilding. In the 1850s, forty-seven whaling ships were using the port of Hobart, many of these having been built locally. As well, the number of trading vessels from full-rigged barques and steamships to small coastal schooners and ketches must have been close to a thousand. Some indication of this number may be gained from the list provided by the late Harry O'May of five hundred and thirty trading craft of from ten to five hundred and sixty tons built in southern Tasmania alone between 1812 and 1947.[3] This also gives some idea of the enormous pool of skills, knowledge and experience of ships and shipbuilding which had been created in the island in those years. Tasmanian shipwrights were renowned for their work wherever these ships sailed. A particularly distinctive and serviceable type of whaleboat made from Huon pine was designed and built by a Hobart builder named Lachlan Macquarie. Many were used by Tasmanian whalers and by those in other colonies. Harry O'May and Will Lawson[4] both refer to these whaleboats. According to O'May's account:

> The bay whaling boats were splendid double-ended craft 32 feet in length, with a beam of from five feet six inches to six feet, constructed of Huon pine, with a neat sheer. They were either clinker or carvel built, with six men at the oars and a head man at the twenty-foot steer oar.[5]

It is fitting that the tradition of shipbuilding is maintained in Tasmania, with a wooden boat-building enterprise preserving the old skills, and the outstanding, innovative work of Incat Tasmania using new methods and materials.

Just as building and shipbuilding relied upon a wide range of skills which made use of the island's timber species, these timbers have been utilised by other craftsmen from the early days of the colony for fine cabinet-making and joinery. At first, timbers such as eucalypts, blackwood, celery-top pine, King Billy and pencil pine were little valued, blackwood often being destroyed during clearing. However, by the 1840s the warm, dark grain of blackwood was gaining popularity for furniture, while Huon pine and the other native pines were used increasingly for their lightness, strength and working qualities in both joinery and cabinet-making. A strong tradition of craftsmanship developed, and both the timber itself and items made from local timbers by Tasmanian craftsmen were prized in the other colonies. Today the tradition is still strong, both in finely crafted products and in the trades. A larger range of timbers is now in use, the beautiful grain, colour and texture of species such as myrtle, horizontal, sassafras and *Banksia* taking their place beside the timbers familiar to craftsmen of earlier years.

13   LIVING WITH THE LAND

In some cases they chose this life and would have been satisfied with no other; their spirits yearned for a place away from their fellows...

Over the period of European settlement a number of people have lived in close proximity to the land and have developed skills and strategies which have enabled them to spend considerable periods, often months at a time, living away from settlements and the resources of society. Some left the camps and straggling huts of the young colony and took the only form of freedom available to them, learning to live in the island's natural environment. Others were hunters who helped the early colonists to survive the lean years that followed the founding of the two main centres. The bushranging gangs also came to develop bush skills and the special knowledge by which they were able to survive for long periods in relative comfort and safety. During the course of the nineteenth and early twentieth centuries there were many whose lives took them far away from human company. The lone stockkeepers and shepherds of the new pastoral runs were the forerunners of the stockmen and cattlemen of later years.

From the 1820s exploring parties pushed out into the remote, unmapped country, opening routes for further settlement and examining the resources of the land. Later, the prospectors followed in their tracks: men who became so accustomed to a harsh, isolated life in the mountains that some could never become reconciled to towns and streets, even in old age. They had much in common with the trappers, those sturdy bushmen who could stoically face the bleak highland winters, and whose lives came close to legend.

All of these men lived close to the land, and in varying degrees in harmony with it. Each developed to a high level the skills essential for survival: to find their way, obtain shelter and sustain themselves for long periods, living upon animals they hunted or trapped. In some cases they chose this life and would have been satisfied with no other; their spirits yearned for a place away from their fellows, where they were at peace with themselves and relied upon no one else. Others accepted bush life because it provided a way of keeping themselves and their families in hard times, or because their occupations took them into the field for months at a time. All, however, had in common a view of the land as a resource. All developed the ability to harness the land and to exploit it in some way. As well, they all belonged essentially to the world of complex social organisation: life in remote places remained an extension of the life they had known and possibly rejected, even for those who lived for the most prolonged periods out of contact with their society. In this their lives and perceptions were profoundly different from those of the Aboriginal people who had gone before them and whose bond with the land was intensely spiritual as well as physical and social.

Almost as soon as the first tents and guard-posts had been erected on the shores of the Derwent and Tamar men began to struggle away into the surrounding hills. Some were convicts simply seeking to escape the daily grind of the work gangs and perhaps seek an opportunity to join the crew of a passing whaler. But others were independent spirits who preferred a life in the wilds. They came to terms with the Aborigines over hunting and living within tribal territories, understanding and observing the complex system of obligations and relationships. Often they took Aboriginal partners, also by negotiation with the tribes, and these women enabled the escapees to live comfortably on the resources of the land as well as to maintain good relations with the tribal clans. The men learned to hunt and forage for themselves, and to use animal skins to make clothing; their understanding of the country, through their closeness to the tribes, was probably greater than that attained by any other white people since that time. There was a close link between these escapees and the hunters who were sent into the grasslands to secure wallaby to augment the diminishing stores of the early colony. Some of the hunters were themselves escaped convicts, or else convicts who had proved themselves adept bushmen and were encouraged to live outside the settlements to bring in regular loads of wallaby meat. It was this hunting on a large scale across the tribal grounds which eventually led to the first serious conflicts between settlers and the Aborigines.[6]

Others who broke away from the cells and convict barracks joined the notorious bushranging gangs, to prey upon settlers in the outlying farms and villages, and on travellers along the colony's bush roads and at isolated inns. Most of these men survived by keeping to the fringes of settlement, living off the selections and the scattered stockkeepers, with whom they often shared a common background. The successful gangs knew the country and learned to live from it, working from bases deep in the mountain valleys and learning their skills from the Aborigines. Gangs such as Brady's and Cash's were hardest to trace because of their knowledge of the land.

Not all of the men who left the early settlements chose to live in the wilder country. Many were drawn to bay-whaling, one of the most successful industries of the first fifty years. Tasmanian waters were a breeding-ground for Sperm and Right whales; so plentiful were the latter that it was at times dangerous for small boats to venture into the main stream of the Derwent. The Reverend Knopwood recorded that he could see seventeen whales on one occasion from the window of his cottage overlooking the river. Bay-whaling stations were set up as early as 1803 in the Derwent and a little later on Schouten Island, but the most active period was between 1824 and 1845, when stations operated along the east coast, the south-east, and as far west as Bramble Cove, Port Davey. Whales had been virtually hunted out on the east coast by 1847. The whales were captured by crews based at shore camps which were usually simple stone or slab huts. After they were secured, the carcases would be towed close inshore for flensing. Oil was extracted from the blubber by boiling it in large iron try-pots along the shore. Like offshore whaling, this was a dangerous though lucrative activity, calling for skill, courage and quick responses. Boats were often swamped or crushed, and loss of life was common. Bay-whaling was a rough and isolated life, with stations in such locations as Freycinet, Schouten Island, Recherche Bay, Cox's Bight and Port Davey. Not only regular whalemen were employed, but the rewards and excitement attracted young men from the farms and other occupations during the off-season.

The same skill and hardiness were evident in the lives of the sealers who formed small, self-sufficient camps among the Bass Strait islands. Fur sealing began even before white settlement of Tasmania, with huge numbers of the animals being slaughtered for their oil and skins. Once the seal colonies had been exploited almost to extermination, the sealers settled to a more regular way of life based on fishing and mutton-birding. The early sealers were recruited from the crews of sailing and whaling vessels, but they were soon joined by escaped convicts, various adventurers and men who wished to evade the law. The sealers' unions with Aboriginal women produced generations of strong, courageous young islanders who were renowned for their skill as boatmen. Their descendants ensured the survival of the Aboriginal people and of the traditional seal-hunting and harvesting of mutton-birds amongst the stormy Furneaux Islands, where the boat-handling ability of their Straitsmen forebears is still maintained.

The rapid spread of the pastoral selections in the 1820s pushed flocks into what were at the time extremely remote districts such as the upper Derwent, Clyde and Shannon, with runs extending well into the highlands. Selectors took up open land wherever they could find it, with active encouragement from the Governor to settle outlying areas. As was the case with sparsely settled parts of the north-west, the Esk Valley and the east coast, it was not possible to leave sheep or stock on unfenced runs at the time of the Black War, and under threat from thylacines, as well as from other settlers anxious to build their own herds and flocks. The only way to protect livestock until fences could be built and the land was more closely settled and secure was to engage stockkeepers and shepherds to mount guard over pastures. In the case of property belonging to a wealthier landowner whose main interests lay in the town, this may have involved two or three men overseeing an extensive area of unimproved land for several years. At first they would be assigned convicts, later men who had earned ticket-of-leave or who were free by servitude. They were little prepared for the work in most cases, having been at best labourers or shepherds on English or Irish farms before they were transported. They were, however, used to a hard life, and this was just as well. Their shelter was a slab or paling hut, or possibly even a sod hut for a time; food consisted of flour for bread or damper, tea, salt pork, occasionally potatoes and onions, and whatever they could kill for fresh meat. This would usually be wallaby or even a beast if the owner were generous—or absent for long enough. From labourers they developed into stockmen. Months and years spent in the saddle checking herds, looking for strays in rough country, riding endlessly through land unchanged since the tribes had been driven off, gave them all the practice that was needed to become excellent horsemen.

'... *taking stock from Mole Creek across the Borradaile Plains into the upper Mersey ...*'
The Paddocks, upper Mersey Valley (author).

The shepherds and stockmen came to know their work. They cared for their horses; they doctored the stock, and each other, when necessary. They faced the threats of fire and flood, of highland snowfalls, of injury, illness and snakes. They kept in with the local bushranging gang and learned to negotiate with rustlers, squatters and encroaching neighbours, and from their own experience they knew the ways of villains and of petty authority. The district constable had probably been a fellow assignee. Even the loneliness of the life did not defeat them. They grew to understand the country, eventually to like it in a patient, resigned way. As the property developed, a more permanent cottage was built on the track from the homestead; a man would find a woman willing to endure the simple life of the back-blocks, and their children would grow up versed in the skills of this life. So the island bred good horsemen.

But they were more than this: they were tough, resilient men and women who weathered hardships without complaint, who could handle the tasks of the farm and knew the bush, and who were generous and dependable in character. Louisa Meredith recalls instances of assigned convicts who worked out their sentences with the one family and then continued as trusted and valued stockmen on the same farm for many years, twenty-eight in one case. Others became managers of properties and then leased their own farms. It was their children and grandchildren who became legendary stockmen, driving sheep from the midlands or the Clyde River properties into the high country, or taking stock from Mole Creek across the Borradaile Plains into the upper Mersey. Cattle and sheep were driven across some of the highest parts of the Central Plateau, ascending Higgs' track from Western Creek and following Ritter's route to the grassy summer runs of the Walls of Jerusalem. It was their wilder brothers who worked Fields' stock on the Middlesex Plains, through the Vale of Belvoir and the Surrey Hills, riding after half-wild cattle amongst the timber and out across the native grass clearings, into Cradle Valley and almost to the foot of Cradle Mountain: rough country where Fields ran ten thousand head. James Calder met some of these stockmen on the Van Diemen's Land Company's road in 1865 and was glad of their guidance along this ill-defined track:

> We had hardly gone a mile [from Surrey Hills Station] when we met Mr Sutherland (the head man of the Messrs Field), accompanied by their entire staff of renowned 'riders' who have the reputation of being the best, the most fearless and dashing horsemen in Tasmania. They were escorting a small herd of wild cattle which they had captured on their ride homewards.
>
> These men in travelling from station to station have more the appearance of a little colony than a mere company of horsemen. A dray with all their baggage follows them wherever they go; and they carry with them everything necessary for their wants.[7]

Calder's final guide on the journey was a very impressive and capable horsewoman, wife of one of Fields's fencers. Other stockmen of the 1890s undertook the epic drive from remote properties near Whales Head (Temma) on the west coast to the mining town of Zeehan. These cattle, which had rarely seen people, were excitable and belligerent. Periodically a mob was rounded up and driven along the coast to the Pieman River. The stockman swam them across the river near its mouth, and then took them over the stock track through the North Heemskirk country. Any traveller on the track was charged by the cattle, the only escape being to dive into a hole or ditch and lie there until the mob passed. By the time they reached Zeehan, the cattle were almost uncontrollable. When they swirled through the town with their wild eyes and tossing horns the streets cleared as townsfolk fled into shops and gardens. It took horsemen of great heart and skill to drive cattle such as these. Men of their time and proud of their ability, they loved just such a challenge.

One of the loneliest situations of those who lived close to the land was that of the trapper. From the middle years of the nineteenth century until the 1950s, numbers of men went out into the forests, particularly in the higher country, seeking the pelts of the red-necked or Bennett's wallaby, the Tasmanian pademelon, the brush-tailed possum and common ringtail. There was a season for taking wallaby and possum, usually May to July,

'A small hut was the centre of operation.'
Trapper's hut, Wurragarra Creek (author).

though in some years the season was varied or closed to allow populations to build up. In these months the fur grew thicker and was of greater value to the clothing industry. In hard times such as the depression years, many trappers would stay out far longer. The peak period for trapping ran from the 1890s to the 1940s, when many men could earn more money from three months' trapping than they could from regular labouring work for a whole year. The main areas favoured by trappers were different sections of the Western Tiers and the western fall of the Plateau above the upper Mersey and Forth rivers. Often snare lines would run far into the high country of the Plateau itself, and a snarer had to be prepared to face severe winter weather in checking his line and carrying the skins back to his hut. These areas supported large populations of game, and they were also readily accessible from the farming country of the north and north-west. Importantly, they could be reached with a cart or packhorse, so that loads of skins could be carried out at the end of a season. Some of the more experienced trappers went far into the mountains, setting their lines around Cradle Valley and Lake Rodway, the Borradaile Plains, the Du Cane Range and Lake St Clair. These were remote and dangerous places in winter, subject to heavy snowfalls and difficult to escape from after a fall, so that a man had to be prepared to survive in extreme conditions.

The trapper usually worked alone; sometimes two men shared a hut, their lines on different sides of a valley. A snare line often extended through the forest for several kilometres and took five or six hours to check. Two or three lines would lead away in different directions. Many trappers visited their areas in summer, putting snare poles and stakes in place on animal pads, so that the game would be accustomed to their presence. A small hut was the centre of operations. This was constructed quickly and usually lasted ten to fifteen years, though many survived for considerably longer, years after their builders had ceased using them. They were built on a sapling frame anchored to four upright posts, one or two of which were sometimes standing tree trunks. Palings and shingles were split the previous year and stacked to dry ready for use. Most trappers' huts did not have the traditional fireplace and chimney at one end, the fire being lit in the centre of the hut so that its heat helped to dry skins stretched out along the walls. The smoke found its way out through a hole left in the gable at one end, or through a roof-hole protected by a raised sheet of iron. Bunks were built at one end, and the hut was gradually furnished by the men who used it hewing stools, table and other items out of wood after they had checked snarelines and pegged out skins for the day. In a favoured locality two huts were built: one solely for living in, of customary design with fireplace at the end and a slab floor; the other, sometimes an extension of the first, was a skin-shed where the skins were dried around the walls by a centrally placed fire on the earth floor. In the hut, the fireplace was built carefully from rocks to allow a good blaze without endangering the paling chimney. Above it, chains were attached to movable spars across the chimney, so that iron pots and billies could be moved about over the fire to heat or simmer. A wallaby stew in the iron cooking-pot was one of the great pleasures of the trapper's life.

The number of men engaged in trapping in a season varied in response to economic conditions, but was probably not more than a hundred at any time. Some spent a good part of their lives in the mountains and were still facing the rain and isolation well into their sixties. They had a deep understanding of the forests and mountains in which they lived, and particularly of the animals on which their livelihood depended. They were weather-wise, and knew from a lifetime of experience the kinds of conditions likely to follow a change. Even when they were caught in the mountains by severe weather they could find shelter or an escape route. A trapper was strong both mentally and physically: a necessity for living and surviving. There are stories of men regularly carrying loads of forty kilograms and more over rough tracks as they brought skins at season's end to a pick-up point for a packhorse or cart to collect.

The names of some of the trappers of the 1900–1950 period are still associated with certain places: Paddy Hartnett and Bert Nicholls with the Du Canes and upper Mersey, Tom McCoy and Basil Steers with the Borradaile and February Plains, the Miles brothers with the north-western Plateau, Reg Dixon with the Walls of Jerusalem, Arthur Youd with the Rogoona country. Fortunately, some detailed accounts of these fine bushmen, their names, their methods and where they worked, have been published in recent years.[8] The way of life of the trappers, their resilience, their knowledge of the forests and their array of skills belong now to past generations, the last of whom have almost vanished. But their lives and work have, like those of the stockmen, had a continuing influence upon current attitudes to the land.

The work of investigating and mapping the more difficult and remote parts of Tasmania took over sixty years to complete. This in itself is a gauge of the complexity of the topography and roughness of the terrain of much of the island. The process began before 1820 and continued to at least 1880, and even then there remained substantial areas about which little was known. The surveyors, geologists, bushmen and others who made up the exploring parties had to learn their craft rapidly, particularly those who ventured into the mountains in the first few decades. For most, it was a matter of learning as they journeyed, often through their own mistakes and lack of knowledge. Men such as Sharland, Hellyer, Wedge, Frankland, Calder and Gould were strangers to the Tasmanian forests when they first led expeditions. Their training and experience had been gained in the English countryside or in India, and was entirely inappropriate for Tasmania. They began by knowing almost nothing of the Tasmanian climate, its rapid changes and the marked effects of altitude; neither did they realise the extreme contrast between the western mountains and the remainder of the island. They knew nothing of the western scrubs and of the ways of finding routes through the different types of vegetation. They had to learn to deal with swiftly rising rivers, prolonged cold, wet conditions and the slow pace of travel through much of the country. Even to survive in this country required new skills; to explore, to map and to cut tracks demanded different attitudes of mind and a very special craft.

Expedition members came from varied walks of life. Sharland and Wedge took soldiers; Hellyer was accompanied by convict servants of the Van Diemen's Land Company, though he relied on men such as Isaac Cutts and Alexander McKay, who had already spent some time on bush work. Calder also drew upon McKay's ability for much of his investigation of new country. By the time Frankland recruited his parties in 1835 he could call upon men with good bush skills and experience. Later expeditions such as those of Gould in the 1860s employed men of the calibre of Ibsen and Burgess who had spent years in the mountains and had gained knowledge of many parts of the island. The bushmen who accompanied exploration and survey parties had a particular liking and background for this work. Most had hunted, or had worked at pining or milling, or had lived close to the forests, and they had acquired bush skills in their youth from an older generation. The body of bush lore grew steadily. Some needed little teaching: James Goodwin, who with Thomas Connelly escaped from Macquarie Harbour in 1826, found his way over some of the wildest country in the island. Later he was assigned to assist John Darke on two expeditions to the Vale of Rasselas. Over the period 1820 to 1860 there developed a breed of very hardy, competent bushmen whose skills and knowledge were specifically adapted to the harsh and beautiful country which nurtured them.

This group of bushmen came to prominence in the era of prospecting, when the great exploration tracks were cut to open the western forests and mountains for mineral development. The leader of a track-cutting party possessed a wide range of abilities relating both to the bush and to people. A few, such as Charles Sprent and Edward Counsel, were qualified surveyors, though most had completed only basic surveying training: they could use circumferentor and prismatic compass, perhaps even a theodolite, and could draft a clear, practical sketch map. The tracks they cut had to remain in use for some years and provide safe access to the country for prospectors who were not familiar with the region and did not have the bush skills or confidence to probe the area without a track within reach. A track also enabled prospectors to pack in supplies and thus remain in the field for long enough to investigate the country thoroughly. The track-maker therefore had a considerable responsibility as an all-round bushman. He went ahead initially and blazed the route of the track for two or three kilometres while the clearing party worked on the previous section. He kept it well contoured, avoiding steep sections wherever possible, and following well-drained ground. He then supervised the cutting and clearing, benching it into hillsides and corduroying over wet patches. Rivers had to be bridged with secure logs and handrails; shelter huts were built at key points. Throughout the cutting operation supplies were replenished, tools replaced and camps staged, all dependent upon the leader's judgement.

More important even than his bushmanship were the personal skills which every leader had to exercise. He was in charge of three or four men whose background was usually timber work or prospecting. The party may have been away for up to five months at a time, even into the depths of winter, with little to break the daily round of hard physical work with axe, saw and scrub-hook, moving camp and provisions, and repairing equipment and clothes. A packer brought in mail and supplies. It was not unusual for cutters to become sick, to sustain injuries or to have disagreements in the close confines of bush camps where clothes and bedding were always damp, the food monotonous and the toil endless. In prolonged bad weather the men of these parties could have a very miserable time. It was up to the leader to keep his bushmen occupied, to maintain a good spirit over a long period and to avoid dissention by recognising the danger signs. On completion, the leader was expected to write a report on the track-cutting work, detailing the methods used for the various aspects of construction and marking, and commenting on the country itself: the types of timber and their value, the potential of the land, and any evidence of minerals. This report was accompanied by a map with the compass bearing of each section of track, as well as sightings onto prominent points when these were visible.

It is little wonder that the prominent track-cutters were highly respected in a society in which physical strength and endurance were often accepted without comment. The names of such men as Robert Ewart, Edward G Innes, Charles Sprent, David Jones and Tom Moore were probably better known in the mining region during the years 1880 to 1910 than were those of financiers, mine managers and politicians. They embodied skills and qualities which had been developed by generations of bushmen throughout the island. The bushman, invested with the stature of men like these, continued to be a figure who, in the perceptions of many people, remained closely identified with the Tasmanian landscape for a further half-century, becoming established in the island's history, its mythology and the self-image of its people.

Many of the prospectors who preceded the track-cutters or who later made use of their tracks were no less competent bushmen. Sometimes a prospector worked for a mining company such as the Mount Lyell Company, or was employed by a syndicate or prospecting association, many of which flourished briefly in the 1880s and 1890s. More often, however, the prospector was independent, or was 'grubstaked' by a local merchant such as F O Henry: supplied with provisions in return for a share in any claim he might register. It was usual for a locality to be prospected by a pair of men or by a small group of three or four who would work along the bed of a stream or examine a section of valley or ridge. Most of the mineral discoveries in the north-east and on the west coast were made by small parties such as these: the Merediths, Donnellys, Moores, McDonoughs, Tom Currie and Con Lynch, Frank Long and William Johnstone, William Bell and James Smith. Apart from easing the loneliness of weeks in the forest, it was easier for two or more to share the heavy tasks of a prospector's work, the hauling of loads of food and equipment, the daily chores and routine of establishing camps. There was always a high risk of illness and injury; a man by himself was completely dependent upon his own resources and very vulnerable if he were disabled. Some prospecting procedures called for the strength of more than one man: the building of a wing-dam to divert a stream was punishing work, as was the sinking of a prospecting shaft or driving an adit. However, there were always some wandering spirits who chose at different times to spend many weeks by themselves. Foremost of these were James 'Philosopher' Smith and T B Moore, while others worked alone at intervals, particularly in the early years of Zeehan and Dundas, when excitement ran high and men were eager to take every chance of finding rich lodes. In 1881 Moore undertook a long journey alone south of Macquarie Harbour that took him into unknown country in the headwaters of the North and Old rivers below the Arthur Range. Over the years he spent lonely months in the West Coast Range and amongst the tributaries of the Gordon and Pieman, with his dogs as his only companions. 'Philosopher' Smith also made many a lone journey in the country south of Black Bluff, where he had several favoured camps, and he ranged as far afield as Cradle Valley and the Surrey Hills. It was on one of these solo expeditions that Smith made his momentous find of tin at Mt Bischoff.

Whether alone or in small parties, the prospectors had to know the land thoroughly, and to develop a whole range of general and specialised skills. It was vital to be able to find a practicable route through dense western forests, to kindle a fire in the wettest conditions, to know the dangers of river crossings and to recognise a good splitting tree for hut palings. Other skills were learned more painfully. Most important of all was a man's ability to 'read' the country, its intricate pattern of outcrop, fold, fault and strata which could provide the essential key to a long-sought lode. The earlier prospectors had experience on gold-diggings in New Zealand and the Australian colonies, but were often unable to recognise the signs of other valuable minerals. Even tin, which many had washed on Blue Tier and other parts of north-eastern Tasmania, was not always identified, and pack-loads of worthless tourmaline, mistaken for tin-bearing cassiterite, had to be dumped at the end of a long, hard track. Only gradually, through the efforts of men such as Charles Sprent, and through courses run in Zeehan, Launceston and Hobart, was better knowledge gained by the ordinary prospector. In the twentieth century, prospecting passed from the realm of the bushman who was prepared to endure the dangers and hardships of a rough and lonely life and who learned most of his skills from others in the field, to become the work of trained professionals who had access to an array of sophisticated equipment.

14 THE SKILLS OF THE LAND-USERS

Establishing the early west coast mines involved a major struggle between the miners and the country itself...

Bonds were close between men who worked together in the forest or the mill, and whole families became involved in the occupation...

BOTH MINING AND THE FOREST INDUSTRIES have long traditions of winning resources from the land in the face of difficulty and danger, through resolve and specialised skills. In both there has been a sense of continuing contest between people and the land implicit in terms such as 'winning' and 'harnessing'. Mining in particular has demanded extraordinary ingenuity and perseverance from men whose daily lives were shadowed by the inherent dangers of their trade. In the east, north and north-east, mining has a long and successful history, with well-established collieries in the South Esk Valley, tin mines scattered throughout the north-east, productive mines at Rossarden and Storys Creek, and goldfields also in the north-east. Until its flooding in 1919, the Tasmania Mine at Beaconsfield returned profitable yields, with nearly-eighty four thousand ounces won in its peak year, 1899. It resumed production in the present century. These fields presented few problems of access. They lay in relatively dry country and could be reached without difficulty from the main northern centres. Rossarden and Storys Creek were perhaps the most remote, perched high in the mountain ridges below Stacks Bluff on Ben Lomond. However, Tasmania's main mineral wealth is found in the mountainous region inland from the west coast where, until 1932, there was no road access and only one railway. Before 1900 this field relied entirely upon shipping. Establishing the early west coast mines involved a major struggle between the miners and the country itself, a process which challenged the strength and resolve of the miners, and came as a final engrossing chapter to the story of the explorers, track-makers and prospectors of the previous half-century.

Mt Bischoff was the earliest mine in the western region, and for a time the richest tin mine in the world. It was located above the headwaters of the Arthur River, in country which had only a rough track to link it with the town of Burnie some eighty kilometres to the north. In order to develop the mine, first a vehicle track was cut so that drays could be hauled over the ridges from the coast. This was followed by a horse-drawn tram and finally by a railway. Much of the initial mining and concentrating plant was brought by the drays so that the mine could begin work, which it did by December 1872, a year after Smith's discovery. From the scattered tents under the mountain a township of paling and shingle soon emerged, the island's first true mining town of Waratah.

The first west coast fields were small alluvial diggings in the valley of the Pieman River. The North Heemskirk tin field was worked by several syndicates totalling perhaps fifty men, in 1876 and 1877. Poor returns here led prospectors to probe the tributary streams, and gold was found in what became known as the Pieman field, where a series of small rushes attracted up to a hundred diggers. There were only two ways of reaching these fields and bringing in supplies: by a stormy and uncomfortable voyage in a small sailing vessel to Macquarie Harbour or the Pieman, or an arduous walk of several days over extremely rough tracks from Waratah or Lake St Clair.

Miners on these early fields often ran short of food or were reduced to fishing for eels or hunting the scarce game. What food they stored went mouldy and rancid, though the miners learned ways of treating it to make it edible. They lived in tents or hastily built bark-roofed huts and worked through the summers alternately in heat or cold, driving rain. On the exhausting trek from the coast at the end of the season many were caught on exposed ridges by bad weather and came close to perishing. Despite the hardships, the miners persevered. Although the early fields failed to prosper, they led to the eventual discovery of richer deposits and to successful mines. By 1881 a bridle track had been cut from Waratah to Corinna, replacing the two exposed mountain tracks.

The first underground mining, on a limited scale, took place at South Heemskirk at a location which offered even greater difficulties for the miners. Here a small lagoon behind a reef was used as a fair-weather port, still called Trial Harbour after the tiny cutter that first sailed into it. A zigzag road was benched into the steep hillside above, and every piece of material for more than twenty mines was dragged up this road, including boilers, stampers, timber and heavy concentrating equipment. On the bleak, rain-swept Heemskirk hills the miners sank shafts and erected winding gear above them, some powered by boilers, others by simple horse-whims or water-wheels. High on the range above the field, a dam was built and a valley flooded to provide water pressure to drive pelton wheels. But the hard work, optimism and expenditure were in vain: despite promising predictions, the field collapsed after three years.

There were mining sites in even more difficult situations. In 1882 Lynch and Currie found gold in Lynchs Creek, south of the site of Queenstown. During the rush that followed, the McDonoughs and Karlson climbed through the forest on the side of the West Coast Range and washed gold in the Linda Valley at what became known as the Iron Blow, sparking a further rush. But the problems of supplying the two fields were staggering. Boats were pushed up the King River by men wading waist- and shoulder-deep in the cold mountain water. Supplies were then packed on men's backs over a high ridge into the Queen Valley; those destined for the Iron Blow were carried over a forest track up the six hundred metre side of the range to the Linda Valley. Eventually a cart track was built from Strahan to the Queen Valley, and the foot track to the Blow widened to a sled track. Over this came iron boiler-plates, stampers, pipes, anvils and all the other heavy material for mining. When the gold-seekers of the Iron Blow sold out to Bowes Kelly and the Mount Lyell company began to mine copper at the Blow, the same problems remained. A fortunate find of silver enabled the new company to build a railway from the mouth of the King River and to set up a smelting plant in the Queen Valley. The entire operation was a triumph of skill and perseverance over immense natural obstacles. The pyritic smelter was designed on a new principle which eliminated the need to bring in expensive coke and coal, and an overhead cable haulage carried ore from the Iron Blow across the heights of Philosophers Ridge and down to the smelter in the forests of the Queen Valley. The railway followed the gorge of the King River, clinging to the sides of cliffs and crossing steep ravines on high timber bridges through extraordinarily difficult country. Abt locomotives were built specifically to climb the steep grades of the watershed, having toothed wheels which were lowered to engage with a ratchet central rail on the steepest sections. In one of history's ironies, this railway has been rebuilt using modern methods, and its stock restored, to enable tourists to view in comfort the great gorge which demanded such labour. The company port of Teepookana was built at the mouth of the King River; from here everything travelled to and from Strahan by barge until the railway was extended to Strahan in 1900.

In 1888, many leases were registered on the silver-lead fields of Zeehan and Dundas, and by 1890 over thirty mines were in various stages of development. Here there were also severe problems involving access and broken country. At first the only link was a packhorse-track through the hills from Trial Harbour, later upgraded to a dray road. Once again the tiny, exposed lagoon had to be used by small steamers unloading mining equipment onto barges in the infrequent calm periods when the seas permitted entry. Everything had to be hauled along the hilly, winding road to Zeehan by dray until a railway was completed to Strahan in 1894. Hundreds of miners, their families and other travellers walked the long miles from Strahan along Ocean Beach and then across the Trial Harbour road to reach Zeehan. Alternatively, many took the equally weary journey from Waratah to Corinna and then south by way of Trial Harbour. Despite these obstacles, miners had explored their leases, sunk shallow shafts and set up much of their machinery by the time the railway was completed. The Zeehan field lay in a basin amongst the hills, in an area of high rainfall. Every mine had to have powerful pumps operating continuously to stop the workings from flooding, and these also had to be brought a considerable distance by ship, and then by rail from Macquarie Harbour. In addition to these problems of isolation, the skill of miners and surveyors was further challenged by the narrow, fractured ore seams which petered out at depth and made the prospects of any mine uncertain.

Through the 1890s the miners moved into the mountainous country further inland. The Curtain–Davis companies mined the precipitous Godkin Ridge beside the Montezuma Falls; the Hercules miners worked an ore-body high on the side of Mt Read after gold prospectors had found promising mineral potential. A township was built not far below the summit, and all necessities carried to it across the mountain ridge until a haulage was completed between the mine and Williamsford. The small Mt Farrell silver-lead mine at Tullah was so isolated that no road reached it for over sixty years; it was served by a narrow-gauge railway, the trams originally drawn by horses.

The sheer determination of the miners and engineers, and their practical ability in meeting the challenges of isolation and difficult country resulted in the development of profitable and enduring mines such as Mt Bischoff, Mt Lyell, Mt Farrell, Rosebery and Renison. Mines such as these gave crucial impetus to the island's economy, and the more recent development of Savage River, Henty, Hellyer and Que River have maintained the contribution of mining. Like the bushmen, trappers and prospectors, miners have added substantially to the continuing tradition of Tasmanians' harnessing the resources of the land. In the struggle to overcome problems of access and topography, the land itself has come to be regarded almost as a hostile entity, an obstacle to progress and wealth. Sadly, the scars of this struggle endure.

When he was sent in 1803 to found a settlement on the Derwent, Lieutenant Bowen's initial instructions from Governor King contained a request to note the specific types and specifications of timber available in the island and to assess their suitability for shipbuilding.[9] Tasmania's timber resources have been utilised ever since, and continue to form an important part of the state's primary production. Harvesting timber has always been a dangerous, exacting occupation, demanding physical strength, courage, fine judgement and very specific skills. It is with the forests and tree-felling that the image of the Tasmanian bushman has been most closely associated. Many communities have depended for their existence upon the island's forests and upon the men who worked in them. The timber industry has been based historically on the two major native timbers: the various eucalypt hardwoods and Huon pine. Many other species are harvested, such as myrtle, blackwood, celery-top pine and the introduced European pines and firs, but since 1820 the hardwood forests have provided the bulk of production. Around both eucalypts and Huon pine have grown different methods, different communities and ways of life. Each has its own distinctive traditions and legends.

Huon pine is endemic to Tasmania. A remarkably durable, easily worked timber, it has been in demand for shipbuilding and joinery since its qualities were discovered in the early years of the colony. It is slow growing and close grained, with a warm, honey colour after exposure and often has attractive figuring. Its natural oil prevents drying and splitting. Although the first Huon pine logs were found near the mouth of the Huon River and the earliest pining took place on the Huon, the west coast has been the major source of pine, particularly the rivers draining into Port Davey and Macquarie Harbour, with some pine also being taken from the Pieman. From 1816, when the pine beds of the western rivers were discovered by seamen and adventurers such as James Kelly, there has been constant harvesting of these ancient trees. The original pining settlements were formed in Port Davey, on Payne Bay and the Spring River, and the piners worked along the three main streams, the Spring, Davey and Frankland. The other large tributary of the Davey contained no pine on its forested banks, hence the name conferred by the piners, the Hardwood. The logs were floated downstream to the settlements, where they were cut into sections and shipped to Hobart, though some timber was used at Payne Bay for building small vessels. Pine was largely worked out in the Port Davey area by the 1880s. While they were cutting along the rivers, the piners lived in unique bark huts known as 'Badger Boxes'. These were of inverted V shape, without vertical walls, and accessible by punt as floodwaters rose to bunk level on occasion, and the billy had to be boiled on top of a stump. The Payne Bay village contained a number of quite substantial cottages with gardens and fruit trees, and generations of families such as the Doughertys, Longleys and Heathers lived in this distant and beautiful corner of the island. There were few visitors apart from the crews of trading ketches which called for pine, the bay-whalers of Bramble Cove and people aboard ships taking shelter. Towards the end these often included prospectors bound for Macquarie Harbour. Those who died at Port Davey had their graves in the small cemetery marked by Huon pine headboards.

The pine beds of the Gordon–Macquarie Harbour area were far more extensive. Small sailing vessels began to brave the treacherous bar at the entrance to the Harbour from 1816, picking up loads of the softwood logs along the lower reaches of the Gordon. One of the main reasons for the establishment of the Sarah Island penal settlement in 1822, apart from its isolation, was that the convict gangs could be employed usefully in harvesting pine and in shipbuilding. Others in the settlement were engaged in such activities as lime-burning for mortar and cultivation of a small area near Farm Cove, as well as tending the gardens on Sarah Island. The convict piners created traditions which were to be continued by generations of piners for well over a century. A convict pining gang lived in the forest for several weeks at a time, being issued with rations at two-weekly intervals during this period, a situation that enabled Goodwin and Connelly to make their successful escape overland in 1823. Pines felled away from the bank of the river were dragged along rough skidways corduroyed with saplings; once in the river they were lashed into rafts, the men working in the water to secure them. The pining gangs worked in the wet forests in all weathers, their clothing saturated for weeks on end. These conditions, as well as the harsh punishments inflicted for misdemeanours, made Macquarie Harbour a place to be feared, and an enduring symbol of the darkest side of the penal system. In this situation men came to hate and revile the west coast forests, the mountains which enclosed their prison and the great, dark river that dominated their lives. The same scenes a century later, and in a very different society, would represent the essence of beauty and tranquillity.

When the penal settlement was closed in 1833, the forests were left to the piners who supplied the small ships. Over a hundred and thirty years these men worked the forests close to the Gordon, King and Franklin rivers, gradually moving further from the Harbour and the main streams. Like the convict timbermen before them, the piners also had to adapt to the cool, wet forests. Instead of hauling the logs along skidways with their own labour they winched them for short distances or else used horses to drag them to the banks, where they were formed into rafts to be taken downstream to the loading points, usually established landing places which still bear their old names, where vessels would pick up loads. In later years the log rafts were towed to Strahan, where they were loaded onto larger ships, avoiding the delay for vessels in sailing up-river. At the landings the piners built solid slab huts where they could dry out after a day's work in the forest. These became the focus of their lives for many weeks while they were 'up the river'. Not only were the piners skilled at their work of felling and moving the great pine trunks; they were also excellent boatmen. The river, powerful and dangerous, was the only road for reaching the forests, so that they had to use it under nearly all conditions. In flood-time the Gordon and its tributaries carry enormous quantities of water from the western mountains, and the piners learned to 'ride' the great river, hazardous though this was. Although they used larger vessels, including small steamers in more recent times, their favoured work-boat was a punt built from pine. These they manoeuvred with consummate skill, reading the river's currents and turbulence from long experience. Travelling upstream against the current was even more difficult, and was often achieved over short distances by 'bushing': hauling the punt along by grasping bushes which overhung the water. With their boats loaded with provisions, they probed the long, difficult tributaries such as the Denison, Franklin and Jane, the piners wading the rapids as they manhandled the boats against the current.

Once there was a settlement on Macquarie Harbour, at Smiths Cove in 1877 and then Strahan in 1883, the piners were able to live more settled lives, with an assured source of supplies and their families living nearby. Sawmills were also set up in Strahan, so that pine could be shipped out in more valuable and economical loads. For a time between the 1880s and 1920s some of the piners lived in their own village at Piccaninny Point, close to the mouth of the King River. Most of these men worked the pine beds and other timber along the King and on the Teepookana Plateau, where Hartwell Conder held leases. An Anglican clergyman, the Reverend Frederick Copeland, recalled rowing to this village from Strahan in the 1890s to baptise the children. He found it sheltered behind a high bank, quite invisible from the harbour:

> ... four or five big huts, one or two of them surrounded by pretty gardens. They looked as though they were below the level of the river, but I was assured it required very high tides before any flooding took place, and that was at very long intervals. It really seemed a charming spot, with its background of trees sweeping upwards and protecting the place from all winds but the north.[10]

*Tree fallers, Don Valley c1870.
Most felling was carried out in this manner (author's collection).*

In the eucalypt forests of southern Tasmania, logging gangs had been at work for over a decade before the piners sailed for the west coast. Beginning on the slopes of Mt Wellington and then moving to the Channel district, the timber settlements spread ever further south to the major inlets of the Huon itself, Cygnet, Port Esperance, Southport and Recherche Bay, then across to the shore of Bruny Island. The timber-cutters moved constantly to exploit timber which stood closest to the shore and therefore involved least difficulty in hauling from the forest. As settlement spread through the island, other forested areas became accessible along the north-west coast, in the eastern highlands and the north-east, below the Western Tiers and in the central highlands. The huge trees of the upper Derwent and Tyenna valleys were being felled by the later decades of the century.

Timber-cutters faced some of the world's tallest trees in a dangerous contest, armed with axe, cross-cut saw, maul and wedge, together with their courage and an array of skills learned from boyhood. Strength and stamina were taken for granted: without them, no man could last long in an occupation which demanded heavy physical work for long hours every day in cold, wet winters or midsummer heat. Skill and judgement had to be sound where a mistake or a careless blow could cost life: one's own or a mate's.

A man working on a shoe[11] may have been up to five metres above the ground to clear the buttresses of a big eucalypt; a badly placed shoe or a slip were sometimes fatal. Misjudgement of a falling tree, or its unexpectedly striking another and sliding back over its stump, or a limb dislodged by the tree's movement: these were just a few of the daily hazards that could be avoided only through experience and caution. Even on 'safe' ground a log being loaded could roll without warning. It is not surprising that timber work had the highest injury rate of any industry.

Judgement had to be exercised in many other ways in the forests. It took experience to know which tree would split easily and cleanly, which might have rot eating into its core, which might be suitable for solid piles and beams needed for a wharf contract. Men worked in pairs or in small teams, and thus depended heavily on one another for both safety and efficiency. A youngster in his teens who had finished the boys' jobs in the mill would learn forest work alongside an older man whose experience added to his own knowledge and skill day by day. Two axemen would cut the same face or opposite faces together; thus a left-handed axeman was always welcome in a timber camp. Sawyers worked together on the cross-cut or the pit-saw, while a whole team would line a log to square it into a beam, a task requiring skill and concentration.

A complex system was put in place to bring logs from deep in the forest to the mill, possibly several kilometres away. The whim-carts of the early mills, which straddled the log and were drawn by horse or bullock, were soon replaced by tramways. In the older or smaller mills, this was a matter of building a temporary track with squared timber rails to a point as close as practicable to the main logging area. Logs were cut into manageable lengths, pulled onto trolleys at loading ramps, and hauled along the tramway to the mill. In larger operations the tramways were solid structures, with light steel rails in many cases. They crossed marshy ground on well-built log spans, and safely carried small locomotives drawing several logs. In crossing a steep ravine, a bridge sometimes had to be built up with three levels of trestles, each beam patiently drawn into place by bullocks. Power was provided for many early mills by a water-wheel, fed from a nearby stream, which enabled large rip-saws to operate. After 1880 small mills were frequently powered by take-off from traction-engines. Once a mill was well established, a boiler was installed to drive the saws and to provide power for the cable-winding gear. Older mills often had upright boilers driving their haulage drums; cable was laid out along a tramway using a horse, and attached to the bogies carrying the logs, which were then drawn back to the mill.

For all of these specialised tasks large numbers of skilled men were employed in milling and its associated operations. Quite apart from the axemen and sawyers in the forest who selected and felled the trees, there were others who cut the log and a group who positioned each section and loaded it. Boilermen drove and serviced the engines and winches. There were men expert at sharpening and setting the saws, and a crew operating the mill itself. Stacking, seasoning and shipping of the milled timber involved further experience. The workforce employed by a mill usually lived in company cottages close to the mill site. Sometimes they were part of a farming or fishing community, but often they were isolated on a river or inlet close to the forests on which they depended, and they invariably developed their own unique society. Bonds were close between men who worked together in the forest or the mill, and whole families became involved in the occupation, generations following one another. Even in recreation, the timber communities strongly supported their entrants in the very closely contested chopping and sawing competitions at local fairs and meetings and at the shows in the larger towns. By the 1890s these events, which arose from the daily working lives of the men ranked in many districts with the major sports and drew a considerable following, with popular heroes and a lively betting ring. This public interest added to the pride and standing of the men in the forests. These traditions live on today in the popularity of chopping and sawing contests and in the love of many Tasmanians for the feel of an axe in the hand. With an island population of one hundred and seventy-two thousand in 1901, when the timber industry, like mining, employed several thousand men, it is not surprising that the image of the bushman of the forests was held in universal regard, and that the contingents of troops which sailed to South Africa in 1900 and 1901 should be called the Tasmanian Imperial Bushmen. Even today, the huge figure of an axeman hewn from a tree trunk, standing beside the Huon River is a potent social image. Thus the abiding myths of a society are created and nurtured.

15   A PRACTICAL PEOPLE

The Mount Lyell and North-East Dundas railways ran through some of the most beautiful forest and gorge country in the west, the latter passing almost through the spray of the Montezuma Falls.

The exciting arc of the Gordon Dam, the wedge of Darwin or the solid walls of Clark and the older structures command attention.

TASMANIANS are singularly practical and innovative. Over two centuries they have overcome the difficulties posed by the mountainous nature of their island, its climate and vegetation, and have harnessed its features for their own use. Generations of people have built, shaped, adapted and transformed the land to control it and utilise its resources. In doing so, the island society has acquired both the skills to create change and the confidence that any challenge posed by the land will be met. What earlier generations achieved in clearing, draining, establishing settlement and agriculture, pulling great logs from the forests and mining the remote and hostile mountains, has created the foundation, shared mythology and cultural direction for those who followed to continue to apply their skills and ingenuity to even larger ventures in extending the material infrastructure. Tasmanians gain a particular satisfaction from overcoming the practical obstacles they encounter in the island's complex landforms.

One of the most immediate problems in a region beset with steep mountain ridges and valleys, is the construction of adequate roads. From the time when convict-built dray roads wound through the midland hills, their bridges and culverts fine and sturdy examples of the stonemason's craft, the island's roads have demonstrated the mastery of engineer and builder. Convict gangs laboured for years quarrying and hauling rock for the Bridgewater causeway, and the base of the swinging span of an earlier bridge remains as a tribute to its engineers, just as the causeway itself still answers the critics of its construction. One of the most difficult sections of highway was the long climb over St Marys Pass on the east coast, its careful grades maintained with deceptive ease on the steep ridges and sidelings. The later road on the nearby Elephant Pass, on less stable ground, was a further sound achievement, despite its liability to landslip damage. More recent roads reflect the same care in design and engineering. Most notable are the two depression roads on Mt Barrow and Mt Wellington, intended both as relief projects in the dark years of the 1930s and as part of the state's tourist network. The Central Plateau posed similar problems, necessitating climbs to an altitude of twelve hundred metres, but the Lake and Poatina highways make good use of ridge and gully to provide safe and attractive access to the highlands. The difficult country of the west coast had its share of challenging road projects. The most memorable is the dramatic section of the Lyell Highway between Queenstown and Gormanston with its sharp bends, frightening drops and vistas of denuded mountainside. A close rival for scenic appeal as well as for engineering competence is the HEC Anthony road south of Tullah, winding about the spurs of Mt Murchison. Less visible, but no less notable for sound design and construction are the thousands of kilometres of HEC and forestry roads through mountain country in every part of the island, roads which take heavy loads in all weathers and which thread through some of the most difficult terrain in Australia.

In the past, Tasmania has been innovative in the construction of railways, particularly the lines in more remote regions. In the early decades of the twentieth century, branch lines were extended to many rural districts, not always for sound, practical reasons. While main lines ran to Smithton in the north-west and north-east to Herrick, there were at the same time subsidiary lines to Waratah, Sheffield and Staverton, Mole Creek, Redpa, Roger River, Nietta, Sorell, Apsley and Kallista. Most of these were uneconomical, but the will and the expertise to build were always strong. In the mountains of the west coast, where until recent years roads were not practicable, the Emu Bay Railway, originally terminating at Zeehan in 1902, was for over thirty years the west's only land link with the rest of the state apart from packhorse-tracks. This line still operates between Burnie and Melba Flat, across wet, mountainous country where substantial bridges are required. Railways connected the port of Strahan with Zeehan and Queenstown, with further lines to Dundas, and from Pillinger to Linda. These lines were essential for the mines to continue operating, as roads could never have been built and maintained economically in such country. The Mount Lyell Railway was itself a wonderful example of railway engineering, with over forty bridges, including the 'Quarter-mile' bridge crossing the stream and floodplain of the King River. There was such difficulty in finding a stable base for the piles of the bridge in mid-stream, that this, added to other problems, forced the contractor to relinquish the project. High timber bridges spanned deep ravines and took

'... railways ran through some of the most beautiful forest and gorge country in the west ... passing almost through the spray of the Montezuma Falls'.
Railway bridge at the foot of Montezuma Falls, 1900 (John Watt Beattie; author's collection).

the railway along the precipitous sides of the King River Gorge. Even now, the slender timber supports may be seen beside the new line, towering among the trees above mountain torrents.

So steep were the gradients on this railway that locomotives had to be specially designed in Germany using the Abt system, to give them greater purchase. The western region played a leading part in the development of the narrow-gauge mountain railway as the most effective means of transport in difficult country. The North-East Dundas Railway was one of the best examples of this type of line, serving mines between Zeehan and Williamsford. The narrow gauge enabled its builders to take it around the sharp folds and spurs of narrow gorges. The deep cuttings and remains of heavy timber bridge abutments of these long-abandoned railways are an enduring tribute to the construction engineers and navvies who built them. The Mount Lyell and North-East Dundas railways ran through some of the most beautiful forest and gorge country in the west, the latter passing almost through the spray of the Montezuma Falls. The builders of railways were so versatile and their promoters so confident, that they would undertake to bring a line through virtually any country, and they competed keenly with one another to do so. In the 1890s there was considerable rivalry between developers in the north and those in the south of the island to exploit the growing mineral wealth of the west coast, and at least nine different railway proposals were submitted to governments. Though a few would have been quite feasible projects, the major problem always lay in securing financial backing. Several proposed lines were surveyed, but only one, the Great Western, reached the construction stage, about two kilometres of formation being completed.

Relatively few inlets on Tasmania's coasts have provided ready-made harbours for vessels larger than trading ketches. This was a severe limitation to an island state dependent upon trading links with other centres. Several ports have had to be constructed to enable regions to develop. Port Frederick, at the mouth of the Mersey, had to be dredged and cleared, and the bar, which in 1828 was only two metres below the surface at low water, had to be deepened progressively so that shipping could enter safely. A training wall was designed by harbour works engineer Charles Napier Bell so that scouring by the river's current would prevent the accumulation of sediment. The same principle had been applied earlier by Napier Bell to the notorious entrance to Macquarie Harbour. The shallow, narrow entrance passage was subject to heavy seas and strong currents which had led to the loss of a number of vessels. The development of the west coast mining fields was hampered throughout the 1890s, as only small steamers could cross the bar and enter the harbour. By dredging the bar and building a training wall on the southern side, Napier Bell used the massive outflow of water to scour the entrance channel. A breakwater at the entrance protected ships from the large seas that roll in from the west and south-west. Similar works projected for the northern side of the entrance were not undertaken. The town of Burnie grew on an exposed coastline, little shelter being afforded by the wide indentation of Emu Bay. A substantial breakwater converted the open anchorage into a secure port, enabling industries such as APPM to become established. Similarly, the port of Stanley has been developed in stages behind its breakwater. Coastal works in other areas have included the Dunally Canal, which was excavated to enable coastal craft to avoid the rough passage through Storm Bay and around Cape Raoul and Cape Pillar, and the extensive pellet-loading facility at Port Latta.

The network of hydro-electric schemes has created widespread and systematic changes in the Tasmanian landscape, and has demonstrated more clearly than any other work the degree of control and utilisation possible with modern equipment and techniques. The sheer scale of the undertaking in relation to the area of the island is itself impressive.

In order to take advantage of the high rainfall of the western and central regions, the elevation of the Central Plateau, and the flows of the major northern, central and western rivers, the interlinking projects have spanned all of these areas. Starting from the first Great Lake scheme in 1917, three generations of workers built one of the most effective and advanced power schemes in the world for the area of land on which it draws and the population which supports it. Through most of its existence the HEC was a commission, known throughout the island simply as 'The Hydro'; its Commissioner was generally regarded as the state's most powerful man. Many families have based their lives upon HEC employment, and successive generations have gained both their livelihood and high levels of satisfaction from their involvement in creating the network. They included Tasmanian-born, other Australians and, from 1947, a large influx of European migrants who came to swell the workforce in the period of postwar expansion. These were people who had immense pride in the outcomes of what was often rough, unpleasant work in conditions that were wet, cold and dreary for long periods. For over seventy years, this large group of diverse people, working on a wide range of tasks under different conditions and living in communities in remote parts of the state, accumulated an immense store of skills and experience, some of which is now being applied to development in other countries. HEC construction workers epitomised for many the qualities most valued by the Tasmanian community: hardiness, practical competence, pride in their work, self-reliance.

The great dams tend to dominate as symbols of the HEC's attainments, monuments to engineers, draftsmen and a large group of specialised workers and administrators. The exciting arc of the Gordon Dam, the wedge of Darwin or the solid walls of Clark and the older structures command attention. Of equal interest, however, and just as advanced in their conception, are the large rock-fill dams such as Rowallen, Parangana and Cethana, the rock hewn from nearby quarries, carefully sorted and stabilised as it was shaped into the structure. Viewing platforms and explanatory diagrams inform the traveller concerning the technology and building strategies, yet few who see them can begin to appreciate the extent of personal commitment, training and experience which occupied the years of their design and construction. Beyond the dams are extensive infrastructure units.

The HEC produced highly skilled tunnelling crews who created the many diversion and other tunnels as part of several systems. The tunnelling machine, the Mole, set distance records at the height of this work. Notable among the achievements of the tunnellers are the Dee, Mossy Marsh and Wayatinah tunnels in the Derwent scheme and Fisher and Parangana in the Mersey–Forth. Amongst other features of the network are hundreds of kilometres of canals such as those near Shannon Lagoon and below Butlers Gorge, the large siphons, power stations, including the underground Gordon station, and thousands of kilometres of transmission lines which march across almost every region. The fine roads, many in areas of high scenic value, have contributed greatly to tourist access, and will be of increasing importance to the state.

To many Tasmanians, it is the HEC projects across the island which are most highly visible and largest in scale, and which have the strongest appeal. They represent not only the complete control and subjugation of the wilder parts of the land, but they also provide reminders of a period in Tasmania's recent past that is seen increasingly as an ideal time: a time of high employment, security, prosperity and material development. Seen in retrospect, it was a period when problems were solved in direct, practical ways, when communities such as those of the HEC retained the virtues and values of the past, and when life seemed far simpler. The HEC took Tasmanians to the high point of the practical culture.

16   LIVING WITH THE MYTH

The culture of the land remains largely as it has always been: one of practical endeavour and achievement.

The Derwent's broad waters and the shapely hills of the eastern shore are constant reminders of the world beyond the city.

TEN GENERATIONS of European Tasmanians have developed a dominant practical tradition of modification and utilisation of the land. It is a tradition which grew originally out of the necessity of establishing the whole complex fabric of a modern society in a small island without regard to any other factor, and which was later driven by prevailing nineteenth-century ideals of progress. Because this process has touched the lives of so many Tasmanian people, it has shaped their cultural identity. The same process has operated, though less pervasively, through the country, forming a central aspect of the Australian self-image. To the Tasmanian, this identity is one based upon acceptance of the land as a testing-ground for strength, ingenuity and masculinity. The figure of the bushman in its many manifestations: surveyor, engineer, builder, miner, logger, hunter ... stands at the core of this identity.

Tasmanians are still closer to the bushman and countryman than are other Australians. Theirs is a provincial society, in which most live physically within more immediate reach of the rural or natural landscape than do their mainland counterparts. Eighty-six per cent of Australians live in urban areas;[12] while the percentage is certainly far lower for Tasmanians, even those who live in Tasmania's cities have a higher level of contact with, and greater knowledge of, the land beyond the suburbs. The island is far less urbanised, with a population of fewer than half a million; its cities are small and still relatively compact, and even within them one is conscious of surrounding hills, trees or fields. It is easy to leave city streets and suburbs and to be in open countryside or mountain foothills within a very short time. Many Tasmanians grew up in the smaller towns and still have family connections with the rural or mining districts, even a sense of belonging to them after years of living in the city. The Tasmanian population is a stable one, with fewer people settling from overseas or from other Australian states, so that a great many spend most of their lives in the island and develop that close attachment to it which is characteristic of all islanders.

Not surprisingly, Tasmanians demonstrate a high level of awareness of their non-urban surroundings. The visual impact of the natural features which surround them is inescapable. It is hard to ignore the dominance of Mt Wellington over Hobart suburbs or to remain insensitive to its infinite variety of light and cloud patterns in the course of the day. The Derwent's broad waters and the shapely hills of the eastern shore are constant reminders of the world beyond the city. Likewise, Launceston's surrounding hills, the gorge or the blue-hazed valley of the Tamar can be seen from most parts of the city. Burnie and Devonport are still sufficiently compact for one to be always conscious of the coast and of the rural countryside which lie close beside them. This physical proximity to the land has made it both easy and attractive for people to spend their leisure time in pursuits away from the towns such as camping, fishing, touring, picnicking, hunting and holidaying in seaside or highland shacks. Thus it is difficult not to identify with the continuing traditions of the land and, unconsciously or otherwise, to accept the culture of utilising the land, seeing it as an extended field for resource and recreation and subject to people's rightful and inevitable control. The culture of the land remains largely as it has always been: one of practical endeavour and achievement.

Attitudes and values which relate to the land are substantially those of a century ago, now given a contemporary form; they are still pragmatic, assertive, masculine. Tasmanians still walk into the forest psychologically, and often literally, with an axe in one hand. Physical strength is still part of the tradition, as it was in the forests of the 1880s. Control is now achieved through the power of hands on a machine rather than through the skilful swing of an axe or the body's weight on a saw; teamwork, resilience, hardiness and the mateship of the camp continue to be prime perceived virtues. The images and ideals are still embodied in those who face natural forces, who drive the great machines, who change the land. The culture is seen in attitudes and perceptions which underlie the process of change: altering natural landscape or long-established farmland is seen almost universally as progress, as development, as the harnessing of nature through human endeavour. The ultimate values of such change are seldom seriously questioned or doubted by the majority of people. Hence a road, plantation, mine, rural housing development, transmission line, is still assessed on material and immediate criteria, and large-scale change is hastened by special legislative processes.

Perhaps the clearest evidence of the strength of the practical culture can be found in the many recreational activities which involve the use of the land. These seek to recapture the perceived independence and self-reliance of the old-time trapper, prospector, bushman, though without the skills and complexity of the original who, after all, lived in a very different world. They possess an element of control and subjugation, of tension between the individual person and the land. Hunting, off-road driving and trail-bike riding are the most obvious examples, with horse-riding, fishing and walking involving some elements of the traditional perceptions. A major distinction between activities of the past and those of today is that with the technologies now available people are infinitely more mobile than their forebears and the effects of their actions upon the land are far more substantial and enduring. The four wheel drive vehicle, the trail-bike, aircraft, forest roading and walking tracks now afford entry to places hitherto secure in their remoteness, while the chain-saw and the wheel effect change on a scale unimaginable to the bushman of old. All assume an inherent right of participants to use the land and to bring about incidental change.

So strong is the inherited culture of land use and control that there are organisations set up specifically to ensure its maintenance in particular activities on the basis that tradition confers a right to continue to use the land in established ways. It is certainly of value to preserve details of historic land use and practices, even though these may not have been generally beneficial, and to celebrate the bushman's virtues of hardiness and generosity as well as the skills associated with bush traditions. What is open to question is the continuation of past activities in the more crowded and pressured conditions of today, and the assumption that because a practice has been carried on for a few decades—and all post-settlement history is brief—this confers a right to maintain the practice.

At the beginning of the third century of European occupation of a small, fragile and uniquely beautiful island, it is time to review all of the traditions and perceptions that have shaped our approach to the land. The skills and qualities of bushman and engineer, and of generations of other practical people, have established a material infrastructure across much of the island. They have wrought substantial changes to its landscape, changes which were largely unavoidable in the context of their times. We who have inherited their traditions continue to change it. If these traditions and the view of the land which has become so deeply ingrained in our island society persist, and continue to direct our treatment of the land, the next half-century will bring significant and irreparable loss of both the ecological and landscape values for which the island is loved by its people and renowned beyond its shores, and upon which it must chiefly rely for its future viability.

Section VI

THE COUNTER-CULTURE: A LAND TO BE CHERISHED

'... nature had put forth her best effort and had produced a scene in beauty far beyond the wildest dreams of art.'

In a *Courier* article of 1850, Surveyor-General James Calder recalled the events and impressions of his 1842 journey overland from Lake St Clair to the lower Gordon with Sir John and Lady Franklin. One of the clearest of his recollections was that of the view westward across the forested valleys and ranges from Mt Arrowsmith, at a time when the forests were still untouched by the wildfires of the prospectors. Calder's comments on these extensive forests convey the attitudes which largely prevailed in the colony during his lifetime and which have persisted since:

> The general character of our landscape is, to my taste, displeasing; for notwithstanding the diversity of surface a mountainous country ever presents, it acquires in Tasmania a disagreeable monotony, from the unvarying hue of our black and interminable forests. Many a scene has its beauty half marred by the constant intervention of these gloomy-looking woods, the trees of which, though individually often handsome, are, in the mass, anything but an agreeable adjunct

to our wild scenery; and the extent of the woodland is mostly so disproportioned to every other object, that it is only here and there that the forest becomes unobjectionable ...

An irrepressible feeling of regret involuntarily overcomes us as we survey the tract now in view, and reflect that all this immense waste is without a single inhabitant. Not the faintest trace of its occupation by man is apparent. No homesteads or roads, no enclosures or cultivation, attest his presence; but, on the contrary, the country could not look more void of animation ...[1]

Eventually, the Linda Track ran close to the heights since named Calders Lookout and descended into the forest-filled depths upon which Calder had remarked so disparagingly, winding through the Franklin, Collingwood, Victoria and Nelson valleys on its way to the west coast mining fields. In 1888 a reporter from the *Tasmanian Mail* followed the Linda Track on his way to cover the rapidly developing mines. His description of those 'interminable forests' reveals a very different attitude in one whose calling brought him into just as close contact with the world of everyday practicality as did Calder's:

> The cut track follows the undulations of the hills about 100ft from the water's edge, below it grow giant ferns in truly vernal bloom, the eye seems to rest on a sea of fern fronds, broken here and there by the moss covered trunks of the myrtle and other trees; the pretty climbing heath with its pendulous, dark red, vase shaped blossom twined its slender stalks round the myrtle trunks, and here and there fallen trees added diversity to the scene, while the babbling of the water below all made music to heighten the effect of the spectacle. A humid climate this, moss grew from everything, and hung in festoons from

some of the lower branches of the trees. Above the track it was the same, while tiny cascades of water fell from every rock. The picture was perfect, nature had put forth her best effort and had produced a scene in beauty far beyond the wildest dreams of Art. It is said the Nelson Valley is gold bearing, but it is to be hoped the sacrilegious pick of the gold digger may never disturb a soil so beautiful, and that nature will not be profaned by sordid, wealth-seeking man.2

The two passages do not simply reflect the differences in temperament and background of two individual men; they also highlight two deep and contrary currents in the developing society of the island, and in particular an emerging sensitivity to the land itself during the course of the nineteenth century.

17   THE ARTISTS' VIEW

Tasmania's reputation had changed from that of a harsh repository for prisoners to a place of considerable beauty and charm.

THE EARLY Van Diemen's Land colony was no place for a landscape artist. Yet eventually it was artists who would create amongst the colonists the first realisation of the island's character and beauty. For almost a generation settlers were preoccupied with the practical tasks of clearing and building. Apart from portrait painters such as Bock, Gould and Wainewright there was little scope for an artist. If the colonists held a common image of the land's future, then that image was a re-creation of the ordered green countryside of the British Isles; they saw little beauty or appeal in the brown grasses and straggly eucalypts of their adopted home, and certainly would not have been persuaded to buy such landscapes. When Joseph Lycett interpreted Tasmanian scenery, he wisely cast it in the form of the English pastoral setting. Lycett had been transported to New South Wales in 1814, and came to Van Diemen's Land in the 1820s. Over a period of three years he painted scenes in the south and in the settled lands of the midland plain, the Tamar and South Esk valleys. Few are readily recognisable or convey any sense of specific place or of the individual character of the land. Trees are rounded to the form of English copses, their sinuous stems bearing no resemblance to those of eucalypts. Forests are clear-edged and restrained, offering no threat. Farmlands are gentle and clearly fertile, while prosperous farmers make their way along the roads on sturdy hacks or stride across their pleasant fields. Such landscapes reassured settlers and spoke to migrants of a country subjugated and docile.

During the first three decades there were people who saw and drew or painted the Tasmanian landscape with far more realism and sensitivity to its form and particularly to its vegetation, but their work was relatively little known. In the north-west Henry Hellyer, the Van Diemen's Land Company's Chief Surveyor and Architect, made numerous sketches in his field books during the course of his explorations between 1826 and 1831. These were intended not only to record the appearance of the topography he was examining, but also to express his own response to specific places. His coastline views from Northdown and from the entrance to Port Sorell[3] are fine, accurate studies though the most detailed and remarkable is the full-circle panorama from the summit of St Valentines Peak,[4] which clearly portrays mountains and forest, and locates the grassed openings of the Surrey Hills. A particularly graphic drawing in his Hampshire Hills road journal of 1827 shows the road party's camp.[5] Masses of straight eucalypt shafts tower over the rough bark shelters of the workmen, while closer at hand giant man-ferns drape fronds across a heap of fallen tree trunks. The slender corridor of road leads off into the forest beyond the camp, fragile beneath the dark canopy. Hellyer was an accomplished artist; had he lived longer, some of his sketches may have been worked into early Tasmanian watercolour landscapes. Even from his brief descriptions of coast, forest and mountains, it is clear that he saw the island's beauty and diversity with a clear vision and without feeling the need to shape what he saw to a set of preconceived images.

Augustus Prinsep and his wife Elizabeth were in Van Diemen's Land for only six months, between September 1829 and March 1830. Although Augustus was weakened by poor health which had necessitated this break in his Indian service, the couple travelled widely in the island; a series of letters describing their travels was published by Elizabeth in 1833, following her husband's death. A number of illustrations were at first published separately, and in a later edition were included with the letters.[6] These are scenes of Hobart, the Derwent River and New Norfolk, and are notable for their accuracy and understanding of the land. The watercolour of the Black Snake Inn (Granton) conveys the rawness of colonial roads, the distinctive shape of Mt Dromedary and the summer brown of the grassy hills above Bridgewater. In both of the New Norfolk paintings the straight and sometimes spindly limbs of eucalypts are faithfully portrayed, as are the separate shapes of trees covering nearby hills: features that troubled early Australian artists. Both illustrations give emphasis to the farmlands which have pushed the forests back into the hills, and present a well-established, ordered way of life.

By the time of John Glover's arrival in 1831, the colony was a little less wary in its attitude to the land. The tragic Black War had ended with the agreement of the Aborigines to be moved away from the Tasmanian mainland, and the settlers were no longer facing constant threat. Pastures had spread and the great push of flocks to the outlying lands had commenced. Though life was still rough and often basic, there were rising levels of prosperity and confidence. At sixty-four, Glover was a professional landscape painter with an established reputation in Britain, his Arcadian treatment of the land reminiscent of the work of Claude Lorraine.

He came as a man of substance whose work and name commanded attention. For his part, Glover was too sensitive an artist not to respond to the bright skies of his new surroundings. He knew at once that Tasmania was essentially different from Europe and he sought to grasp that difference and respond to it. This involved a process of turning from the softness, dim shades and classical figures of convention and accepting the light which radiated from the Tasmanian countryside. He began to master the strange new shapes of the eucalypt, whose presence pervades the landscape, and in this lay perhaps his greatest success. Glover was a painter of the pastures, the open or lightly wooded country that Calder had extolled, which stretched across the midland plain and along the valley of the South Esk, a country which lay close to his home, 'Patterdale', at the foot of Ben Lomond. His paintings offer symbols of prosperity in the contented cattle and distant homestead, but the hills beyond are native Tasmanian hills, their scattered, open woodland becoming denser as the flanks rise.[7] In his best works, Glover's trees have the true eucalypts' individuality, with twisting bark, open crowns and pleasant asymmetry. Some of his Nile paintings depict Aboriginal people going about their normal activities, though by the time of his arrival the survivors of the Black War were being removed to Flinders Island. Even so, he did meet Aborigines on several occasions. The Nile district, where Glover had settled, had been a favoured hunting and living area of the Ben Lomond Tribe, and the evidence of their lives: their tools, weapons, huts, even the ashes of their fires, would have been familiar across the countryside. Glover clearly sensed their continuing presence in this land and felt it fitting to incorporate scenes from their lives, including corroborees.[8] One of Glover's strengths lay in his recognition of the quality of Tasmanian light and in his ability to convey this in works which respond to a range of conditions, particularly the effects of the low sun and the reds and golds of late afternoon.[9] One of the most striking landscapes is that of Stacks Bluff from the South Esk Valley;[10] in its fine treatment of cliff structure, timbered hills and foreground trees it captures the essence of Tasmanian mountain country and looks forward to Prout and Piguenit.

Despite his reputation, Glover sold few paintings in Tasmania, although his output was constant and work despatched to England in 1835–6 was well regarded. Virtually any mediocre European landscape or copy was more attractive to colonists than was the work of local artists. However, when his paintings were dispersed cheaply after his death in 1849 they gained belated recognition, presenting for the first time the island's features, its light, distance and form, treated by a respected artist as fit subjects for landscape. The artists who followed benefited from the influence of Glover's work and standing.

The foremost figure of the group of artists which emerged in Hobart in the 1840s was John Skinner Prout. He had emigrated at the age of thirty-five, far younger than Glover had been, but still having attained notable success as an artist and lithographer in Britain. Skinner Prout spent three years in Sydney before difficult conditions there forced a move to Van Diemen's Land in 1844. He was deeply impressed by the island and toured extensively, going as far afield as Lake St Clair, Great Lake and Flinders Island, putting together material for his two volumes of *Tasmania Illustrated*.[11] A few months after his arrival in Hobart he gave two series of lectures, both of which proved popular. One response to the increasing interest in art was the formation of a sketching club which conducted excursions to various scenic spots, favourites being the ferny glens in the foothills of Mt Wellington. A second venture was the staging of Hobart's first exhibition of art, held in the Legislative Council Chamber in January 1845. The organising committee included Prout, Francis Simpkinson, Bishop and Mrs Nixon, Peter Fraser and G T W B Boyes. This exhibition was extremely successful, and was followed by a second in May 1846 in the Exhibition Rooms.

John Skinner Prout (1805–1876): *Mt Wellington, Hobarton, 1846*, watercolour and chinese highlights, 27 x 37.4, Purchased 1962, AG515 (TMAG).

Art in the colony had gained a respected leader, public acclaim and the blessing of the colonial establishment.

Drawing and watercolour painting were considered to be creditable accomplishments amongst educated people, so that many of the community were capable of responding to the mastery and enthusiasm of such an established artist as Skinner Prout. Some had learned the skills of accurate pencil and brushwork as part of their professional training, among them Lieutenant Simpkinson RN, attached to the Rossbank Observatory, and the Surveyor-General, George Frankland. During these years sketching and painting scenes from the Tasmanian landscape became accepted to the extent that many colonists came to regard their surroundings with a fresh perception. This marked a significant change in attitude over the two decades; henceforth there would always be people who could value the land for qualities beyond its economic worth, and who could communicate this value to others.

A close working relationship developed between Skinner Prout and Francis Simpkinson. Though they differed in background, age and experience, they were clearly drawn to each other by a common delight in their surroundings and the challenge of capturing in their work the essence of the island's scenery. Simpkinson was a gifted amateur who painted for the sheer enjoyment of the task, and to record his time in a distant and attractive land. Prout, the elder man, was a professional artist, living by his painting, teaching and publishing. Undoubtedly each influenced the other. Simpkinson's paintings have a freshness, a freedom from convention, to which Prout responded. Many paintings were created as they worked side by side, studying and discussing the tones of mountain and water, the play of light along a shoreline or the ever-changing skies.

Prout's paintings express a strong sense of place; not simply of the tranquil and colourful, but of the commonplace as well. The various Mt Wellington views demonstrate a range of responses to the mountain's commanding presence from differing vantage-points and in varying conditions of light and weather. He could convey the starkness of fire-scarred gums on the mountain, their blackened trunks crowding about the corridor of the track, their leafless branches arching above.[12] By contrast, he captured in other paintings the power of tall forest, with the stately shafts of big trees dwarfing a woodcutter's shingled hut.[13] Like Simpkinson, he was attracted by the sense of space and the tonal range of the east coast, a view from Little Swanport focussing attention on the distant Maria Island framed by wind-blown casuarinas.[14] Skinner Prout's work was accessible and well known to those in the colony who were responsive to its cultural life and whose views were influential. Locally acquired paintings and his two volumes of lithographs ensured that his work remained available to later generations, to influence the way in which they in turn saw their own land.

Francis Simpkinson's watercolours remained little known apart from works displayed in the exhibitions of 1845 and 1846. With Skinner Prout, he rambled through what were then the pristine forests of Mt Wellington and he, even more than Prout, was drawn to the shaded, rocky glens and deep fern gullies.[15] He was fascinated by the sandstone cliffs and colourful formations above the Derwent at New Norfolk, the subject of several sketches and paintings. In the same way, the granites of the Freycinet Peninsula were viewed from many different angles, their fine slabs and buttresses rising proudly from the water. The excursion to Lake St Clair in 1845 was quite venturesome for men with little bush experience, as the lake had first been reached by an exploring party only ten years earlier, and the track to it was still extremely rough and hard to follow. Simpkinson and Prout produced a number of studies, notably of Mt Ida and Mt Olympus.[16] It was not simply the grandeur of the mountains far from human activity which concerned the two artists, however. The bleached, frost-killed forest of the Nive and the intricate shapes of fallen trees beside the shore of Lake St Clair were also subjects of interesting treatment. Simpkinson made a close study of the eucalypt in all its variety, ranging from the great trunks of the southern forest near Port Cygnet[17] to the forested slopes of the Derwent Valley above Plenty.[18] He sketched the twisted white limbs of dead trees beside the river[19] and the delicate tracery of smaller shrubs on the Domain.[20]

The major contribution of Glover, Prout and Simpkinson was to show the colonists of Van Diemen's Land their own surroundings in such a way that they awakened to their beauty and variety. As Browning's Fra Lippo Lippi saw it:

... We're made so that we love
First when we see them painted, things we have passed
Perhaps a hundred times nor cared to see;[21]

This was not achieved by painting only the sublime and tranquil, nor by idealising or glamorising their subjects. Their success lay in the freshness and clarity of their vision: their subjects were the recognisable daily surroundings of the settlers' lives. They were the cultivated valleys backed by forested hills, the shingled cottages on remote selections such as The Den, and the established homesteads of successful landowners. They were the small villages, the roads, the probation stations and projects where work gangs laboured. The artists revealed to the people of mid-century Hobart their own city in its splendid setting, the fine sandstone buildings, gardens, docks and shipping, and above all the great mountain in its many moods and seasons.

Their influence had gained from the changed cultural climate of Sir John Franklin's governorship between 1837 and 1843: the Franklins gathered around them people who were generally cultivated and urbane, in particular those who were accomplished in the arts and sciences. The influence of their work was, of course, restricted to a relatively small circle of those with sufficient interest to concern themselves with art and in a position to do so. It was greatest upon those who were themselves amateur artists: the sketching club members and those who attended the lectures and exhibitions. But it was an influence that spread across the years; Tasmanians' view of their own country had begun to change.

One of the most influential Tasmanian artists and writers of the second half of the century was Louisa Anne Meredith. Her achievement lay in bringing many of her fellow colonists to view their surroundings more sympathetically, and in giving them a better knowledge of both the land and its wild creatures. She brought at least some of her readers to begin to value whatever was native, and not to see their Tasmanian landscape and animals as inferior to those of Home. Louisa was twenty-eight when she came to Van Diemen's Land late in 1840, having won critical acclaim in Birmingham for her journal articles, poetry, reviews and paintings. She had published three books, including a collection of poems and two volumes on English flowers which were illustrated with her own paintings.

Louisa and Charles Meredith had lived for a time in New South Wales, which in drought conditions they found dusty and unattractive. By contrast, the Hobart of Sir John and Lady Franklin was a place of coolness and beauty. They also found the cultural climate to some extent in harmony with their own tastes, as the Franklins attempted, with indifferent success, to raise the level of interest in literature and learning in general. Following their arrival, the Merediths stayed for a time in New Town, which was then a village on the outskirts of Hobart, surrounded by farmland.

After the dry plains of New South Wales, the green fields, wide reaches of river and wooded hills were attractive beyond anything Louisa had thought possible. On the final part of their journey the couple travelled to the east coast across the very rough track from the Coal River Valley to Little Swanport. Louisa found the eucalypt forest along this route monotonous and unappealing, the trees strange and untidy with their dead limbs and hanging strips of bark. However, once the party reached the coast, the scenery was to their eyes far more fresh, open and varied. Apart from short interludes at Port Sorell and Launceston and her last years in Hobart, the greater part of Louisa Meredith's life was spent on the east coast, at first in the district close to Waterloo Point (Swansea) at the head of Great Oyster Bay where Charles's father and his family were settled on the 'Cambria' property, and in later years at locations further south.

It was the east coast that Louisa Meredith came to love and about which she wrote. Her writing had a wonderful vitality and crispness and she had the gift of being able to create vivid impressions of places, people and events and of the native animals of her adopted home. She never tired of gazing across the wide sweep of Great Oyster Bay towards the fretted line of the Hazards, Freycinet and Schouten Island, and at the distant blue heights of Maria Island, the subject of one of her most attractive sketches. Between the 1850s and 1890s Louisa produced four books which described her surroundings and also portrayed them through her drawings. *My Home in Tasmania* (two volumes) was published in London in 1852, copies selling well in Tasmania, while the two editions of *Our Island Home*, 1879 and 1881, were published jointly in London and Tasmania. Again, the last series of *Bush Friends*, a limited edition of 1891, was available in Hobart. Through these books, as well as through her talks and her influence in many community bodies, Louisa Meredith succeeded in bringing the colour, form and variety of the Tasmanian landscape to the reading public of the colony. Her delightful style appealed to the reader and her drawings and paintings of Tasmanian scenes, and of plants, flowers and wild creatures brought to some their first real knowledge of the richness of their own land.

Louisa and Charles Meredith shared a deep concern for the animals and birds of the Tasmanian bushland about which Louisa had written so much. They were often distressed at the way in which these creatures were hunted and killed indiscriminately. During his years in parliament Charles successfully introduced some of the first laws for the protection of native animals and birds.[22]

The 1840s and 1850s were rich years for Tasmanian landscape painting. Apart from major figures such as Glover, Skinner Prout and Simpkinson, many other gifted artists, among them Mary Morton Allport, Bishop Nixon, Knut Bull and Henry Gritton, exhibited in this period. It was a pioneering time, which saw the Tasmanian landscape firmly accepted both by artists and by discerning colonists. No longer did the Hobart or Launceston merchant follow only his nostalgic longing for the English scenes of his youth in choosing a painting. He was now prepared to live with at least some of the light, tranquil views of the farmlands, hills and stately eucalypts of this country upon his walls. For increasing numbers, this was the country of their youth. This also reflected a growing pride in the island which was linked in 1856 to its new name of Tasmania, and there was pride also in their own success, often reflected in a commissioned painting.

By the 1860s, however, established painters no longer made their homes in Hobart, preferring the exciting gold-rich cities of the other colonies; the local artistic community fragmented and lost some of its former vitality. It was in this changing, uncertain climate that the best known of Tasmania's landscape painters grew to maturity.

William Charles Piguenit was Tasmania's, and Australia's, first native-born artist of importance. Born in 1836, the son of a convict father and free mother who followed her husband to Van Diemen's Land, Piguenit had a good general education by local standards, but received no formal training as an artist. In 1849 he joined the Survey Department and mastered the skills of draughtsmanship, the standard of his work earning praise ten years later from Surveyor-General James Calder. In 1860 he became friendly with fellow survey draughtsman Frank Dunnett, who had studied as an artist in England and had also tutored in Hobart. Dunnett's advice and influence were invaluable for a young man who lacked other avenues of training. Dunnett, like Piguenit himself, admired the grander aspects of Tasmanian scenery, and it was to the elemental world of the western mountains that Piguenit turned for the subjects of some of his most acclaimed work.

Piguenit was described by his friend Colonel Legge as '... a painter whose life's aim was to make known the beauties of his native country.'[23]

Of particular importance in forming his unique view of the island's landscape was his participation in several expeditions into the little-known mountain country of western and south-western Tasmania. These took him into some of the wildest and most inspiring scenery in Australia and helped to develop the sense of awe and majesty which became a central element of his painting. Where Glover, Prout and Simpkinson had brought before Tasmanians the beauty and subtlety of the island's open landscapes, its coasts, its tall and elegant eucalypts and its complex patterns of light, Piguenit sought to convey the character of the wild and remote mountains. He saw the power of the country in brooding mist, dark lakes and the dominance of lofty peaks.

Piguenit's position on the staff of the Survey Department enabled him to take part in James Scott's expedition overland from the Huon to Port Davey in 1871. The party travelled up the Huon River, along the Arthur Plains and down the Spring River to Payne Bay, the route of McKay's old track, and one which provided wonderful views of the gray quartzite peaks of the Arthur Range and the ranges to the south. Several days were spent at Port Davey and a visit was made to the gorge known as Hells Gates on the Davey River. Piguenit made many sketches of scenery along the route, some of which were later used as bases for paintings, several different works sometimes emanating from one sketch. One of the best known paintings resulting from this expedition was that of the Arthur Range from The Razorback, showing the array of peaks of the great range, including Federation Peak, and the broad sweep of the Arthur Plains.[24] In August 1871 the sketches were displayed in the reading room of the Public Library, and the public could see for the first time an accurate portrayal of the mountains and gorges of the mysterious south-western region. The display proved extremely popular; it was a major step both in Piguenit's career as an artist and in his quest to reveal the quality of Tasmania's mountain scenery.

Scott made sure that Piguenit accompanied his second expedition in 1873, a journey to Lake St Clair and along Gould's track past Lake Petrarch to the Eldon Range. This took him amongst Tasmania's highest mountains and into the region of some of the grandest scenery, particularly Lake St Clair, Mt Olympus and the dolerite peaks of the Du Cane Range. He would return several times over the next fifteen years to absorb the atmosphere of this wonderful lake under different conditions, and its spirit would infuse some of his best known work. In 1874 Piguenit resigned from the Survey Department after twenty-three years' service and devoted himself to building his career as an artist. He was still eager to accept a place in Scott's third excursion, again to the south-west, in November 1874. This time the party followed McKay's track to the western end of the Arthur Range as they had done in 1871, but Scott then turned north-west to Lake Pedder, where they camped for a few days. Piguenit was delighted with this lake, as visitors have been over the years since, sketching the peaks of the Frankland Range from the white quartzite beach. Scott's plan was to continue north around The Sentinels and cross the Wedge Plains to the Vale of Rasselas, returning to the settled districts by way of the Dawson Road on the Florentine River. This route had been followed by Wedge's party seventeen years earlier, and led through relatively clear country. Unfortunately, in that time before accurate maps, Scott veered east into dense forest near the foot of Mt Wedge, where the party encountered horizontal scrub.[25] Eventually they returned to their Huon camp, hungry and tattered.

Thirteen years elapsed before Piguenit undertook his fourth journey into the highlands; by this time he had moved to Sydney, though he made regular trips back to Tasmania. In 1887 he joined a group led by C P Sprent and consisting of a number of prominent young Hobart men, among them his friends Robert Johnston and James Walker. The intention of the party was to walk the Linda Track from Lake St Clair to the west coast, inspect the new mining districts and return either by boat from Strahan or by foot to Waratah. When they reached the Cardigan River Piguenit decided to leave the group, together with Colonel Legge, and to spend more time in the St Clair–Arrowsmith area. He was fascinated by the mountains of this region, especially Frenchmans Cap, and was quite content to forego a visit to the mines. For several days the two men walked and climbed in the King Williams and the mountains about Lake St Clair, and many of Piguenit's sketches of Frenchmans Cap, Mt Gell, King William I and Olympus were made at this time.

As early as 1876 Piguenit's work received public acclaim. The *Mercury's* critic in that year published a sixty-three line commentary on his painting of Mt Byron and Lake Petrarch, describing it in the most favourable terms. The final comment was prophetic:

We see a fine career opening out for this rising young artist, and if he fulfils his present promise we shall find him enjoying a more than colonial reputation, with a chance of all the undefinable possibilities beyond.[26]

Piguenit achieved outstanding success in his aim to bring to as wide a public as possible the grandeur and beauty of the Tasmanian landscape, as he did later with the mountain gorges and broad inland vistas of New South Wales. His work was exhibited frequently in the Australian capitals and in New Zealand between 1866 and 1915, though he has always remained closely identified with his native Tasmania.

The landscapes which drew public attention and in which Piguenit expressed his strong feelings for Tasmania are, generally, his mountain paintings. This does not detract from the number of wonderful coastal and rural works that he created, such as his 1887 oil *Faith, Hope and Charity Islands, Port Esperance, Tasmania* which embodies some of the major qualities of his art: the sense of space and distance, the tranquillity and range of tones. But it is clear that the mountains evoked his deepest responses. Like Prout's, Piguenit's works which have the greatest fidelity to both the form and the character of the highland country are those that were executed simply and rapidly, retaining the freshness of the artist's experience, rather than those which evolved through a more attenuated process. Many of the latter were charged with a Romantic atmosphere of brooding or suffered from a distortion of the subject in order to intensify their impact which, while they appealed to contemporary tastes, lost their immediacy and sense of place. His oil *A Mountain Top, Tasmania, 1886*, is one of his finest mountain paintings. It is powerful and evocative, with the weathered dolerite monoliths and small pool seen against a background of gathering cloud. Sunlight, deep shadow and drifting mist all contribute to the interplay of elemental forces. Piguenit excelled in conveying the subtle tones and scale of mountain scenes in works given much lighter treatment, such as his 1873 sketch of Lake St Clair in pencil, pen and ink, and watercolour.[27] Most interesting of the early watercolours was that of the Arthur Range[28] from his journey to Port Davey. This revealed for the first time the characteristic gray ranges and golden-brown button grass plains of the south-west with their sharp ridge forms and pattern of softer colours. Twenty-three years later the photographer John Watt Beattie described these plains and their mountain background as being '... from a purely artistic point of view the loveliest landscape in Tasmania.'[29]

Other scenes were presented in clear, accurate impressions with pencil and watercolour: Mt Gell,[30] Frenchmans Cap,[31] Mt Rufus,[32] all sketched during the journey along the Linda Track in 1887. Of particular interest are the monochrome oil paintings of the western mountains, paintings which give emphasis to the lines of peak, ridge and valley. These brought to public notice the remote fastness of Lake Pedder and the Frankland Range,[33] Mt King William,[34] the Murchison Valley[35] and Eldon Bluff.[36] Through his focus upon the unaltered and dramatically beautiful parts of the island, Piguenit not only created awareness of new aspects of the landscape; he also conveyed the strength of his own love for this land. In this he looked across the decades to the work of Spurling III, Truchanas and Dombrovskis, and ensured his own relevance in a world in which so much was to change.

Piguenit preferred to show the Tasmanian landscape, especially the mountains, in a calm, often sombre atmosphere, with still, reflecting waters and drifting mists, suggesting a storm approaching or clearing. This may in part have helped to create the aura of mystery which the western mountains preserved in the imagination of Tasmanians until well into the twentieth century. In many of his paintings Piguenit also showed his ability to portray the characteristics of the different eucalypts, as can be seen in the white gums on the Cracroft River[37] and the stand of blue gums near Huonville,[38] continuing the recognition of the character of the eucalypt in landscape which distinguished the work of earlier artists.

By the 1880s those Tasmanians who were familiar with the galleries and attended exhibitions, who took note of paintings and who read the comments of critics and reviewers not only knew the artists who had captured the many facets of landscape, but had also become aware of the exceptional qualities of that landscape. It was possible to sense that in this island lay a variety of scenery which was unlike that of any other part of Australia, and which made it a place of particular value. The Tasmanian landscape artists of the colonial period had also brought the countryside, mountains and streetscapes of the island before people in the other colonies, and by the closing decades of the century Tasmania's reputation had changed from that of a harsh repository for prisoners to a place of considerable beauty and charm.

18 A PROCESS OF RECOGNITION

'I am struck dumb, but oh, my soul sings.'

THE TRADITION of fine landscape painting continued into the twentieth century, but for the majority of people awareness of the quality of the Tasmanian landscape came with the growth of photography. As early as 1843 Daguerreotype portraits were being taken, first by G B Goodman and later by the artist Thomas Bock and his son Alfred.[39] This type of photography did not lend itself to landscape work, though a few street scenes were recorded. In the mid-1850s the improved Chromatype process became available, enabling paper prints to be made from glass plates. The partners John Sharp and Frederick Frith pioneered the production of panoramic prints of towns, printing a five-section panorama of Hobart taken from the Domain late in 1855. Mounted copies of this were sold and found a ready market, as did Frith's views of streets, buildings and scenery around Hobart from 1857. Over the next few years the Frith brothers, Frederick and Henry, travelled to the other Tasmanian centres, producing panoramas and street views of Launceston, Deloraine, Stanley and other towns. Copies of these were popular for display in homes, and also for sending to families and friends overseas. The Frith brothers displayed Chromatype scenes in their Launceston and Hobart galleries, most of them views of towns, farms and picturesque countryside, and they also offered for sale albums of these views. Other photographers in the 1860s and 1870s followed the lead of the Friths in landscape work, Samuel Clifford in particular building up a very large collection of landscapes. Photography brought to ordinary Tasmanians a much broader knowledge of their own towns and countryside, and inevitably created a sense of its beauty, history and wealth of fine buildings and streetscapes. The major drawback of wet-plate photography for landscape work lay in the cumbersome developing equipment that had to accompany the photographer, usually in a horse-drawn coach or a railway carriage. Thus photographers were generally restricted to areas within easy reach of road or rail. Morton Allport still managed to take stereoscopic views of Lake St Clair and of mountain scenery near the Calder Track on Mt Arrowsmith in February 1863, while Piguenit and Paul Recochet also took early wet-plate photographs of the lake.

The introduction of gelatine dry plates revolutionised landscape photography. It allowed faster exposure, and exposed plates could be stored for later developing. The photographer was therefore free to move away from roads and into the more remote regions of the island. The glass plates could also be used to make positive transparencies or 'magic lantern' slides, which were an invaluable aid for lectures. There were many capable photographers of the 1880–1920 period who worked in both town and countryside, but the two acknowledged leaders in this field were John Watt Beattie and Stephen Spurling III. Their studies of Tasmania's mountains and coastline, its farmlands and rivers, and of the island's rich built heritage went far beyond simply creating awareness of these assets. They prepared the ground for the preservation of some of Tasmania's most valuable historic and scenic features.

John Beattie is more closely associated with the Tasmanian landscape, the streetscapes of towns and cities and the island's visible history than is any other photographer. He alone of the earlier artists and photographers took a public stand to advocate that some areas of particular beauty be given legislative protection, and to express concern at the effect of industrial development on the natural environment. Soon after his arrival in Tasmania as a nineteen-year-old in 1878, Beattie began photographing rural landscapes in the Derwent Valley close to the family farm at Mt Lloyd. His interest soon turned to the wilder regions: in 1879 he travelled the rough cart track to Lake St Clair, where he spent several days and took a number of dry-plate photographs of surrounding mountains. From this period of his life stemmed John Beattie's love of the Tasmanian landscape, the countryside, towns and villages; a love that was expressed throughout his life in thousands of photographs as well as through his writing and many series of illustrated lectures. In 1882 Beattie was employed by the Anson brothers, themselves capable landscape photographers, and in 1891 he purchased the business, building it over the years into a large and successful enterprise.

Like Piguenit before him, Beattie was thoroughly at home in the majestic and beautiful country of the central mountains and the west coast. He wrote of himself late in his life:

> I have been essentially an outdoor man, I love the bush, and nothing gives me greater delight than to stand on the top of some high land, and look out on a wide array of our mountain giants. I am struck dumb, but oh, my soul sings.[40]

Also like Piguenit, Beattie undertook many journeys into lesser-known areas. He visited the west coast mining fields on three occasions, the

Gordon River twice, Port Davey, the Pelion district, Mt Field, the Hartz Mountains and the Freycinet Peninsula. Often he walked or rode on horseback many miles along rough tracks in bad weather, carrying heavy, bulky camera and plates, as well as the usual camping equipment. Despite conditions which often prevented photography for days on end, he invariably returned with outstanding studies of the western country. On the visit to Pelion in April 1901, Beattie had ridden Innes's long track from Liena across the February Plains. When the weather broke he was confined to the small Pelion hut for several days, fortunately with the prospector and miner George Renison Bell for company. The packers could not get through and food supplies ran low. A typical diary entry reads:

> *April 16 - Fearful night of wind, snow, thunder and lightning. Everything white. Snowed all day.*[41]

In the end Beattie shouldered his swag and took to the track, camera in hand, walking back to Liena in two stages with prospector Harry Andrews as guide. In spite of the snow, rain and high wind, the photographs he did manage to take are impressive, and several were published in the *Weekly Courier* later that year,[42] including a fine study of Pelion West and attractive views of Lake Ayr and Mt Oakleigh.

Beattie was an untiring publicist for the land. He kept a detailed journal of each excursion, with comments on weather, scenery, tracks, mining activity and similar ventures, and on his return he compiled lectures for the Royal Society and any other interested body. Sets of glass plates—'slides'—were prepared both to illustrate the lectures and for sale, each set on sale being accompanied by a printed commentary. A Royal Society lecture would normally occupy a full evening's program. The lecture presented after his first west coast tour in 1898 was illustrated

'On a still day the reflections are indescribable...'
Grass Tree Bend, Gordon River (Stephen Spurling III; AOT).

by seventy slides, and dealt with the history of Macquarie Harbour, the scenery of the west, and the progress of mining developments.[43] In describing Port Davey, Macquarie Harbour and other places of great beauty, Beattie drew attention to their tourist potential, seeing this as one of the island's foremost economic assets.

Beattie was deeply conscious of the devastating effects that different kinds of industry were having on landscape values, particularly in the west, lamenting on one occasion that when the North Mount Lyell Railway was completed the lovely King River Valley beneath the peaks of the West Coast Range would have its solitude destroyed by the 'shriek of the locomotive'.

His dismay at the destruction of the forest around Mt Lyell was expressed strongly and prophetically:

> ... what lover of nature can stand unmoved and contemplate her glories swept away by the tide of humanitarianism, - the axe and the horrid sulphur fumes ... the Company are cutting down the timber in great quantities for use in their works, and in a few years the highlands of Lyell will be bare, desolate wastes.[44]

On a later visit to the west coast in 1908, Beattie was so concerned at the damage that pining would continue to cause to the ancient forests along the Gordon that on his return to Hobart he called for the government to extend the protected area. Already a strip along each bank to a depth of five chains (one hundred and fifty metres) had been proclaimed a reserve, but Beattie considered that this was too little to prevent further damage over a wide area as the piners moved back from the main stream, a situation likely to be hastened by the projected construction of a mill beside the Gordon. He advocated extending the reserved area upstream for twenty-six miles, taking it a mile above the Franklin, and widening the strip on each bank as far as the skyline. Beattie was exceptional in that in a matter such as this he could see beyond short-term gain to long-term values, and he recognised even then the importance of retaining the ancient Gordon forests in their original state:

> Apart from the aesthetic side of the Gordon's attractions, its scientific aspect, as contributing a unique display of our West Coast flora, must become apparent to all, and should alone warrant beyond question its rigid protection.[45]

In the same way, in 1903 Beattie actively supported the proposal to reserve the whole of the Freycinet Peninsula and Schouten Island, illustrating with his photographs a paper by J F Mather which influenced the government to withdraw the Peninsula from sale. He later proposed that a plan for managing the area be drawn up, though no action was taken to implement this.[46] In other illustrated lectures he drew attention to the potential for tourism of the Hartz Mountains and the Mount Field high country.

Beattie's photographs and lectures had a wide public audience, both within Tasmania and far beyond. Processes had been developed for producing good quality newspaper and magazine prints and his photographs were frequently published in photographic supplements as well as illustrations for articles. Through this medium, and through the exhibitions and lectures, Tasmanians became familiar with the island's mountain scenery, its farming landscapes, lakes and rivers, and the quality of its extensive heritage of fine buildings. In speaking to Beattie's 1908 Royal Society address, the Tasmanian Statistician, Robert Johnston, who had known Beattie for many years, paid tribute to the wide influence of his work:

... it was due to his hard work and careful selection of subjects that the world knew so much of the beauties of Tasmania.[47]

The tradition of landscape photography was strengthened in the early decades of the twentieth century by a number of capable amateur photographers as well as by professionals such as Stephen Spurling III. Photographic clubs flourished in the cities and also in some of the major towns, and cameras and dark-room equipment became progressively cheaper and easier to use. Apart from Beattie, Stephen Spurling was the best known of the landscape photographers, his work also gaining wide circulation.

Stephen Spurling was seventeen years younger than Beattie, the third generation of his name.[48] His work extended through the period from 1902, when he took his place in his father's business, to the mid-1930s. Spurling's major interest lay in landscape photography, to which he devoted himself almost exclusively. Like Beattie, he delighted in visiting the remoter parts of the island, though he tended to concentrate on the Plateau, the Cradle Mountain–Lake St Clair region, the west coast and the northern farming districts, working from his studio in Launceston. In 1921 Spurling wrote:

> Tasmania is a land of scenic contrasts, where weather-beaten mountain ranges with foaming torrents contrast with peaceful midland farms, gloomy forests with smiling wheatfields, wave-lashed coasts with placid rivers—and the lure of the camera leads one on from scene to scene, and so each year there are a few more negatives to be treasured.[49]

He ascended snow-covered Ben Lomond in 1902 and a year earlier recorded very early scenes along the Gordon and Franklin rivers. In 1905, Spurling made only the fifth recorded ascent of Cradle Mountain, in company with three other Launceston men, and the first photographs of the mountain to be published were probably taken on this occasion.[50]

In 1913 he made an excursion to the Windermere–Pelion district, at that time subject to prospecting activity, where some of his finest studies of mountains and lakes were taken. Spurling's work included beautifully composed streetscapes in the northern towns, scenes of the tranquil northern farmlands and many coastal studies. Like Beattie, Spurling was deeply impressed by the beauty of the Gordon River, of which he took some of the earliest photographs:

Never will I forget my first impression of this magnificent stream ... The charm of the river is undoubtedly the magnificent setting provided by the steep gorges through which it winds, the hills on both sides being clad from water's edge to lofty summit with a wealth of verdant foliage. On a still day the reflections are indescribable.[51]

His photographs sold in large numbers as postcards, but their broadest public circulation, as was the case with Beattie's, came through the

'... where some of his finest studies of mountains and lakes were taken ...'
Lake Windermere, 1913 (Stephen Spurling III; author's collection).

illustrated journals such as the *Weekly Courier*. Large format prints were used extensively by the Tourist Department, by the Tasmanian Government Railways, the Launceston Tramways and private operators. Chris Long estimates that Stephen Spurling's collection originally contained over three thousand plates of Tasmanian landscape.[52]

Amateur photographers continued Spurling's fine tradition into the 1950s and beyond, the most prominent of the northern group being Frederick Smithies and his friend Herbert J King. Both were adventurous spirits as well as competent photographers. A noted climber and walker, Smithies was drawn particularly to Cradle Mountain and its surroundings, photographing features of the country and recording its moods over many years, dating from the time of Gustav Weindorfer. He was a member of the Cradle Mountain Reserve Board and of the Scenery Preservation Board from the 1920s until their termination in the 1970s. He made several journeys by foot, motorcycle and car to different parts of the west coast, including one through the trackless country of the Eldon Range and the Murchison Valley, another into the Spires region and an early ascent of Frenchmans Cap. He screened his lantern slides widely, raising funds for church and charities, as well as publicising Tasmania's scenery. King was a keen motorcyclist and covered thousands of kilometres of remote roads and tracks. He and Smithies made the first overland motorcycle trip to the west coast, by way of Corinna.

The work of Tasmania's foremost landscape photographers reached a very wide range of the community, and made a strong appeal to people at a time when most did not have the means to travel to out of the way places or to see the countryside other than by bus or train. Their photographs continually drew attention to the scenic beauty of the island and influenced many Tasmanians to value their surroundings. In a time when the state remained relatively free from urban sprawl and industrialisation, they created a strong impression of the unspoiled surroundings and attractive way of life of the island community. A further dimension was added by the depth and interest of the state's history which were conveyed by many of the photographs, especially those of Beattie. Like the painters, the photographers saw the land as far more than a field for human development; although they recorded much of the mining and industrial history, they also established the appeal of the land in its own right, and its value as an asset which people could simply experience and enjoy. The landscape photographers conveyed the dramatic character of the mountain country and of the remote west coast, but they were also able to capture the unique scenic quality of the island as a whole, and many of their most memorable studies were taken along the more sheltered coasts, on the still reaches of rivers, in the farming country and in the streets of the cities and towns. To them, Tasmania was a wonderland and their work made an eloquent appeal for its appreciation and protection.

From the 1920s compact cameras were available to everyone with an interest in photography or who simply wished to record. With the growth of skiing, touring and bushwalking there were many who were attracted to the outdoors and developed competence as photographers. Wilderness photography, however, grew from the 1950s with the advent of low-cost thirty-five millimetre colour film which could produce high-quality slides for small home projectors. This enabled amateur photographers to capture the subtle colours of rainforest, the tones of sun and shadow on mountainsides and a wide range of skyscapes. Of seminal influence was the work of Olegas Truchanas, whose patience, dedication and artistic ability created photographs of extraordinary beauty. His photography marked a new direction in this field, and he was followed by a generation of outstanding wilderness photographers such as Peter Dombrovskis, Martin Hawes, Rob Blakers and Chris Bell, whose work was distributed widely in posters, diaries and calendars. This photography was a potent agent in the fight to protect the Tasmanian forest and mountain country through the turbulent years of the 1970s and 1980s. The posters produced from Peter Dombrovskis' photographs of the Franklin River are credited with having played a crucial role in the success of the campaign to prevent the flooding of the river. Landscape photography in its more comprehensive form tended for a time to be overshadowed by wilderness photography, with the notable exception of the excellent work of Owen Hughes, whose two books present a broad range of landscape studies from all parts of the island.[53]

Tasmanians have been made aware over a period of one hundred and sixty years of the beauty and character of their island, evoking a wide range of responses. Many in the community have accepted that the land is attractive without considering that this confers any obvious advantage upon the state apart from its being a pleasant place to spend their lives. Certainly there has been little awareness of any contradiction between the ethics of land use and development, and its aesthetic qualities. Some, including governments, have come increasingly to regard the state's scenic appeal as an economic asset which forms the basis of an expanding tourism industry, and which can be developed accordingly. A few in each generation have been deeply moved by images of the island's fragile and complex landscape. They have realised, as did the artists and photographers themselves, just how rare and valuable it is in an increasingly crowded and industrialised world, and have felt a need to protect and nurture it, so that the island may retain its essential character into the future.

19 THE PERSONAL QUEST

'... a man who set out to use and change the land to suit his own purpose, but was gradually absorbed by it ...'

'He used to say that the creek sang to him, and verily, I believe it did.'

THERE HAVE ALWAYS been people upon whom the Tasmanian landscape has had a profound effect. They have recognised some quality in the limitless combinations of mountain and forest, coast and river, field and village, to which their own spirits have reached out and formed a deep and lasting attachment. Some were people whose lives took them into the untouched fastnesses of the mountains. Others worked in the forests or lived in urban, farming or coastal regions of great beauty. They were people who held a vision of the land far beyond its usefulness or potential for exploitation. Intuitively, they saw the land, or at least certain parts of it, as existing in its own right, free of man's authority, with a claim to remain undisturbed. Such people were few in number, but the strength of their vision and conviction often gave them a powerful and persuasive voice.

Even in the years when the use and alienation of land were unquestioned, there were men and women who, because they spent much of their lives in remote places, came to be both knowledgeable about and sensitive to their surroundings. Paddy Hartnett spent many years as a trapper, ranging the wild and beautiful country of the upper Mersey Valley and Du Cane Range. He built his huts beneath the great mountain crags, beside mossy stream banks and in groves of pines and snow gums. In his later years it was more often as a guide to ramblers and walking parties that he set forth with his swag and his bowler hat, and today the Overland Track follows the old pack-track close to his Du Cane hut. Hartnett had a genuine love for the mountain country, and was one of the first to suggest that the area between Cradle Mountain and Lake St Clair should be reserved. Even earlier, Tom Moore passed his adult life amongst the ranges and tangled scrubs of the west coast as a prospector and track-cutter, but his eyes were trained not simply to see the mineral prospects of this country. He wrote papers on the evidence of glaciation, sketched many of the plants and insects and sent specimens to prominent naturalists such as Baron von Mueller. In the early years of scenic reserves, the first rangers were men whose practical skills had been acquired in a wide variety of occupations. They were poorly paid and had little security of tenure, and they were expected to undertake difficult, uncomfortable work in isolated situations. Yet a number became legendary for their intimate knowledge of their surroundings and for the care and attention they gave to their reserves. One of these men, and perhaps the best known, was Albert Fergusson, known universally as 'Fergy', who managed a small accommodation resort at Lake St Clair and acted as ranger between 1930 and 1947. He guided parties, operated the boat, cut and maintained tracks and generally regarded the southern half of the Cradle Mountain–Lake St Clair Scenic Reserve as his own territory, passing on to those who walked with him his own love of the country. At the Cradle Mountain end of the Reserve, members of the Connell family also had a long association with 'Waldheim', the forest home of Gustav Weindorfer, Lionel Connell having taken over management of the small lodge after Weindorfer's death in 1932. Other family members served as rangers both in the north and south of the Reserve until the 1960s. In the Mount Field National Park the first ranger was Will Belcher, a position he held for seventeen years. He was responsible for building a number of huts, marking tracks, meeting and guiding parties. He and his packhorse 'Runic' were a friendly and familiar sight to hundreds of visitors who toiled up the long climb from Ellendale for a skiing or walking vacation. Will demonstrated the same pride and ownership of the Park as did 'Fergy' and the other early rangers. It was men such as Will Belcher who taught many people the value of conserving plants and animals and caring for the country, long before this was a widely accepted issue.

Some of those who have been close to the spirit of the land have lived for much of their lives in relative isolation, extending traditional bush hospitality to travellers and at the same time communicating their knowledge and understanding of the wild places. Some of their names have permanent places in the island's history, while others remain in obscurity. One of these solitary figures was Johnny Ahrberg, for thirty-eight years ferryman at the Pieman Heads. Johnny was originally a Swedish seaman who had sailed on his country's ships to most parts of the world during his twenty-five years at sea, before surviving the wreck of the steamer *Devon* on the Macquarie Harbour bar. He then tried his luck prospecting on the western fields, and finally accepted the post of government ferryman in 1899. After the mining boom subsided, and roads and railway replaced the coastal track, there were long years when Johnny saw hardly another soul, having for company only his dog, Tiger, his horse, his hundreds of phonograph records and his books. Though a hermit, he loved to yarn to his rare visitors by the hour. E T Emmett recalled an evening spent in his cottage, built from the remnants of Sutton's old hotel:

'Yarns - they fell from his lips like ripe mulberries
from a shaken tree...'
Johnny Ahrberg, ferryman of the Pieman (John Watt Beattie; AOT).

Yarns - they fell from his lips like ripe mulberries from a shaken tree. He has roamed the world, battled with the seas on many ships, roystered in mining camps of the early days of the wild west, and gathered up a host of experiences.⁵⁴

Johnny Ahrberg had time in the lonely years before his death in 1937 to come to know the Pieman and its wildlife. He would not hear of anyone shooting wild ducks on the river, or the quail or wallaby along its banks, or even catching mullet off the jetty. All 'his' creatures had a right to live in freedom and safety, and some of his visitors heeded his views long after they had met him.⁵⁵

Far away in the Vale of Rasselas, Ernie Bond lived alone for nearly eighteen years. In the early 1930s, the heady days of the Adamsfield diggings, he and his father had been osmiridium buyers for overseas companies in the little town of tents and paling huts. While prospecting in 1934, Ernie and his friend Paddy Hartnett discovered a patch of alluvial soil in the Vale near the foot of Mt Wright. He, Paddy and Bill Powell leased four hundred hectares and built a three-room house, 'Gordon Vale', which was later extended and also supplemented by several outbuildings. The partners' intention was to establish a farming and grazing property in the Vale which would serve additionally as a base for prospecting and trapping. Had the Adamsfield osmiridium field continued beyond the late 1930s and proved richer, prospects would have been better for the venture, with an assured market for fresh produce close at hand. However, when much of the big timber had been cleared from the rise and a section of the plain enclosed with post and rail fences, it was obvious that their estimates of the land had been far too optimistic, and that farming the Vale would never prove profitable. Ernie remained as the sole occupant, leaving only for occasional winter holidays in Hobart and prospecting trips along the Boyes, Holley and Pokana rivers to the west. Farming was limited to keeping a few head of stock and growing fruit and vegetables on the rich soil of the rise. 'Gordon Vale' lay off the beaten track, being some three hours' walk north from the Adamsfield track where it crossed the Florentine River, and even that track carried little traffic. The bridge across

'... *love and understanding of that severe and beautiful country...*'
James and Jessie Wilson of Steppes (John Watt Beattie; AOT).

the Gordon at the Great Bend endured for only a few years, its loss in a bushfire closing the track for carts and increasing the Vale's isolation. The homestead soon became known to walkers, partly through its position and magnificent setting below the peaks of Mt Wright and the Denison Range, but largely through the character of Ernie Bond himself. A big, genial man with a deep, rumbling voice, his generosity and hospitality were legendary. Visitors were treated to wallaby stew, fresh vegetables and home-made bread with butter and wild honey, and in summer strawberries, raspberries, gooseberries and other fruit, usually garnished with cream while the cow survived. Around the huge fireplace of an evening Ernie produced his delicious and very potent honey mead, brewed from the honey of wild bees. The talk would go on often into the early morning, while rain beat upon the shingled roof and the wind swayed the great ringbarked trunks which towered over the house. Like Johnny Ahrberg, Ernie had a rich fund of stories, most of them of Adamsfield days, of his prospecting trips into the remote valleys north of the Gordon, of years crowded with people, and of the creatures which he encountered in his daily life. His is the not uncommon story of a man who set out to use and change the land to suit his own purpose, but was gradually absorbed by it and grew close to its own spirit. The first Hobart Walking Club party visited 'Gordon Vale' at Easter 1935, before the house was fully completed, and from that time, apart from the war years, the Vale was a regular destination for walkers. Most came away with a strong impression both of the man and of the country with which he was so closely identified, an impression which they have retained clearly over the intervening years.

    High on the lonely road that winds from Bothwell to Great Lake is a district known as The Steppes, on the fringe of the Central Plateau lake country. Here in 1863 James Wilson and his wife Jessie settled on a remote selection, and James soon afterwards accepted the post of Police

Superintendent for the lakes district. The Scots couple remained on The Steppes property for the remainder of their lives and brought up their five children to the ways of high country life, a life which necessitated being largely self-sufficient. Jessie developed a close interest in the creatures of the surrounding bushland, particularly the birds, about which she was so

'... he seemed to embody the very spirit of the country ...'
Deny King of Port Davey (Tom Coles, published by courtesy of Janet Fenton).

knowledgeable that she became widely known as 'the Lady of the Birds'. She observed closely the habits of each species throughout the year, and would put out food for them in the hard days of winter when snow covered the ground. The Wilsons' five children grew up with their parents' love and understanding of that severe and beautiful country, often travelling with other property owners from the district to camp at the southern end of Great Lake. Two daughters remained at The Steppes: Mary taught at the district primary school for many years until her death in 1936, and Madge took over management of the store and post office from her mother, running it for thirty years. The Wilsons of both generations maintained the tradition of bush hospitality, and no traveller called without enjoying their wonderful home-made bread and other delights. Madge was an artist as well as a naturalist and made fine wood carvings of local plants and flowers, now held in a Bothwell church, as well as re-creating in watercolours scenes from the natural world which she knew so well. Madge died in 1975; the concern of Jessie, Madge and other family members for the birds, animals and plants of The Steppes over a period of one hundred and twelve years is kept alive very fittingly by the sanctuary which surrounds their historic home. More important still is the influence of the Wilsons' lives upon the many hundreds of travellers with whom they came in contact, and who learned so much about the high country from them.[56]

Another family which gained a place in the memories of travellers both for their friendliness and knowledge of their surroundings, is that of Denis King of Port Davey. The Kings lived for many years at Melaleuca Inlet, in one of the most isolated locations on the mainland of Tasmania. Denis's father, Charles King, had begun prospecting at Port Davey in 1930, as a supplement to his farm on the Huon. When he worked his own claim a few years later, Denis went with him to Port Davey. After service in World War II, Denis built a house at Melaleuca, where he and his wife Margaret lived from 1949.

The airstrip, completed in the mid-1950s, reduced the family's isolation; they had a schooner in which they sailed periodically to Hobart, and also maintained daily radio contact. Their daughters, Mary and Janet, spent much of their childhood in this beautiful and often turbulent corner of the island. After Margaret's death in 1967, Denis was often alone, his daughters able to return to Melaleuca only in their vacations. Visitors were always welcome, and in summer months increasing numbers came to the area as its colour, variety and interesting natural history became better known. They came by yacht, by aircraft, or over the long tracks from Scotts Peak and Cockle Creek. Many were themselves naturalists who sought to benefit from Denis's considerable knowledge of the botany of the south-wes

'... a man who had a deep spiritual bond with the country...'
Gustav Weindorfer of Cradle Mountain (John Watt Beattie; AOT).

while others were there simply to absorb the magnificent scenery of the mountains and waterways. Denis's quiet humour and his understanding of all aspects of the Port Davey country created a lasting impression upon those who met him: to many he seemed to embody the very spirit of the country.[57]

Of all those who have lived alone in the remoter regions of Tasmania, who have come to love and understand the land and its conditions, and who have generated in others a love and respect for its wild spirit, none has attracted greater interest than Gustav Weindorfer. Weindorfer was already a competent naturalist before he came to Tasmania, having carried out collecting excursions and published papers in Victoria in the early 1900s. His first two visits to Cradle Mountain in 1909 and 1910 were deeply moving experiences for him: he described the country as resembling his native Carinthia (Austria) with its forests, lakes and lofty snow-covered peaks. For the rest of his life this would be his spiritual home, and for many years the focus of all his activities. He realised that if other people were to experience the beauty of this region accommodation facilities and a road would have to be provided. Governments would assist only if the potential of the country for tourism could be demonstrated. He would have to build a house and attract tourists by his own efforts. At first this was to be a summertime venture, separate from his farming; by 1913 he had completed the main section of 'Waldheim', doing most of the work himself, and was ready for his first party of visitors. After his wife Kate's death in 1916, 'Dorfer' moved to 'Waldheim' permanently, having sold the farm at Kindred. The long winters in isolation were hard and lonely for a man fond of companionship, particularly during the war, and the occasional visitor was greeted warmly. He kept very detailed meteorological records and notes on animal and bird life, and he continued to correspond with a wide range of specialists in different fields of natural history, sending specimens of plants to overseas institutions. His original goal had been to have the Cradle Mountain area declared a reserve, and largely through his constant efforts and those of his friends this was achieved by 1922, though the Reserve Board was not appointed until March 1927.

Visitors to 'Waldheim' found, amid the peace and grandeur of the mountains, a man who had a deep spiritual bond with the country. Although he was obliged by financial necessity to remain there, and often endured periods of intense loneliness and frustration, he belonged there and whenever he talked to people about Cradle, as he did frequently at 'Waldheim' and on his lecture tours, he spoke of the land itself, his feeling for it evident in every phrase. When he died in May 1932, his vision remained with the number of people who were left to continue the work that he had begun.

People such as Deny King, Weindorfer, the Wilsons, Ernie Bond and Johnny Ahrberg were eminently practical; they were not simply dreamers. Like thousands of their contemporaries they gained their livelihood from the land, and they would not have considered themselves exceptional. What set them apart was not their considerable knowledge, nor the time they spent in close daily contact with their surroundings. They possessed a reverence for the land which transcended their other qualities and affected those with whom they came into contact. This reverence is perhaps most clearly seen in an incident in Weindorfer's life, recounted during his burial service by his friend Archdeacon Atkinson:

> We had gone into the pine forest along the creek at the back of the house. He used to say that the creek sang to him, and verily, I believe it did. When we came to the heart of the forest, he showed me a fallen tree. We could see that a giant of former days had fallen. Removing his hat and raising his hand to heaven, he said, "This tree was growing in this valley before Our Lord came to the

earth." He bowed his head and for a moment he was silent ... I see him now as I saw him then, a man of simple and beautiful faith, humble in the presence of the maker of that tree.[58]

One of the most significant developments in the growth of public awareness of the Tasmanian landscape and of the factors which had a bearing on it was the increase in popularity of walking as a recreational pursuit, especially after the 1950s. There had always been people who enjoyed venturing away from the settled parts and experiencing the qualities of unaffected places for themselves since George Bass ascended Mt Wellington in 1798, but most found it difficult to gain access to mountains or remote coastline, and had to be content with visiting the better known resorts and listening to the accounts of surveyors, trappers, prospectors and others whose occupations took them further afield. In Britain and on the continent walking tours were popular throughout the nineteenth century, and to some such as the poet William Wordsworth and his sister Dorothy, walking was an accepted part of their way of life. In the late eighteenth century mountaineering, as well as walking, was well established, with capable guides available in most Swiss, French, Austrian and Italian alpine resorts. By contrast, in Australia, even in the 1950s those who walked for pleasure were regarded as eccentric.

Until the early 1900s, walking through the mountain regions of Tasmania had been the province of naturalists such as P E de Strzelecki, R C Gunn, and Joseph Milligan, or of those who were fortunate enough to join sponsored excursions led by men of the standing of J R Scott and C P Sprent. There were people, however, who were so enthusiastic and determined to see the country that they overcame all barriers to travel and accommodation. Graeme and Frances Cox in 1890 undertook an extensive walking tour of the west coast, from Devonport through Emu Bay to Waratah, thence to Corinna on the Pieman and along the track to Trial Harbour. They were in Zeehan on 'Pegging Day', and witnessed the ingenious system of allocating ownership of the town blocks. From Trial Harbour they walked the length of Ocean Beach to Strahan, continued to Mt Lyell and then along the Linda Track to the Derwent, climbing Mt King William on the way. Their journey home took them through bushfires in the hottest season of the year, but they thoroughly enjoyed their experience. Graeme and Frances were no novices to walking long distances; they had previously visited Lake St Clair and had toured extensively in other countries. They were intrigued by the curiosity their walking enterprise created among fellow travellers along the tracks.[59]

In 1907 Ronald Smith, son of James 'Philosopher' Smith, undertook the first of many walking excursions to Cradle Mountain. He and Weindorfer walked the country in every direction during Weindorfer's years at Cradle, and Smith built his own cottages in the valley: 'Crater House' below Crater Lake, and its successor near the Dove River. The two men marked tracks, mapped prominent features, and shared with their friends the delight they found in this mountain paradise.

By the outbreak of the First World War in 1914, many people, men and women, were spending their weekends and vacations on walking tours away from the towns, some in response to the publicity given to the mountains by the photographs of Beattie, Spurling and others. Walking as a form of recreation was also becoming popular at that time in New South Wales and Victoria, aided by the activities of Field Naturalists clubs and by the growth of the Scouting movement and other organisations for young people with their emphasis on self-development and vitalism. Geoff Chapman, who made his first mountain walking excursion in 1921, recalled:

I can suggest that lawyers, clerks, civil servants, teachers and many others tramped far and wide well before the early twenties when I came on the scene.[60]

Among the early walkers Chapman refers to were Cecil Murray, Mac Urquhart, Leonard Livingston, Jack Murray, V C Smith, Leicester McAulay, Alan Giblin and Doug Anderson. The walkers of the 1920s and early 1930s undertook treks into challenging areas such as the Arthur Range, Precipitous Bluff, Port Davey, The Spires, The Walls of Jerusalem and the Du Cane Range. Geoff Chapman himself achieved the first ascent of Mt Anne, in 1929. All of these places were far more difficult to reach in the 1920s without the access roads and tracks which exist today, and equipment was heavier, more cumbersome and less waterproof. The accepted carrying method was a rolled swag, with purpose-made rucksacks becoming available in the early 1930s. 'Paddy' Pallin's sturdy lightweight walking equipment created something of a revolution amongst walkers in the 1930s, replacing the old surplus army gear. In describing the approach to Mt Anne, Chapman paid tribute to the efforts of a group of pioneer walkers known as the 'Anners', who devoted much time and effort during the 1920s to clearing the Port Davey and Weld Valley tracks to the foot of Mt Anne,[61] and mapping the main features of the south-west. Until the 1960s, walkers were still using the old Mines Department South-West Sketch Map which had been compiled largely from reports of prospectors, geologists and bushmen over a period of fifty years.

An early walking club, the Sunday Trampers, functioned quite informally in Hobart from 1920 to 1933, its members taking part in short walks within close range of the city. The Hobart Walking Club was founded in 1929, and from its inception members planned walks to the mountain areas as well as to coastal and local venues. A number of the experienced southern walkers such as Geoff Chapman joined the new club, and for several years there was an annual club walk through the Cradle Mountain–Lake St Clair Reserve. The popularity of walking and the formation of walking clubs brought together people whose interests centred upon the natural environment: artists, photographers, naturalists, geographers and historians ... From the mid-1930s, and particularly following the Second World War, walking attracted a strong following. Most simply enjoyed a pleasant form of recreation which offered variety and social contacts. For some, however, walking became a vital element, a way of life; they sought unchanged, often remote parts of the country, not for the physical challenge, though this enhanced the sense of isolation, but rather in a spiritual response to the land itself. They recognised the qualities of the Tasmanian landscape and for years of their lives they explored the places in which those qualities were evident in their many different forms. Some of the more committed walkers attained skills and understanding equal to those of men who worked in the mountains and forests for their livelihood. Their concern for the places they visited was reflected in their ability to adapt to the conditions they encountered and in their intimate knowledge of the past and of the natural history of the country. Not all walkers became members of clubs, but these bodies made it easier to organise and join excursions; they brought together people of similar interests and encouraged the interchange of information. Importantly, the walking, Field Naturalist and other outdoor organisations provided a collective voice for concerns about the land and about the ways in which the land was used. From such gatherings came some of the first real challenges to hitherto unquestioned land-use assumptions and practices.

20 VALUES IN CONFLICT

It's very difficult to make a case for beauty, when there are facts and figures standing against you.[62]

WITH GROWING AWARENESS of the qualities of the island's landscape, the complexity and fragile nature of its ecology and the changes being brought about by the processes of development, it was inevitable that conflict would eventually arise between those who viewed the land in different ways. Such a conflict is always damaging, resulting as it does in a polarisation of attitudes and the distortion of views and intentions.

At first the opposition to large-scale development which altered the land was almost imperceptible. Throughout the nineteenth century it was generally accepted that the land must be tamed, that industry, agriculture and the harnessing of resources should override all other considerations. The occasional expressions of concern and dissent such as Beattie's were isolated and attracted little public attention There was no perceived conflict between operations such as the clearing of forest and mining on one hand, and appreciation of the aesthetic appeal and ecological fabric of lake and mountain on the other. The land and its resources were, after all, virtually inexhaustible. People who worked all their lives in the countryside or forest were often foremost in their praise of its beauty; some cared deeply for the land and made every effort to protect it as a resource. The major guiding principle which was inherited from the nineteenth century was that of utilisation: the land was there for man's use, and whatever its other qualities, its economic value was of prime concern. This principle would continue to underlie the attitudes of individuals, institutions and governments throughout the following century and beyond.

As early as the 1880s it was recognised that there were places of particular interest and popular appeal which should be protected for recreational and tourist use. These were all of limited size and ready access, and included such amenities as sports grounds and picnic areas. One notable inclusion on the list in 1885 was the Russell Falls Reserve, which had already become a popular tourist destination. Towards the end of the century a number of organisations were working to have areas of significant size and importance reserved for their aesthetic qualities as well as for their natural and historical associations. The Royal Society and the Tasmanian Field Naturalists Club were the most prominent of these: the Royal Society had in fact been lobbying unsuccessfully for many years for the creation of state scenic reserves.[63] The Tasmanian Improvement and Tourist Association was formed in 1893 to further the interests of the steadily developing tourist industry and promote access to scenic areas. Other bodies, such as the Royal Ornithologists Union, the Railway Exploration League and the Australian Natives Association were also active in voicing their concerns. The first major step in preserving Tasmania's landscape came in November 1915, when the Earle government passed the *Scenery Preservation Act*. Under this Act, all scenic reserves were administered by the Scenery Preservation Board, a body which remained in existence until 1971, when it was superseded by the National Parks and Wildlife Service. The Scenery Preservation Board was a creature of government and reflected prevailing attitudes to the land. Although it fought valiantly on some issues, its powers were severely limited and it was provided with few resources. Always chaired by the Surveyor-General of the day, its members were drawn largely from the public service: the heads of the Engineering and Railways departments and a representative of the Tourism Department. Later the HEC was also represented. As well, there was provision for three members of the public who were actively concerned with aspects of the state's scenic amenity. A separate body, the Animals and Birds Protection Board, administered matters concerning wildlife.

With the establishment of the Scenery Preservation Board the way was clear to declare larger reserves, each of which could be controlled by a subsidiary board responsible to the Scenery Preservation Board. In 1916 Freycinet Peninsula and Mt Field were gazetted, as well as the Port Arthur Historic Site. These were followed by Cradle Mountain–Lake St Clair, which was given scenic reserve status in 1922 and administered for nearly forty years as two independent jurisdictions, each with its own board. It was not declared a park until 1940. There was no possibility, given the utilitarian and economic imperatives of the time, that aesthetic and ecological values could be equated with practical considerations: the land itself had no inherent rights. Surprisingly, the *Scenery Preservation Act* of 1915 initially declared the reserves inalienable, but this condition was amended in 1921 and 1938 so that timber, mining and grazing leases could be granted and the reserve status revoked whenever necessary. Reserves were regarded as 'flexible'. In any case, before an area could be considered for reservation it had to pass the scrutiny of all relevant departments and be declared 'waste' land. It also had to justify classification on its economic potential for tourism development.

In 1946 the major reserves were declared national parks. By 1972 there were ten significant areas with national park classification, as well as many road reserves and scenic reserves whose security was far more tenuous. The Tasmanian community came to accept that these were places of particular value, a concept which impinged even upon those who did not visit them and who had little concern for the outdoors. Those who came to know the parks, however, placed great faith in the security which national park status afforded, though this security was apparent rather than a legislative reality. Any perceived threat to a park was bound to create strong resentment. From the 1970s there was also a growing realisation that far more of the state was of considerable aesthetic and ecological value and merited the same kind of protection as the land within park boundaries.

When open conflict over land-use values did arise, its unlikely source was the Scenery Preservation Board itself. Although it operated under government statute and scrutiny, and consisted substantially of representatives of departments concerned with land use, the Board took its role of scenery preservation seriously, and was prepared to resist what it saw as threats to the statutory integrity and scenic values of the parks. In 1938, when a resumption of wolfram mining in the Pelion area was planned, the Board took a stand against the Mines Department before being forced to give way in the following year. In 1940, the HEC proposed to raise the level of Lake St Clair by constructing a dam near the Derwent outflow. Again, although the Board had no power to resist the might of the HEC, it tried vainly to obtain a commitment to stabilise the new shoreline and to remove timber that would be killed by the rising water.

The Board's major fight, however, took place between 1946 and 1950 in response to the government's pressure upon it to release an area of some 1620 hectares of forest in the Florentine Valley at the request of Australian Newsprint Mills. The area in question lay within the western boundary of the Mount Field National Park, and contained a majestic forest of mature mountain ash. This conflict highlighted the values and priorities of both the practical land-users and of those who sought to protect land which was important for other reasons. At the beginning of postwar expansion, with the shadow of the 1930s depression still darkening people's memories, a move to allow a major company to prosper and provide employment by gaining access to prime forest was seen as being of great and immediate benefit to the state. Besides, it was argued, the forest in question was not close to roads or accessible to tourists, whereas an equivalent area near the Russell Falls could be added to the Park in exchange, and this would include a range of forest species close to existing roads and tracks. The Scenery Preservation Board and those in the community who supported its stand also saw the values of the land clearly. There was already concern that the rate of forest clearance in the state was very high, and far exceeded the pace of re-afforestation. The section of the Park in dispute held some of the finest mountain ash forest remaining in the state, and therefore possessed aesthetic and ecological values far beyond its economic return as newsprint pulp and building timber. No area offered in exchange either north or south of the Park held forest of this quality or extent: forest at which future generations might gaze in wonder. The Board also saw a particularly dangerous precedent being established, in that land which had been recognised as worthy of preservation in a national park could be resumed whenever it was desired for exploitation by logging, mining or other commercial interests. In the end, however, there could be only one outcome. The Cosgrove government, after a stormy parliamentary session in 1949, passed the National Park and Florentine Valley Bill, changing the Park boundary. The practical values of development had held sway over the wider, more enduring, though less clearly defined values of the land itself.

In 1962, when the HEC under the Reece government proposed the construction of two large water impoundments in the heart of the south-west, the community's reaction was far more widespread and well organised than it could possibly have been two decades earlier. There was increasing awareness of environmental concerns, and a readiness to challenge the assumption that material progress and development should always take precedence over natural and aesthetic considerations. Many people had come to know the south-west and other remote areas of the state and there had been repeated moves to have the south-west formally protected, resulting in the creation of the Lake Pedder National Park in 1955. The spiritual and visual values of such a large, unspoiled area were clear, as was its compelling ecological and recreational importance. The ribbed, quartzite beach of Pedder and the gray Frankland peaks were seen far beyond Tasmania through the colour slides of Olegas Truchanas and other photographers, and people in distant places felt something of the magic of this lovely region. Many saw it as unique, and belonging to the nation as a whole. Resistance was focussed through such bodies as the South-West Committee, the Save Lake Pedder Action Committee and the political party United Tasmania Group. Thousands of ordinary people joined protests, lobbied politicians and displayed posters and stickers. Even some of those not sympathetic to the cause of saving the lake were uneasy at the growth of the HEC and at its apparent ability to gain unrestricted support from governments for its huge and expensive schemes. The efforts to save Lake Pedder failed, and the lake, together with thousands of hectares of south-west wilderness were inundated in 1972. The new Whitlam Federal Government, coming to power in 1973, would not reverse the process, and the Gordon Power Scheme Stage I was finally opened in 1979.

There were major outcomes from the Lake Pedder flooding. These illustrated the extent to which the community had become polarised over the treatment of the land, especially the west and south-west. The conservation movement became more closely organised, the Tasmanian Wilderness Society and the Conservation Trust maintaining pressure to have the remainder of the south-west protected, and for protection to be extended to other areas of value in the state. It was also evident that those who believed in development and land use in all regions would design more effective strategies, concerned at perceived threats to employment and to the structures and future plans of the HEC. Most politicians, employees' organisations and associations of business leaders actively supported continued implementation of hydro-industrialisation. There would be no reconciliation.

When Stage II of the Gordon Power Scheme was announced in 1978, there was already the potential for deep and bitter conflict, and no political leader of that time had either the will or the ability to attempt to reconcile the holders of opposing views through processes of genuine consultation or open public debate. For five years a battle was waged over the construction of dams which would drown both the lower Gordon and lower Franklin rivers. Those who opposed these dams identified two central issues. The Gordon and Franklin were among the last wild rivers in south-eastern Australia, and their deep gorges wound through some of the most dramatically beautiful country in Tasmania. These should be saved at all costs. Beyond this was a basic issue of asserting the right of some country to remain free from development not because it had other economic potential, but because it had intrinsic value in itself through its landforms, its aesthetic qualities, its remoteness from any developed area or road, and its ancient and complex fabric of life-forms. A further factor had by this time begun to affect the view of the land, in the rapid expansion of knowledge of the Aboriginal prehistory of the island. It had been discovered that south-west Tasmania possessed Aboriginal sites of inestimable value, which revealed the way of life of people during the height of the Pleistocene ice-age. One of the richest of these sites, Kutikina (Spirit) Cave on the lower Franklin, would be submerged by the new scheme, as perhaps would other sites yet to be discovered. The Tasmanian Aboriginal community had begun to gain strength and insight into their own past from the caves of the southwest, and they entered the conflict with the moral force of their ancient bond with the land.

Public awareness of the implications of the scheme was greater in 1980 than it had been even at the time of the Pedder conflict. There had been far more attention drawn to the qualities of the south-west by photographs, lectures and media reports, while many had visited or flown over parts of it. There had been more research on its ecosystems and aspects of its natural history, and there were by this time growing numbers of young people with tertiary training in the natural sciences who could speak critically and with authority about the effects of the scheme on the land and its life-forms.

With equal fervour and sincerity, the Lower Gordon Scheme was supported by the government, business and industrial interests, unions and many of the workforce. They felt strongly that the land and its resources were there for the community to use in any way suited to its needs. Their views were shaped by the practical ethic which had always guided Tasmania's destiny, and they were deeply distrustful of any argument based upon ill-informed aesthetics and 'emotional' objections about ecology and the value of land for future generations. They were proud of the accomplishments of the long-established structure of the HEC which, to many, represented the cutting-edge of the state itself. For them, the loss of a relatively small area of land, attractive though it may be, was more than compensated by the provision of work and the assured source of power which would meet the state's needs into the future. And, after all, there would be two attractive man-made lakes when it was finished, with first-class access roads and lots of tourist potential. There was still an abiding faith in the ideal of hydro-industrialisation which had resurrected Tasmania after the depression and promised a prosperous future. When the Lowe government attempted to modify the scheme to save the Franklin River, its ranks divided and it was swept from office.

The conflict rapidly moved further away from rational debate: the opposing sets of values were held so strongly that they were virtually irreconcilable. It parted friends, divided families and left resentments which in many cases never healed. There were times when anger was released in physical violence. It produced an array of misconceptions and facile rationalisations. Those opposing the dams were painted as impractical middle-class idealists from leafy suburbs, or as young work-shy students or drop-outs who knew nothing of the realities of life. Those who supported development, on the other hand, were seen as insensitive to the environment, their lives focussed upon purely material concerns, and determined to push development at any price. Such views were, of course, simplistic. There were people who held very passionate views on both sides; there were many others who tried sincerely to see the merits of each argument, who valued the land and its remarkable beauty, and yet saw the value of clean power development. But the climate rarely favoured objective discussion. The issues involved the whole nation; for the first time Tasmania was recognised as having a unique landscape, an asset that belonged not just to Tasmanians, but to the country as a whole. This recognition was formalised in the Fraser government's offer to compensate Tasmania if the scheme were not proceeded with. As well, the issues were clearly universal: the debate applied with equal force to land-use values throughout the country. Rallies reminiscent of the Vietnam War years filled the streets of the capital cities and protesters from a wide range of backgrounds and occupations streamed into the island from every other state. Press and publicity networks were used extensively by both sides. The compelling posters presenting the aesthetic values of the rivers, many featuring photographs by Peter Dombrovskis, were pivotal in shaping community responses, as were the arrests of one thousand three hundred and forty people on the Gordon River and at the Crotty Road. The debate itself could never be won or lost. A change of federal government in 1983 and a decision by the High Court of Australia ended construction of the dams, but they did little to resolve the opposing attitudes and values of the two cultures which had generated and sustained the conflict. The surface issues were settled, but the underlying substance of contention was not addressed, and remains two decades later.

Inevitably, conflict over land use continued through the 1980s and 1990s, decades of increasing economic hardship for the island, the main focus swinging back to the state's forests. The remaining areas of old-growth and other native forest were being cleared at an increasing rate to satisfy expanding woodchip export markets. Governments desperate to develop any resource to underpin the island's shaky economy imposed drastic legal sanctions to discourage anti-logging protests and again there were violent confrontations and arrests. The report of the Federal Government's Helsham Inquiry into the Lemonthyme and Southern Forests, upheld by the High Court in 1987, brought about an uneasy truce in the forests, but large-scale clearance continued to be a subject of basic disagreement in land-use values. It impinged upon other land issues: when the Wesley Vale pulp mill proposed for the rich farming country of the north-west was resisted, the same kind of conflict flared again. The mill's rejection at federal level on the grounds of its unacceptable effluent treatment system did nothing to mollify the antagonism which those who saw it as an icon of development felt for the conservationists they were convinced had blocked it.

In 1997 a Regional Forest Agreement was signed between the state and Commonwealth governments after a period of public consultation. The Agreement was intended to meet three main requirements: to provide resource security for the industry for a period of twenty years, to eliminate the grounds for future intervention by the Commonwealth, and to end the continuing conflict over forest clearance. These aims were commendable, and the Agreement should have been an enlightened and welcome document. Those who were involved in the process of drawing up and publishing background material, collating responses and interacting with organisations and individuals in the community worked competently and diligently to produce an outcome which would be largely acceptable to all who had an interest in the island's forests. The process drew upon the efforts, knowledge and experience of a large number of people in a range of occupations and disciplines. Through the Agreement an effort was made to protect ecological values by reserving sample areas of different forest species, plant communities and habitats, particularly those of plants and animals known to be rare or threatened. Recognition was also given to aesthetic, historical, archaeological and recreational concerns, as well as to links between communities and forests, and to traditional users.

The Agreement failed to meet the hopes and expectations which many people held for it. Its major flaw was seen to be the constraint placed upon its conception, that the final document was required to guarantee continuity of timber resource at a minimum of the current harvesting level, with provision for an increase in this level over the term of the Agreement. This left the Agreement open to the charge that it was a meretricious document: that it had the appearance of openness and objectivity in its public consultation, but in reality its outcome was fore-ordained, and its major use by government and industry would be to silence criticism of forest policies and practices thereafter with the retort: 'You had your say; abide by the umpire's decision.' It was clear that the process could not go back to basics; those managing it were not free to begin by looking at the whole question of the state's future direction, the vital place of the natural environment in that future, the role which forests would play in projecting the state's image and in the kind of development its tourism industry would undergo over the next two or three decades and beyond. There were other doubts raised about the credibility of the Agreement in the months after it was signed. Sample areas of different vegetation types and habitats had been set aside, but these were generally very small, especially when edge-effect is taken into account, and isolated from larger areas of undisturbed forest. It was evident that old-growth eucalypt forests had been largely excluded from permanent reserves and were still to be subject to large-scale clearance. The national parks, of course, contain very little of the spectacular tall forest for which the state is renowned, so that it was seen as important that a high proportion of this should be protected. In hindsight, the beneficiaries of the Agreement appear to have been the large timber companies rather than the small, locally-based millers. More disturbing were suggestions that some experts' recommendations were set aside. It was also of concern both in Tasmania and beyond that the standards of environmental protection eventually provided by such a major document, which will influence management of the state's forests over such a long and crucial period, fall well short of the internationally recognised JANIS criteria.

An extraordinary opportunity for reconciling the two traditional cultural streams had thus been lost. If the Regional Forest Agreement had been permitted to be more daring and more visionary, there may well have been an end to the conflict of the past three decades.

The new century has brought no peace to the land. A move was made in 2004 by a giant timber harvesting corporation to challenge with court writs those who spoke out against the widespread clearance of native forests. A further pulp mill proposal in 2005 re-established former battle-lines and demonstrated that those who direct the island's course still cling to the old practical certainties, continuing the large-scale transformation of remaining forests.

The closing years of the second century of white settlement have been marked by major differences in the ways in which people regard Tasmania's landscape. The land itself is still subject to constant alteration, but even after two hundred years there is no overall policy for the retention of aesthetic or environmental values throughout the island, no structure which can scrutinise and take responsibility for these values, and no defined vision of their place in the island's future. A relatively small section of the community continues to act as advocate for the land's scenic and natural values. Governments protect some areas on a piecemeal basis in response to particular pressures while disregarding the same values elsewhere in pursuing other agendas. The wider community accepts the reality of the state's unique qualities, yet in day-to-day practice does little to preserve them, and is still largely bound to the development ethic of the nineteenth century. The island's landscape, its fragile ecology and its built heritage rate highly on a world scale, but it is inevitable that in the course of the next half-century they will be further degraded through inaction, disagreement and lack of direction.

IN RETROSPECT: 2014

Over the period 2006 to 2014, tensions have remained between those who support large land-altering development and those committed to protecting the island's natural and aesthetic values.

In a time of economic downturn, forest-based industries have been affected by adverse trends on world markets, resulting in a major reduction in forest harvesting. The long-running conflict over clearance of high conservation native forest was resolved in 2013 following dialogue between industry representatives and conservationists over three hard years, culminating in the Forest Peace Agreement, subsequently ratified by the Tasmanian Parliament. This landmark Agreement was later annulled by a newly elected State Government, raising the possibility of a return to the angry past.

A new Commonwealth Government, with state support, has attempted to excise a significant area of old-growth forest from World Heritage protection, an action without precedence.

The mountains, valleys and extensive rainforests of the Tarkine region, between the Arthur and Pieman rivers, highly recommended for protection for its natural values and as one of the last habitats of the Tasmanian Devil, has been thrown open for mining.

Tasmania's foremost employer, the tourism industry, relies even more heavily on the island's natural beauty and its clean, green image to maintain its place in national and international markets.

SECTION VII

LANDSCAPE OF THE FUTURE

21   LANDSCAPE OF THE FUTURE

The island belongs to the whole of Australia in specific ways,
for qualities that set it apart and place it on a different
plane of value from any other region.

Time is short, but it is not too late to secure the future of this
beautiful and fragile island.

THE TASMANIAN TOPOGRAPHY has been formed by complex processes over vast geological epochs and its fragile and varied plant and animal communities have evolved shielded from large-scale intrusion and competition by their isolation. Over nearly forty thousand years the Aboriginal population influenced some of the vegetation patterns, but established a sympathetic relationship with the land, their care founded upon deep, complex and enduring bonds and upon the needs of a small and scattered community. Today's Tasmanians have thus inherited one of the most beautiful and ecologically valuable islands in the world, an island already substantially altered over the brief period of white occupation. It is essential that its landscape and ecological integrity be preserved into the future, both for their own sake and for the spiritual and economic well-being of Tasmanians for generations to come. We, as a community, must create our own spiritual affinity with the land.

Landscape is Tasmania's most valuable commodity. It follows that its care and preservation must occupy a central place in any vision of the state's future direction. Whatever we aspire to can be created only around the beauty and variety of this island. If we value the land we will care for it and relate to it with sense and sensitivity as our Aboriginal predecessors did for nearly two thousand generations. The present is a crucial time in our occupation: decisions made now will have far-reaching consequences both for the land and for ourselves. We can continue to allow it to be degraded by piecemeal and short-term policies and practices, or we can protect the land as our major spiritual and economic resource. If we recognise the asset we possess, and decide that the island's landscape as a whole is worthy of preservation, there are implications that will challenge current attitudes and practices.

There is much to be learned from the past. We should be aware of the two strong and often conflicting streams within the community: the practical culture of shaping and building, and the strong, widespread response to the island's natural and man-made beauty. Both cultures are essential and each must complement the other. No community can afford the conflict which has developed between them and which continues unabated, flaring periodically around issues concerning land use. Accepting the preservation of the land and its values as central to a vision of the state's future does not imply that the natural and built environments should or can remain unchanged, a situation that nature itself precludes. But it does mean acceptance of an obligation to manage future change in keeping with clearly defined landscape values.

Commitment to the land brings into question issues as fundamental as the state's economic direction. In the past Tasmania has been forced to compete with larger, more populous states with their greater industrial strength, but although Tasmania's per capita production value has exceeded theirs, its economy has largely failed to overcome the impediments of position and size. It is wiser to compete in fields in which this state holds the advantage; since the late 1990s it has begun to re-assess its economic direction and must continue to do so. Its future lies not in large, resource-based industrial ventures, nor in the export of unprocessed materials, but in using the appeal of the island itself far more effectively: its landforms, way of life, freedom from pollution and crowding, the openness of its vistas. These are areas in which it really can compete without compromising its own surroundings. Industries based upon the education, skills and initiative of its people will, with sound management and planning, complement the island's natural qualities.

Understandably, there remain mind-sets from the past, entrenched attitudes which are difficult to change and which run counter to any new perception of the land. Tired old clichés that depict land protected from inappropriate development or exploitation and preserved for the future as 'locked up' are still repeated thoughtlessly. Traditional terms such as 'growth' and 'development' need to be re-interpreted; today's world can no longer afford the indefinite expansion of industries, buildings and infrastructure. Even 'sustainable development' often masks processes that result in long-term alteration of the land. Tasmanians will need the courage to break with elements of the past which are no longer appropriate and accept the challenge of development and growth applied to small, high-technology industries that utilise sophisticated skills and do not depend upon resources torn from the land or upon occupation of large areas of coast or countryside but exist in harmony with the land. This will be genuine progress.

There will always be a place for traditional resource-based industries. Tasmania has a history of achievement in fields such as mining and timber harvesting, but for a future in which the land is a central element of concern, such industries must accept change. Mining has come a long way from the destructive processes of the past and has begun to shed the image which has in retrospect blighted the boom period of the late nineteenth and early twentieth centuries. The bare mountainsides above Queenstown and Waratah still remind us of the damage of those years. Now there are strict environmental controls to protect landscape and ecology, and requirements for the rehabilitation of mining sites; smelting, concentrating and other processes often take place now well away from the mines themselves. Even so, there are still some areas which are too fragile and sensitive for any mining to take place, as ultimately the welfare of the land is of greater importance than any mine.

Forest industries have also begun to respond to landscape and ecological concerns since the 1970s. However, the nature of large-scale forest harvesting is at odds with the concept of an island whose present major industry and future viability depend heavily upon the quality of its landscape and the integrity of its ecology. Currently, only a small proportion of the state's native forest is now protected in permanent reserves. It is frequently claimed by politicians and by timber industry proponents that forty per cent of Tasmania is protected from logging: a claim which misleads. The land protected by national parks, the World Heritage Area and permanent reserves consists largely of alpine plateau, moorland, button grass plains, mountain vegetation, coastal scrubs and heaths, and some rainforest. The majestic old-growth and tall forests, which are now virtually unique in Australia, have been largely excluded from protection, except for samples set aside under the Regional Forest Agreement. The Agreement between federal and state governments in 2005 to protect further areas of forest of high conservation and landscape value, notably in the Styx Valley and Tarkine, was a promising gesture. The increasing number of visitors who are being drawn to the island are better informed and more discerning than those of previous generations. Many come to see the remaining tracts of extensive forest clothing our valleys and mountainsides; to them the images of log-truck, bulldozer and chain-saw are out of place. One must question the judgement of placing a mountain of woodchips in the midst of a city, in a state whose major growth industry is nature-based tourism. There is growing pressure throughout the nation to end the practice of clear-felling native forest, as well as the export of woodchips and of whole logs, and plans need to be put in place now for the phased closure of these sections of the industry. This would allow time to retrain those displaced, particularly for work in caring for the forests and catering for greatly expanded eco-tourism which will involve the forests and employ people skilled in forest management.

It is time now for a plan to be developed that charts the desired future of the Tasmanian economy and defines the place of the land in this future. Not only is the plan itself important, establishing as it would vital guidelines and principles for decisions in decades to come, but the process by which such a plan is evolved would also have great value for government and community. In the past, governments of all persuasions have tended to view only the horizon of a term of office; there has been relatively little long-term directional planning of the kind undertaken in the 1930s when the state embarked on hydro-industrialisation. Since the late 1990s a clearer vision of the island's economic future has been created. The economy has been placed on a sounder footing, with considerable emphasis on the tourism industry, and there is in the first decade of the new century a greater degree of optimism than has been felt for many years. There has, however, been no corresponding change in attitudes to the land itself. Native forest is still being cleared at a rapid rate, and both forest and farmland are being replaced with extensive areas of plantation. Coastline and countryside continue to be alienated by development with little apparent restriction.

It is generally argued by those who advocate a future built upon the continuation of resource-based industries and alteration of the land, that to move away from this tradition and base the state's future more firmly upon tourism and other land-friendly industries will be detrimental to the economy and to prospects of employment. However, tourism in its many forms is already one of the largest and most rapidly developing industries, with a growth rate of over five per cent. With sensible marketing and organisation the potential for further growth is considerable.

Tourism already employs very large numbers; it is the most labour-intensive of all major industries and the one in which employment is least likely to be adversely affected by developing technology. The land is, of course, the most vital asset in the future development of tourism. Even now, seventy-seven per cent of tourists visit natural areas: forests, coastline, mountains, rivers. It is not simply the aesthetic qualities of natural scenery, however, that attract visitors. Tasmanians should be aware of the strength of the total impression created by the combination of so many different facets, in its history, farmlands, streetscapes, open spaces and unspoiled coast and countryside. Above all, there is the wonderful impression of a people free of the stresses of more crowded regions. Capably managed, these assets will bring steadily increasing numbers of visitors and the economic benefits that come with them.

Employment is a crucial and sensitive element in any discussion of changing economic and cultural directions. In a rapidly changing world, a community can no longer cling even to the 'safe' traditional areas of employment. The common catch-cry is that the industries which change the land must be fostered and protected because they are large providers of employment. In Tasmania these have shed considerable numbers of employees over past decades, as have other major industries. The nature of employment itself is changing steadily; as has been pointed out recently, seventy per cent of the job categories in 2020 have yet to be invented. Given adequate time and planning, people can be retrained and communities assisted. The state must surely have learned from the scaling down of the HEC.

It may be necessary to re-evaluate essential elements of Tasmania's relationship with the Commonwealth. Because it will always have a relatively small population and industrial base, the island should not be expected to compete directly with the larger states in the same ways or be assessed by the same criteria. Tasmania brings to the nation qualities which no other region possesses; it is unique and valuable on a world scale, and its special attributes need to be given due recognition to balance its economic disadvantages. The island belongs to the whole of Australia in specific ways, for qualities that set it apart and place it on a different plane of value from any other region. This is a proper role and does not imply that the state should be mendicant in any way. Rather, it recognises that Tasmania should receive a level of financial support that will enable it to maintain landscape values throughout the island, develop its infrastructure and offer employment opportunities without having to quarry and degrade the very features which make it such an exceptional and valuable part of the nation.

Above all, landscape values must be protected into the future. This is not simply a matter of maintaining and extending the World Heritage Area, national parks and the various reserves, vital as all of these are. It is the quality of the island as a whole that is of such paramount importance, for depending upon its landscape quality the state's economic health will strengthen or else steadily decline; the quality of life of its community will be pleasant and fulfilling or will become spiritually diminished. Even now, many Tasmanians have little awareness of the impact of their surroundings upon their inner lives. But those who journey elsewhere and return are certainly aware. With the implementation of sound marketing strategies in the decades ahead Tasmania will attract very large numbers of visitors: many times greater than those of today. They will come to experience both the natural and man-made features of an unspoiled island. They will come to absorb the peace of open, attractive countryside uncluttered by urban spill, and that rarest of gems, primitive forest still in its timeless beauty. Such an influx creates potential dangers. One of the severest challenges will be to provide access to much of the land without allowing it to become adversely affected; to avoid the garish lodges and hectares of car parks, and to ensure that no development undermines either the aesthetic or ecological values of an area. There will be inevitable compromises. Information centres, huts, chalets, hotels and restaurants, access roads and viewing points, boat-ramps and marinas, and all the other infrastructure of a high-volume destination will have to be provided, but in every case a development must be required to meet the most stringent standards appropriate to its site. Otherwise we devalue the very commodity upon which we depend.

In preserving the land, the community will need to accept disciplines and restrictions which to many will prove irksome and difficult, even unacceptable by present standards. Such measures will be possible only if the majority of people understand their purpose, share a belief in the goals they seek to achieve and are prepared to support them individually. Proposals put forward in the past have often been viewed with concern. It has been argued, for instance, that coastlines should be virtually free of further development for a distance of five hundred metres from the shore. Most planners now consider that hillsides, ridge-tops and other highly visible areas should remain free of buildings. One of the more difficult restrictions for a community to accept, yet one of the most vital, is the limitation applied elsewhere on building beyond suburban and town boundaries. If this measure were adopted to retain landscape quality, the concept of rural-residential zoning and the practice of selling blocks from farms would disappear, and prevent further encroachment of houses upon farmland, bush and coastline. It is a requirement in many countries, and even in parts of Australia, that new buildings should be in harmony with prevailing streetscape styles and community atmosphere in sensitive localities, and that lake, sea and river shores should be free of shacks and houses. Shacks may in future be restricted to serviced villages. A permit system to limit track use and resultant damage has already been instituted by the Parks and Wildlife Service, and it has also been suggested in the past that particularly vulnerable areas and places that have been subjected to overuse be listed for voluntary avoidance. Off-road vehicles are coming under stricter control, aided by responsible owners' organisations. In a country anxious to preserve its natural vegetation and wildlife habitats there is increasing resistance to the cutting of firewood, and this practice may have ceased in a few years' time. Such limitations upon personal and community freedom will prove acceptable only if they can be seen as safeguarding the appeal of the island as it continues to build its foremost industry, reversing the damage of past generations and preserving those features that the community values. The state's recent history has demonstrated that measures which one generation regards as extreme restrictions upon its rights and freedoms are seen by the next as sensible and necessary means of protecting the natural and cultural environment.

One strategy already proposed for coordinating the care of the land is the formation of an Environmental Protection Authority, having an overview of ecological and aesthetic concerns which are at present the responsibility of several different departments—or of none. To be effective, an Environmental Protection Authority would need a clear perception of the state's future, and both the freedom and the statutory authority to act without political interference or pressure from vested interests. It would also need access to a wide range of experience and expertise. It should even be possible for a body of this kind to gain such a level of respect in the community for its integrity, independence and understanding that it can resolve conflicts over ecological and practical concerns which have in the past proved so intractable and divisive.

No plan to protect the Tasmanian landscape and maintain its range of values can hope to succeed without a high level of public participation and support. It is not solely the province of experts; ordinary people have to care about the land and understand its importance to themselves, their children and to unnumbered generations to come. In a populous, tense and technologically enmeshed world, our surroundings will acquire a value undreamed of today. It will take wisdom and perceptiveness for the community to recognise this.

Education is one avenue to achieving community support and understanding. Already much is being done both in the classroom and in various forms of practical involvement to enable young people to become responsive to the land and knowledgeable about it. The earth sciences have a particularly important part to play in this process, but it should form a continuing thread in all learning from the earliest years. Practical projects at primary and secondary levels include participation in activities such as revegetation, land restoration and landscaping, the study of ecological systems and water monitoring. These form a good beginning, but the process has considerable potential for expansion, both in the range of projects and in the numbers involved. Also important is the complementary role of studies in writing, the visual and creative arts and photography to train the senses to recognise and value the aesthetic qualities of both the natural and built environments.

The decade of the 1990s brought a substantial increase in community participation in land rehabilitation and protection. Excellent work is being carried out by Land Care groups throughout the island, focussing on problems specific to their own localities. Other organisations are concentrating on the eradication of exotic plants such as gorse, blackberry, pampas grass and ragwort with considerable success, especially on the west coast. There are groups which are concerned with coastline and with wetlands, with the protection of the habitats of native animals and birds, the propagation of indigenous plants and the health of streams and catchments. A vital area of need in a country stripped of much of its vegetation is being addressed through the efforts of Greening Australia. Increasing numbers of people who do not belong to specific land organisations demonstrate their concern by turning out each year for the hard and unglamorous work of clearing rubbish from bush and shorelines. Despite the achievements of these and many other voluntary groups, there is still far to go before the community as a whole develops an ethic of care for the land, and sees all land as important.

There are grounds for optimism. Tasmanians are justly proud of the practical achievements which have built the island's industries and infrastructure over two centuries, and which reflect an innovative and independent society. The extraordinary beauty and uniqueness of Tasmania have deeply affected many in every generation, and have created a strong sense of belonging in the community. The island's future well-being depends upon the coming together of these two features of its people, which should so richly complement each other; central to their merging is an acceptance that the care of the land must be our foremost priority. Such an acceptance would change the community's cultural balance and halt the erosion of ecological and landscape values that has continued since white settlement. A change in culture as profound as this will take courage, foresight and love of country beyond the reach of most communities. It would stand as a landmark and a guide on a world scale. Time is short, but it is not too late to secure the future of this beautiful and fragile island.

ENDNOTES

Section I
SHAPING AN ISLAND

1 *Athrotaxis cupressoides*
2 *Diselma archeri*
3 *Richea scoparia*
4 *E. coccifera*
5 *Donatia novazealandiae*
6 *E. subcrenulata*
7 *Acacia melanoxyn*
8 *E. ovata*
9 *E. amygdalina*
10 *E. obliqua*
11 *Melaleuca squarrose* and manuka *Leptospermum scoparium*
12 *Nothofagus cunninghamii*
13 *Atherosperma moschatum*
14 *Melaleuca ericifolia*
15 *Dicksonia antarctica*
16 Captain J. Rolland, 'Report on a Journey', Nov–Dec 1823, Colonial Secretary's Office 1/95/2276/AOT.
17 Lieutenant C.B. Hardwicke, 'Remarks upon the North Coast of Van Diemen's Land', Legislative Council Journals 16, 1861.

18	*E. regnans*
19	*E. viminalis*
20	Henry Hellyer, 'Journal of Operations in opening a Road from Emu Bay towards the Hampshire Hills,' Jul–Aug 1827, VDL Co papers, AOT.
21	*Lagarostrobos franklinii*
22	*Athrotaxis selaginoides*
23	*Richea pandanifolia*
24	Abel Tasman, *Journal*, 1642, entry for 2 Dec, trans. from Swart's edn., quoted in J. B. Walker, *Early Tasmania* (4th imp.), Hobart, 1973, p. 234.
25	*Banksia marginata*
26	*Acacia sophorae*
27	*Acacia verticillata*
28	*Macropus giganteus*
29	*Aquila audax*
30	*Haliaeetus leucogaster*
31	*Thylacinus cynocephalus*
32	*Sarcophilus harrisii*
33	*Dasyurus viverrinus*
34	*Dasyurus maculatus*
35	*Dromaius diemenensis*
36	*Arctocephalus doriferus*
37	*Macropus rufogriseus*
38	*Bettongia gaimardi*
39	*Thylogale billardierii*
40	*Potorous apicalis*
41	*Vombatus ursinus*
42	*Trichosurus vulpecular*
43	*Pseudocheirus peregrinus*

44 *Petaurus breviceps*
45 *Cercartetus lepidus*
46 *Tachyglossus aculeatus*
47 *Ornithorhynchus anatinus*
48 *Rattus lutreolus*
49 *Hydromys chrysogaster*
50 *Notechis ater*
51 *Denisonia coronoides*
52 Augustus and Elizabeth Prinsep, *The Journal of a Voyage from Calcutta to Van Diemen's Land*, London, 1833; fasc. edn.: Melanie Publications, Hobart, 1981.

Section II
A VARIED TAPESTRY

1 J.E. Calder, 'Topographical Sketches' No. 4, *The Mercury*, 9 Feb 1860.
2 Ibid.
3 Ibid.
4 Ibid.
5 W.A. Tully, 'The Western Country', *The Mercury*, 27 Apr 1859.
6 Ibid.
7 J.B. Walker, 'Account of a trip to the West Coast in 1887', RST manuscript collection, Rs 5/1(2)b, UTA.
8 Ibid.
9 Alfred Taylor, 'Ten years on the Ouse–Zeehan Telegraph Line', *Postal Telegraph Journal*, 24 Nov 1900, reprinted in *Tasmanian Tramp*, no. 22, 1976.
10 J.L.A. Moore, Ouse–Henty River Railway Survey, Lands and Surveys Department 9602b/152 AOT.

11 W.H. Twelvetrees, 'Journal of Geological Exploration on Southern Portion of Great Western Railway Route', Department of Mines, 1908. See map of the 'Great Western Survey' which accompanies this journal. See also 'The Great Western Railway and Electric Ore Reduction Bill', Reports of Select Committees, PP 80 of 1896 and 71 of 1899.
12 Mt Dundas is the exception with its dolerite cap.
13 James R. Scott, *The Mercury*, 5 Apr 1871, AOT.
14 J.E. Calder, quoted in *Walch's Tasmanian Guide Book*, Hobart, 1871.
15 Ibid. Other passages are taken from the same source.
16 H. Butler Stoney, *A Residence in Tasmania*, London, 1856, facs. edn., Melanie Publications, Hobart, 1982.
17 Patsy Adam-Smith, *There was a Ship*, Melbourne, 1983.
18 Stoney, *A Residence in Tasmania*.
19 Ian Brand, *Penal Peninsula*, Hobart, 1978.
20 James R. Scott, 'Port Davey in 1875', RST P&P, 1875.
21 This was the extensive Toolumbunner mine on the southern slope of the Gog Range above the Mersey River.
22 Bill Leitch, *Hearts of Oak*, Huonville, 1990.
23 S. Bennett (ed.), 'A Home in the Colonies', Edward Braddon's letters to India from north-west Tasmania, 1878, THRA P&P, 1980.
24 *E. delegatensis*
25 *E. dalrympleana*
26 *E. gunnii*
27 *Phyllocladus aspleniifolius*
28 K. Kiernan, 'The Extent of Late Cenozoic Glaciation in the Central Highlands of Tasmania, Australia', *Arctic and Alpine Research*, vol. 22, no. 4, 1990, pp. 341–5.
29 E. Derbyshire, 'Pleistocene Glaciation of Tasmania: Review and Speculations', *Australian Geographical Studies*, 10, 1972, pp. 79–94.

30 *Microcacrys tetragona*
31 *Leptospermum rupestre*
32 *Hakea lissosperma*
33 *Telopea truncata*
34 *Bellendena montana*
35 *Cyathodes petiolaris*
36 *E. pauciflora*
37 John Beamont, 'Mr Beamont's Journal, taken on his Tour to the Western Mountains, Van Diemen's Land, Dec 1817', Historical Records of Australia, p. 589.
38 Max Banks (ed.), *The Lake Country of Tasmania*, RST, 1973.
39 J. Calder, 'Topographical Sketches' No. 3, *The Mercury*, 27 Jan 1860.
40 Max Angus, *Simpkinson de Wesselow*, Hobart, 1984.
41 Walker, 'Account of a Trip...'
42 John McPhee, *The Art of John Glover*, Melbourne, 1980.
43 Stoney, *A Residence in Tasmania*.
44 George Clark letter to Martha Clark, 22 Mar 1913 (private collection).
45 *Anodopetalum biglandolosum*
46 *Anopterus glandulosus*
47 John C. Darke, *Peak of Teneriffe* (account of his explorations), LSD 1/91/441 2656/1, p. 52, AOT.
48 Ibid., p. 50.
49 Simon Cubit, *Snarers and Cattlemen of the Mersey High Country*, Launceston, 1987.
    James R. Scott, map of Upper Mersey, 1849, Westmoreland F11/12, Lands Titles Office, DPIWE.
    James Sprent, Map of Tasmania, 1859. AOT.

Section III
KINSHIP AND MANAGEMENT

1 The remains of scale-fish have been found in the lower levels of Rocky Cape South Cave, indicating that fish formed a significant part of the diet until about five thousand years BP.
2 Josephine Flood, *Archaeology of the Dreamtime*, Sydney, 1983, 1995. Fine, sharp awls shaped from animal bones have been found in the earlier deposits of Rocky Cape South Cave.
3 Captain James Kelly, 'First discovery of Port Davey and Macquarie Harbour', RST P&P, p. 163.
4 N.J.B. Plomley, *The Baudin Expedition and the Tasmanian Aborigines, 1802*, Hobart, 1983, p. 202.
5 This reduction in the area of open grassland in the Surrey Hills is evident when Hellyer's sketch from St Valentines Peak is compared with photographs taken prior to clear-felling.
6 Lyndall Ryan, *The Aboriginal Tasmanians*, Brisbane, 1981, Sydney, 1996.
7 For discussion of edible plants, see: N.J.B. Plomley, *The Tasmanian Aborigines*, Launceston, 1993; and N.J.B. Plomley and Mary Cameron, *Plant foods of the Tasmanian Aborigines*, Records of the Queen Victoria Museum, 1993.
8 A clear drawing of one of these craft was made by Baudin Expedition artist C. Lesueur. See Plomley, *The Baudin Expedition and the Tasmanian Aborigines, 1802*.
9 Sketches from the Baudin and Bligh expeditions in Plomley, *The Baudin Expedition and the Tasmanian Aborigines, 1802*, pp. 33-4.
10 James Bischoff, *Sketch of the History of Van Diemen's Land*, London, 1832.
11 Hellyer corres. with Curr, 1 Nov 1828, VDL Co papers, AOT.
12 J. Jorgensen, 'Journal of Discoveries in VD Land and Death of Mr Lorymer', Manuscripts in the Mitchell Library, CY Reel 216.

13 Plomley, *The Tasmanian Aborigines*, p. 62.
14 Ibid., p. 61.
15 *Taraba: Tasmanian Aboriginal Stories*, retold by Rosemary Ransom, DECCD, Hobart, 1977.
16 J.G. Cowan, *The Elements of the Aborigine Tradition*, Melbourne, 1992, p. 72.
17 Ibid., p. 45.

Section IV
TWO CENTURIES OF PROGRESS

1 *Tasmanian Year Book 1968*. This area includes 350,000 acres granted to the Van Diemen's Land Company and allows 12,000 acres for 1822, for which returns were not available. The total would, in fact, have been far greater.
2 Louisa Anne Meredith, *My Home in Tasmania*, vol. I, London, 1852.
3 Thomas C. Just, *Tasmaniana! A Description of Tasmania and its Resources*, Launceston, 1879, SLT (Tasmaniana).
4 Bennett, *A Home in the Colonies*, p. 158.
5 Ibid., p. 176.
6 George S. Perrin, 'Report upon the Systematic Conservation and Management of the Woods and Forests of Tasmania', PP no. 57 of 1887, AOT.
7 Edward A. Counsel, 'Timber Industry of Tasmania', PP no. 48 of 1898, AOT.
8 George S. Perrin, 'Tasmanian Forests: Their Conservation and Future Management', PP no. 48 of 1898, AOT.
9 Charles P. Sprent, 'Recent Explorations on the West Coast of Tasmania', Royal Geographic Society of Australasia (Victorian branch), P&P vol. 3, 1883, pp. 61–3, AOT.
10 Colonel W.V. Legge, 'The Highlands of Lake St Clair', RST P&P, 1887.

11 *Tasmanian Year Book 1968*, p. 591.
12 Ibid., p. 221.
13 'Harvesting and Regeneration of Forests in the Environmental 70s', APPITA 26th General Conference, Hobart, Mar 1972.
14 Forestry Commission of Tasmania, *A Manual for Forest Landscape Management*, Hobart, 1990.
15 ABS figures published by the Sustainable Development Advisory Council (SDAC) in *State of the Environment*, vol. 1, 1996. The SDAC noted that the ABS no longer includes very small holdings in these figures.

SECTION V
POWER OF A MYTH:
THE PRACTICAL TRADITION

1 Robin Boyd quoted in *Priceless Heritage*, National Trust of Australia (Tasmania), Southern Section, Hobart 1971, p. 16.
2 Prinsep, *The Journal of a Voyage* ...
3 Harry O'May, *Wooden Hookers of Hobart Town/Whalers out of Van Diemen's Land*, Hobart, 1949/1978, pp. 67–82.
4 Will Lawson, *Blue Gum Clippers and Whale Ships of Tasmania*, Hobart, 1949.
5 O'May, *Wooden Hookers of Hobart Town*, p. 28.
6 For a discussion of early hunters and bush dwellers, see James Boyce, 'Journeying Home', *Island* magazine, autumn, 1996, pp. 38–63.
7 Calder in *Walch's Tasmanian Guide Book*.
8 Cubit, *Snarers and Cattlemen of the Mersey High Country*, and *A High Country Heritage*, Launceston, 1988.
   Nic Haygarth, *A View to Cradle*, Canberra, 1998.
   Tim Jetson, *The Roof of Tasmania*, Launceston, 1989.

Ned Terry, *Identities and History of Tasmania's High Country*, Launceston, 2005.
9   Referred to in Leitch, *Hearts of Oak*.
10 Rev. F.G. Copeland, Twenty-six articles on life on the West Coast, 1894–1901 SLT (Tasmaniana).
11 A 'shoe' is a narrow board placed in a cut in the side of a tree to enable an axeman or sawyer to work at a required height.
12 ABS figure for 1997, published Jun 1998.

Section VI
THE COUNTER-CULTURE:
A LAND TO BE CHERISHED

1   James E. Calder, 'Some account of the country between Hamilton and the Frenchman's Cap', *Hobart Town Courier*, 21 Sep 1850, AOT.
2   'A Trip to the West Coast', no. II, *Tasmanian Mail*, 28 Apr 1888, AOT.
3   Henry Hellyer, 'Journal of the Advance Party of the Van Diemen's Company in Exploring for a Location, 17 May–15 Jul 1826', VDL Co records AOT.
4   Henry Hellyer, 'Panoramic Sketch from the Summit of St Valentine's Peak, 14 Feb 1827', VDL Company Records, AOT.
5   Henry Hellyer, 'Journal of Operations in opening a Road from Emu Bay towards the Hampshire Hills'.
6   Prinsep, *The Journal of a Voyage*
7   *View of Mills Plains, VDL*, 1833.
8   *A Corrobery of Natives in Mills Plains*, 1832.
9   *My Harvest Home*, 1835.
10 *Ben Lomond from Mr Talbot's Property*, 1834.
11 J. Skinner Prout, *Tasmania Illustrated*, vol. 1: first four parts Jun 1844 to early 1845, reissued late 1845; vol. 2: Dec 1846.

12 *On Mt Wellington, Hobarton, the Ascent*, 1847.
13 *Mt Wellington, Hobarton*, 1846.
14 *Maria Island from Little Swanport, Van Diemen's Land*, 1845.
15 *The Cataract Glen, Mount Wellington, VDL, Nov '47; Fern Tree Valley, Hobarton, VDL Nov '46; Wellington Falls, NW Bay River, VDL, Mar '45*.
16 *Mount Ida, looking across Lake St Clair (Van Diemen's Land)*, 1845. Prout's sketch from the same spot is similar, though muted in tones.
17 *The road from Oyster Cove to Port Cygnet Van Diemen's Land, Jany 11th '48*.
18 *Near New Norfolk, VDL, Oct 14th '48*.
19 *On the Derwent at New Norfolk VDL*.
20 *In the Domain, Hobarton*.
21 Robert Browning, *Fra Lippo Lippi*, lines 300–2.
22 Vivienne Rae Ellis, *Louisa Anne Meredith: A Tigress in Exile*, Hobart, 1979.
23 Colonel W.V. Legge, 'W.C. Piguenit: An Appreciation of a Tasmanian Artist', 1915 RST Papers, UTA.
24 *The Arthur Range, Tasmania*, 1871(?). It is also possible that this painting was based on a sketch made during the Lake Pedder journey of 1874, which initially followed the same route.
25 Described with great feeling by Robert Johnston in the introduction to his *Geology of Tasmania*, Hobart, 1888, which is illustrated with lithographs of Piguenit's sketches.
26 *The Mercury*, 23 Sep, 1876.
27 *Lake St Clair* (Sketch No. 2).
28 *The Arthur Range, Tasmania*, 1871.
29 Quoted by J.B. Thwaites in *Tasmanian Tramp*, no. 23, p. 73.
30 *Mt Gell, Western Highlands, Tasmania*, 1887.
31 *The Frenchman's Cap, from Road on Flank of Mt Arrowsmith*, 1887.
32 *Mt Rufus from Stream near Iron Store, Mt Arrowsmith*, 1887.
33 *Lake Pedder, Tasmania*, 1891.

34   *Mt King William from Lake George, Tasmania*, 1891; *The King William Range*, Tasmania, 1891.
35   *The Valley of the Murchison*, 1880.
36   *Eldon Bluff and Lake Augusta, 1880*.
37   *On the Craycroft, Tasmania*, 1878.
38   *The 'Huon Belle' Range from near Victoria, Tasmania*, 1879.
39   I am indebted to the excellent research of Chris Long in his *Tasmanian Photographers, 1840–1940*, THRA and TMAG for these details of early photography in Tasmania.
40   Thwaites in *Tasmanian Tramp*; Tassell and Wood, *Tasmanian Photographer*, QVMAG (Launceston).
41   RST P&P Sep 1901, p. xxxii, RST UTA.
42   *The Weekly Courier*, 3, 17 and 24 Aug 1901, 27 Dec 1902, AOT.
43   RST P&P 1899, p. xxxix–xl, RST UTA.
44   Tassell and Wood, *Tasmanian Photographer*, p. 9.
45   RST P&P 1908, p. 34, RST UTA.
46   Tim Bonyhady, 'The Artist as Activist', *Imagine Nature*, Tasmanian School of Art in Hobart, 1996.
47   RST P&P 1908, p. 34, RST UTA.
48   For details of Stephen Spurling III, see Long, *Tasmanian Photographers, 1840–1940*, pp. 106–7.
49   *Harrison's Photographic Journal*, 2 May 1921, p. 12.
50   Notes made by Major R.E. Smith, Smith Papers, AOT.
51   *Harrison's Photographic Journal*, p. 13.
52   Long, *Tasmanian Photographers 1840–1940*.
53   Owen Hughes, *For the Love of Tasmania*, Launceston, 1985; *The Best of Owen Hughes' Tasmania*, Launceston, 1992.
54   E.T. Emmett, 'A Walk through No-Man's Land', *Tasmanian Tramp*, no. 1, Feb 1933.
55   R.E. Hingston, *The Advocate*, 17 and 24 Apr 1976.

56 For details of the Wilsons, see J.B. Thwaites, 'The Steppes—Life in Tasmania's Lake Country', *Tasmanian Tramp*, no. 22. 1976.
57 For an account of Deny King's life, see Christobel Mattingly, *King of the Wilderness*, Melbourne, 2001.
58 Quoted by Dr G.F.J. Bergman, *Gustav Weindorfer of Cradle Mountain*, Hobart, 1959.
59 Frances Cox, 'A Lady's Walking Tour on the West Coast', *Tasmanian Mail*, 29 Mar 1890, AOT.
60 Geoff T.F. Chapman, 'Looking Back Along the Track', *Tasmanian Tramp*, no. 20, 1972.
61 Geoff T.F. Chapman, 'Mount Anne', *Tasmanian Tramp*, no. 2. 1933.
62 Max Angus, 'Time Frame', ABC TV, 1 May 1997.
63 Gerard Castles, 'Handcuffed Volunteers – A History of the Scenery Preservation Board in Tasmania, 1915–1971', BA (Hons) thesis, University of Tasmania, 1986. I am indebted to Gerard Castles' work for much of the detail of this section.

BIBLIOGRAPHY

Books

Adam-Smith, P. *There was a Ship*. Melbourne: Nelson, 1983.
Angus, M. *Simpkinson de Wesselow*. Hobart: Blubber Head, 1984.
The World of Olegas Truchanas. Hobart: Publication Committee, 1975.
Banks, M. (ed.). *The Lake Country of Tasmania*. Hobart: RST, 1973.
Bennett, S. (ed.). *A Home in the Colonies*. Hobart: THRA, 1980.
Bergmann, G.F.J. *Gustav Weindorfer of Cradle Mountain*. Hobart: author, 1959.
Berndt, R.M. and C.H. *The World of the First Australians—Aboriginal Traditional Life, Past and Present*. Canberra: Aboriginal Studies Press, 1964, 1999.
Bethell, L.S. *The Story of Port Dalrymple*. Hobart: Tasmanian Government, 1956.
Binks, C.J. *Explorers of Western Tasmania*. Launceston: Mary Fisher, 1980.
——. *Pioneers of Tasmania's West Coast*. Hobart: Blubber Head, 1988.
Bischoff, J. *Sketch of the History of Van Diemen's Land*. London:1832.
Bonyhady, T. *The Colonial Earth*. Melbourne: Melbourne University Press (The Miegunyah Press), 2000.
Borschmann, G. (ed.). *The People's Forest: A Living History of the Australian Bush*. Blackheath, NSW: The People's Forest Press, 1999.
Brand, I. *Penal Peninsula*. Hobart: Jason Publications, 1978.
Brown, T. and Kolenberg, H. *Skinner Prout in Australia 1840–48*. Hobart: TMAG 1986.
Collins, P. *God's Earth*. Melbourne: Dove, 1995.
Cowan, J.G. *The Elements of the Aborigine Tradition*. Melbourne: Element Books, 1992.

Cubit, S. *Snarers and Cattlemen of the Mersey High Country*. Launceston: Regal Publications, 1987.

———. *A High Country Heritage*. Launceston: Regal Publications, 1988.

Ellis, V.R. *Louisa Anne Meredith: A Tigress in Exile*. Hobart: Blubber Head, 1979.

Flanagan, R. *A Terrible Beauty*. Melbourne: Greenhouse, 1985.

Flannery, T. *The Future Eaters*. Melbourne: Reed Books, 1994.

Flood, J. *Archaeology of the Dreamtime*. Sydney: Angus & Robertson, 1995.

———. *Rock Art of the Dreamtime*. Sydney: Angus & Robertson, 1997.

Forest Resources Tasmania. *Forest Trees of Tasmania: Field Guide*. Longreach: 1979, 1981.

Gee, H. and Fenton, J. (eds.). *The South West Book*. Adelaide: ACF, 1978.

Haygarth, N. *A View to Cradle*, Canberra: author, 1998.

———. *Baron Bischoff: Philosopher Smith and the Birth of Tasmanian Mining*. Launceston: author, 2004.

Howitt, A.W. *The Native Tribes of South-east Australia*. (1904), Canberra: Aboriginal Studies Press, 2001.

Hughes, O. *For the Love of Tasmania*. Launceston: author, 1985.

———. *The Best of Owen Hughes' Tasmania*. Launceston: author, 1992.

Jetson, T. *The Roof of Tasmania*. Launceston: author, 1989.

Johannes, C.E. and Brown, A.V. *W C Piguenit 1836–1914*. Hobart: TMAG, 1992.

Johnston, R.M. *Geology of Tasmania*. Hobart: 1888.

Just, T.C. *Tasmaniana!*. Launceston: 1879.

Kirkpatrick, J. *A Continent Transformed*. Melbourne: Oxford, 1994.

Lawson, W. *Blue Gum Clippers and Whale Ships of Tasmania*. Hobart: The Shiplovers Society of Tasmania, 1949.

Leitch, B. *Hearts of Oak*. Huonville: Forestry Tasmania, 1990.

Long, C. *Tasmanian Photographers 1840–1940*. Hobart: THRA and TMAG, 1990.

Lowe, D. *The Price of Power*. Melbourne: Macmillan, 1984.

Mattingley, C. *King of the Wilderness*. Melbourne: Text Publishing, 2001.

McPhee, J. *The Art of John Glover*. Melbourne: Macmillan, 1980.

Meredith, L. *My Home in Tasmania* (2 vols). London: John Murray, 1852.

Mulvaney, J. and Kamminga, J. *Prehistory of Australia*. Sydney: Allen & Unwin, 1999.

O'May, H. *Wooden Hookers of Hobart Town/Whalers out of Van Diemen's Land*. Hobart: Tasmanian Government, 1978.

Page, M. *The Eucalypts of Tasmania*. Launceston: author, 1998.

Passmore, J. *Man's Responsibility for Nature*. London: Duckworth, 1974.

Plomley, N.J.B. *The Baudin Expedition and the Tasmanian Aborigines 1802*. Hobart: Blubber Head, 1983.

——. *The Tasmanian Aborigines*. Launceston: QVMAG, 1993.

Plomley, N.J.B. and Cameron, M. *Plant Foods of the Tasmanian Aborigines*. Launceston: QVMAG, 1993.

Priceless Heritage. Hobart: National Trust of Australia (Tasmania) Southern Section, 1971.

Prinsep, A. and E. *The Journal of a Voyage from Calcutta to Van Diemen's Land*. London: 1833.

——. Facsimile Edition. Hobart: Melanie Publications, 1981.

Radford, R. and Hylton, J. *Australian Colonial Art 1800–1900*. Adelaide: AGSA, 1995.

Reynolds, H. *Fate of a Free People*. Melbourne: Penguin, 1995.

Robson, L. L. *A History of Tasmania*. vols 1 and 2, Melbourne: Oxford, 1983, 1991.

Ryan, L. *The Aboriginal Tasmanians*. Brisbane: University of Queensland Press, 1981; Sydney: Allen & Unwin, 1996.

Stoney, H.B. *A Residence in Tasmania*. London: 1856.

——. Facsimile Edition. Hobart: Melanie Publications, 1982.

Taraba: Tasmanian Aboriginal Stories. retold by Rosemary Ransom, Hobart: DECCD, 1977.

Tasmanian Conservation Trust. *Tasmanian Mammals: A Field Guide*. Hobart: 1987.

——. *The Forest Book*. Hobart: 1984.

Tasmanian Year Book 1967 onwards. Hobart: Tasmanian Government.

Terry, N. *Identities and History of Tasmania's High Country*. Launceston: 2005.

Terry, R.R. (ed.). *Handbook: The Central Plateau of Tasmania*. Hobart: Lands Department Tasmania, 1982.

Walch's Tasmanian Guide Book. Hobart: 1871.

Walker, J.B. *Early Tasmania*. 4th imp. Hobart: Tasmanian Government, 1973.

NEWSPAPERS, JOURNALS, PERIODICALS

The Advocate, Burnie
Australian Geographical Studies
Imagine Nature, Tasmanian School of Art in Hobart; University of Tasmania
Island Magazine
The Mercury, Hobart
The Tasmanian Mail, AOT
Tasmanian Tramp, Hobart Walking Club
The Weekly Courier, AOT

PAPERS, MANUSCRIPTS

Castles, G. 'Handcuffed Volunteers: A History of the Scenery Preservation Board in Tasmania, 1915–1971'. BA (Hons) Thesis, University of Tasmania, 1986.

Derbyshire, E. 'Pleistocene Glaciation of Tasmania: Review and Speculations'. *Australian Geographical Studies* 10, 1972.

House of Assembly Papers (AOT)

Kiernan, K. 'The Extent of Late Cenozoic Glaciation in the Central Highlands of Tasmania, Australia'. *Arctic and Alpine Research*, vol. 22, no. 4, 1990.

Legislative Council Journals (AOT)

Royal Society of Tasmania Papers and Proceedings. RST and University of Tasmania Library.

Van Diemen's Land Company Papers (AOT)

Walker Papers. RST and University of Tasmania Library

Public Documents

Department of Parks, Wildlife and Heritage, DELM:
Tasmanian Wilderness World Heritage Area Draft Management Plan, 1991.
Management Plan, 1992
Management Plan, 1999

Tasmanian Public Land Use Commission:
Background reports, proposals and recommendations relating to the Tasmanian Commonwealth Regional Forest Agreement.

Tasmanian Sustainable Development Advisory Council:
Publications compiled by the State of the Environment Unit, Land Information Services, DELM:
State of the Environment Tasmania, Vol I (1996): Conditions and Trends.
Vol II (1997): Recommendations.

INDEX

A

Aboriginal people, 129, 135, 142,
  146, 152, 163, 171
  art, 178-9
  conservation, 177
  fire management, xv, 10, 16, 26,
    75, 118, 166
  food, 30, 86, 148, 168-9
  impact of white settlement, 44,
    61, 72-4, 76, 83, 86-7, 160-1,
    167, 174, 176, 183, 188, 190,
    243, 245, 297
  paintings of, 135, 160, 298
  population and distribution, 168
  prehistory, 74, 148, 159,
    162-3, 348
  shelters, 173
  spiritual bond with the land, 42,
    175-6, 180, 182-3, 242
  stories, 176-7, 179
  tools and implements,
    171-2, 175
  totems, 181
  tracks, 172
  use of the land, 21, 25-6, 106,
    159-62, 180, 357-8
  see also Ben Lomond Tribe;
    Big River Tribe; Black War;
    North Midland Tribe;
    North Tribe; North-east
    Tribe; North-west Tribe;
    Oyster Bay Tribe; Port
    Davey Tribe
Adam River, 153
Adamsfield, 108m, 153, 329, 331
Adamsfield Track, 330
Adamsons Peak, 14, 36m, 143-4
Adventure Bay, 174
Ahrberg, Johnny, 327, 329, 331, 336
Allport, Mary Morton, 306, 314
Anderson, Doug, 339
Angus, Max, 72
Animals and Birds Protection Board,
  343
Anne River, 108m, 142
Anson brothers, 314
Antarctic plate, 7
Anthony River, 57
Arm River, 111
Arthur Plains, 139, 142, 145, 308

Arthur Range, 13, 36m, 58, 92, 139, 142, 164, 256, 308, 311, 339, 408m
Arthur River, 108m, 151, 227, 260, 408m
Arthurs Lake, 120, 126, 227, 408m
Arthurs Peak, 70
Arve River, 142
Arve Valley, 144
Asbestos Range, 24, 36m, 74, 136
Atkinson, Archdeacon, 336
Australian Natives Association, 342
Australian Newsprint Mills, 206, 344
Australian plate, 7
Australian Pulp and Paper Mills, 206, 280
Australian Pulp Mills, 206
Avoca, 134–5

B
Babel Island, 73
Badger Head, 18
Balfour area, 172
Ballawinne Cave, 164
Balmoral Hill, 77
Balmoral Moor, 121
Banks Strait, 18, 408m
Barn Bluff, 63, 150
Barn Bluff Copper Mine, 150
Barren Tier, 119
Barrington district, 59
Bass, George, 337
Bass Strait, 5, 7, 18, 30, 408m

Bass Strait islands, 244
Bassian Plain, 9, 136, 176
Bathurst Harbour, 36m, 76–7, 79
Baudin, Nicholas, 161, 166, 174, 179, 188
Bay of Fires, 26, 408m
Beaconsfield, 94, 212, 260, 408m
Beamont, John, 125
Beattie, John Watt, 311, 314–21, 323, 338, 341
Beehive Canal, 52
Beehives, The, 47
Belcher, Will, 327
Bell, Charles Napier, 280
Bell, Chris, 323
Bell, George Renison, 316
Bell, William, 256
Ben Lomond, 14, 36m, 55, 59, 94, 134–6, 169, 260, 298, 320
Ben Lomond Tribe, 135, 169
Big Caroline Rock, 76
Big River Tribe, 26, 44, 82, 86, 118–19, 125, 132, 169, 172
Black Bluff, 19, 36m, 41, 59, 61–3, 256
Black War, 245, 297–8
Blackburn, James, 236
Blackwood Creek Track, 101
Blade, The, 69
Blakers, Rob, 323
Blue Peaks, 120
Blue Tier, 94, 98, 257
Bluff Cave, 164
Blumont, 17, 90

Blythe River, 172, 192
Bock, Alfred, 313
Bock, Thomas, 295, 313
Bond, Ernie, 153, 329, 331, 336
Borradaile Plains, 246–7, 250, 252
Bostock, Robert, 82
Bothwell, 148, 227, 331, 333
Bowen, Lieutenant, 264
Boyes, G.T.W.B., 299
Boyes River, 330
Braddon, Sir Edward, 95, 195–6, 198–200
Brady, Matthew, 148, 243
Bramble Cove, 76, 78, 244, 266
Branxholm, 98
Break O'Day Plains, 136
Breaksea Island, 76, 170
Breona, 122
Bridgewater, 224, 238, 276, 297, 408m
Bridport, 90, 408m
Brighton, 24, 225
Bronte, 47, 129
Bruny Island, 170, 179, 227, 270, 408m
Bull, Knut, 306
Bureau of Rural Sciences, 210
Burn, David, 46
Burnie, 206, 208, 225, 260, 277, 280, 284, 408m
Burns Plain, 45–6
bushrangers, 54, 83, 241, 243, 247
Bushy Park, 98, 132
Butlers Gorge, 221, 282

C

Calder, James, 38, 45–8, 52, 59–61, 129, 140, 248, 252–3, 292–3, 298, 307
Calders Lookout, 45–7, 49, 293
Calders Track, 46–7, 314
Cambridge, 224
Candlestick, The, 67
Canoe Bay, 67
Cape Barren Island, 73, 408m
Cape Bernier, 72
Cape Grim, 26, 61, 170
Cape Hauy, 66–7
Cape Paul Lamanon, 28
Cape Pillar, 68–9, 280, 408m
Cape Portland, 26, 72
Cape Raoul, 68, 280, 408m
Cape St Vincent, 76
Carboniferous period, 31
Cardigan River, 309
Carlton, 224
Cascades, The, 63
Cash, Martin, 243
Castle Crag, 124, 149
Catagunya Lake, 220
Cataract Hill, 93–4
Cathedral Mountain, 123, 148
Cathedral Plateau, 124
Cathedral Rock, 69
Caveside, 88
Celery Top Islands, 77
Central Plateau, The, 7, 9, 15, 19, 26, 31–2, 36m, 82, 88, 101–2, 104, 106, 109–13, 115–23, 125–6, 130, 136,

145, 148, 165, 169, 172, 190, 205, 216, 221, 227, 247, 250, 252, 276, 281, 320, 331
Cethana Dam, 282
Cethana, Lake, 220
Channel district, 227, 270
Chapman, Geoff, 338–40
Chapter Lake, 123
Chasm Creek, 105
Cheyne Range, 36m, 42, 44, 53
'Cheynes Mountain', 46
chromatype process, 313–14
Chudleigh, 81, 88, 98
Circular Head, 26, 172
Citadel, The, 141
'City of Ochre', 82
Clarence, 225
Clarence Lagoon, 145
Clarence River, 50, 127, 129
Clark Dam, 221, 281
Clark, W.J.T., 47, 129, 275
Clifford, Samuel, 314
Cloister Lagoon, 123
Clumner Bluff, 220
Clyde River, 108m, 125, 132
Clyde Valley, 26, 54, 61, 125, 245
Coal River Valley, 24, 305
Cockle Creek, 334
Collingwood River, 46, 49
Collingwood Valley, 50–1, 202, 293
Collins Bonnet, 92
Collins Cap, 92
Collinsvale, 131

Commonwealth Creek, 150
Complex Ores Ltd, 218
Conder, Hartwell, 268
Connection Range, 92
Connell family, 327
Connell, Lionel, 327
Connelly, Thomas, 54, 152, 253, 266
Conservation Trust, 347
convicts
    assigned to selectors, 245, 247, 253
    bushmen, 145, 243
    bushrangers, 243
    escapees, 44, 46, 243, 245
    masons and bricklayers, 236–7
    shepherds, 83
    work gangs, 46, 67, 91, 129, 142, 188, 206, 234, 242–3, 266–7, 276
Copeland, Reverend Frederick, 268
Corinna, 261, 263, 322, 338, 408m
Cosgrove government, 345
Cosgrove, Sir Robert, 217
Counsel, Edward, 199–200, 203, 254
Cowan, James, 180–1
Cox, Graeme and Francis, 337
Coxs Bight, 78, 173
Cracroft River, 108m, 312
Cracroft Valley, 142, 163
Cradle–Du Cane ridge, 111
Cradle ice-cap, 111
Cradle Mountain, 9, 12–13, 36m, 55, 63, 248, 320, 322, 326–7, 334–6, 338, 408m

Cradle Mountain–Lake St Clair
  National Park, 52
Cradle Mountain–Lake St Clair
  Reserve, 340, 343
Cradle Mountain–Lake St Clair Scenic
  Reserve, 326
Cradle Mountain Reserve Board, 322
Cradle Valley, 248, 250, 257
Crater Lake, 338
Crescent Mountain, 70
Cressy, 24
Cretaceous period, 6, 14
Cunningham, convict, 145–6
Curr, Edward, 59
Currie, Tom, 256, 262
Curtain-Davis companies, 263
Cutts, Isaac, 253
Cuvier Valley, 202
Cygnet, 137, 270

D

Daguerreotype portraits, 313
D'Aguillar Range, 27
Dairy Plains, 17, 36m, 81, 84–5
Daisy Lakes, 114
Dale Brook, 87, 103, 105
Damascus Vale, 118
Darke, John, 54, 145–6, 152, 253
Dasher River, 59
Davey River, 78, 150, 265, 308
Davie Brothers tramway, 51
Davies, Lieutenant Arthur, 129
Dawson Road, 153

Dazzler Range, 136
De Wesselow, Francis Simpkinson,
  59, 72, 94, 126, 128, 134–5, 299,
  301–3, 306–7
De Witt Island, 170
Dee River, 132
Dee Tunnel, 282
Dell, Sergeant, 95
Dell Track, 106
Deloraine, 17, 61, 81, 85, 88–90, 313,
  408m
Deloraine Bridge, 82
Dempster Plains, 202
Den, The, 303
Denison, Governor, Sir William, 129
Denison Range, 152, 331
Denison River, 268
d'Entrecasteaux, Bruni, 161, 188
D'Entrecasteaux Channel, 14, 18, 408m
Derby, 212
Derwent Basin, 128
Derwent Bridge, 129
Derwent estuary, 18
Derwent outflow, 344
Derwent River, 67–8, 108m, 131–2,
  134, 140, 145, 148, 160, 166, 190,
  219, 242, 244, 264, 283–4, 297, 408m
Derwent Power Scheme, 282
Derwent Valley, 14, 32, 44, 68,
  96–8, 129, 131–2, 134–5, 137,
  145–6, 165–6, 169, 183, 189, 224,
  244–5, 270, 302–3, 315, 338

Derwent Valley Railway, 50
Devils Gullet, 220–1
Devonport, 225, 284, 338, 408m
Dial Range, 36m, 41, 63, 74
Dixon, Reg, 252
Dolomieu Point, 67
Dombrovskis, Peter, 311, 323–4, 350
Don, The, 192
Donaldson River, 154
Donnelly family, 256
Doughboys, The, 170
Dougherty family, 266
Dove River, 338
Du Cane Hut, 149, 326
Du Cane Range, 123–4, 127–8, 250, 252, 308, 326, 339
du Fresne, Marion, 166
Dublin Plains, 105, 121
Duck Reach, 217
Duck River, 192
Dunally Canal, 280
Dundas, 58, 214, 256, 263, 277
Dunnett, Frank, 307
Dunrobin Bridge, 153

E
Eardley-Wilmot, Governor, 61
Earle government, 342
eastern Plateau, 19, 119
Echo Point, 128
Eddystone Point, 26
Eldon Bluff, 311

Eldon Range, 13, 36m, 55, 63, 308, 322
Elephant Pass, 276
Elizabeth Town, 25
Ellendale, 98, 327
Emmett, E.T., 328
Emu Bay, 25, 61, 172, 280, 338
Emu Bay Railway, 57, 277
Emu River, 25
Environmental Protection Authority, 365–6
Esk Valley, 59, 134–5, 183, 245
Esperance, 270, 310
Esperance River, 137
European settlement in Tasmania, xv, xvi, 12, 15–16, 20–21, 42, 66, 74, 78, 88, 91, 98, 129–30, 135, 145, 148, 151, 155, 160, 166–7, 187–9, 192, 194–6, 203, 205–6, 209, 216, 218, 224, 227, 228, 233, 235, 241–4, 270, 353, 367
see also penal settlements
Evans, George, 77
Ewart, Robert, 255

F
Farm Cove, 266
Farsund, 73
Fatigue Hill, 46, 49
Feather Falls, 124
February Plains, 172, 252, 316
Federation Peak, 308
Fergusson, Albert, 326
Fern Tree, 92, 225

Field family, 149, 167, 247–8
Field, William, 84–6
Fingal, 135–6
Fish River, 111, 120, 148
Fisher Bluff, 113
Fisher River, 221
Fisher Tunnel, 282
fishermen, 73, 101, 119, 122–3
Fitzgerald, 153
Flat Witch Island, 170
Flinders Island, 72–4, 160, 179, 190, 298–9, 408m
Flinders, Matthew, 76
Florentine Divide, 147
Florentine River, 153, 309, 330
Florentine Valley, 53–4, 147, 163, 165, 344
Flowerdale, 17
Ford Hill, 82
Forestier Peninsula, 28
Fortescue Bay, 18, 66–7, 408m
Forth River, 29, 60–1, 108m, 138, 196, 201, 219, 250, 282
Forth Valley, 9, 111, 147, 149–50
Forth, village, 195
Forty Lake Peak, 118
Fossey, Joseph, 85
Frankland Beaches, 128, 221
Frankland, George, 54, 140, 145, 152–3, 221, 252–3, 301
Frankland Range, 13, 36m, 139–41, 309, 311, 346
Frankland River, 27, 78, 265

Franklin, 91
Franklin, Lady Jane, 45–6, 292, 304
Franklin River, xiii, 42–4, 49–52, 108m 152, 167, 218, 222, 267–8, 318, 320, 324, 341, 347–9, 408m
Franklin, Sir John, 45–6, 52, 76, 92, 292, 304
Franklin Sound, 18, 73
Franklin Valley, 43, 50, 163, 293
Fraser government, 349
Fraser, Peter, 299
Frederick Henry Bay, 71
Frenchmans Cap, 13, 36m, 42, 46–50, 52, 167, 205, 309, 311, 322, 408m
Freycinet Peninsula, 14, 72, 98, 205, 244, 302, 305, 316, 319, 343, 408m
Frith, Frederick, 313–14
Frith, Henry, 313
Furneaux Islands, 72, 166, 245, 408m

G

Gallagher Plateau, 144
Geeveston, 200, 206
Gell Plateau, 44 see also Mount Gell
Gell, Reverend J.P., 46
Giblin, Alan, 339
Giblin River, 150
Gibson, David, 82
Gisbournes Hut, 150
Gladstone, 94, 212
Glenora, 98
Glenorchy, 225

Glover, John, 22, 59, 135, 160, 297–9, 303, 306–7
Godkin Ridge, 263
Gog Range, 98
gold exploration, 47, 90, 94, 193, 212, 215, 257, 262, 264, 293
Gondwana, xv, 6–8, 19
Gondwana plate, 6
Goodman, G.B., 313
Goodwin, James, 54, 145–6, 152, 253, 266
Gordon Dam, 275, 281
Gordon forests, 318
Gordon Power Scheme, 221–2, 346–7
Gordon Range, 53, 147, 152
Gordon River, 18, 27, 45, 108m, 39–41, 151–4, 164, 221, 256, 266–7, 316–18, 320, 331, 347, 350, 408m
Gordon Vale, 153
Gordon Valley, 27
Gormanston, 276
Gould, Charles, 167, 215, 252–3, 295
Goulds Sugarloaf, 42
Goulds Track, 308
Granton, 131, 224, 297, 408m
Granville Harbour, 227
Great Lake, 19, 26, 111–12, 120, 122, 125–6, 148, 218, 220, 227–8, 299, 331, 333, 408m
Great Oyster Bay, 72, 98, 169, 305, 408m
Great Pine Tier, 112

Great Western Railway, 51, 152–3, 279
Great Western Road, 85
Great Western Tiers, The, 17, 24, 81, 98, 101–2, 104, 109, 250, 270, 408m
Greening Australia, 367
Greens Creek, 178
Gretna, 134
Gritton, Henry, 306
Guncarriage Island, 73
Gunn, Ronald Campbell, 47, 337
Gunns Plains, 63, 138, 408m

H

Hamilton, 98, 132
Hampshire, 19, 208
Hampshire Hills, 25, 296
Hardwicke, Captain Charles 24–5
Hartnett, Paddy, 149, 153, 252, 326, 329
Hartz Mountains, 36m, 93, 143–4, 316, 319
Hartz Track, 105
Hastings, 200
Hawes, Martin, 323
Hazards, The, 36m, 72, 305
Heather family, 266
Heazlewood River, 154
Heemskirk, 27, 201, 213, 261
Heemskirk, South, tin field, 75
Hells Gates, 166, 308
Hellyer, Henry, 25, 59, 63, 88, 167, 174, 252–3, 264, 296
Helsham Inquiry, 350
Henry, F.O., 256

Henty–Anthony Power Scheme, 57, 220
Henty River, 57, 264
Hercules Mine, 214, 263
Herrick, 277
Higgs family, 87
Higgs Track, 103, 120, 247
High Plains, 132
Higher Plateau, 112–14, 116–20, 122–3, 125
Hobart, 23, 48, 91, 93, 96, 190, 224, 236, 238–9, 257, 265, 284, 297, 299, 303–7, 309, 313–14, 318, 329, 334, 339, 408m
Hobart Walking Club, 331, 339
Hobbs, Lieutenant James, 24, 76
'Hole in the Wall', The, 69
Holly River, 330
Holy Trinity church, 236
Howells, Humphrey M., 120, 148
Howells, John, 121
Howells Plain, 120, 148, 220
Hughes, Owen, 324
Hunter, Henry, 236
Hunter Island, 170
Huntley, 153
Huon estuary, 18, 91, 206, 238
Huon Plains, 139, 222
Huon River, 91–2, 108m, 137, 139–44, 148, 222, 265, 273, 307, 309, 333, 408m
Huon Valley, 14, 91, 131, 137–8, 141–3, 145, 201, 270, 307

Huonville, 91–2, 312, 408m
Huskisson River, 154
Hydro Electric Commission, 52, 149, 219, 227, 277, 281–2, 343–4, 346–8, 363
see also Derwent Power Scheme; Gordon Power Scheme; Henty-Anthony Power Scheme; Lower Gordon Power Scheme Hydro Electric Department, 217

I

Ile du Golfe, 170
Innes, Edward D.B., 153,
Innes Track, 316
Invermay flats, 94
Iron Blow, 215, 262
Iron Store, 50, 52
Ironstone Creek, 92
Ivanhoe, 134

J

Jane River, 268
JANIS criteria, 352
Joe Page Bay, 76
Johnson, Samuel, 152
Johnston, Robert, 309, 319
Johnstone, William, 256
Jones, David, 255
Jorgenson, Jorgen, 174
Julian Lakes, 120
Junction Lake, 122–5, 148
Jurassic period, 6, 15

K

Kallista, 277
Kelly, James, 76, 166, 262, 265
Kentish Plains, 17, 59
Kia-ora Falls, 149
Kimberley district, 138
King, Charles, 333
King, Denison (Deny), 79, 332–4, 336
King family, 333–4
King, Governor, 264
King, Herbert J., 322
King Island, 160
King River, 18, 46, 108m, 151, 213, 262–3, 267–8, 277, 279, 317
King William Plains, 129, 152
King William Range, 36m, 42, 44, 51, 123, 152, 221, 309
King William Saddle, 52
Kingston, 225
Kinvara, 134
Knole Plain, 25
Knopwood, Reverend Robert, 244
Kutikina (Spirit) Cave, 164, 348

L

Labyrinth, The, 205
Lady Lake Hut, 123
Ladys Bay, 200
Lake Antimony, 120
Lake Augusta, 26, 112, 114, 120, 221
Lake Australia, 43
Lake Barrington, 220, 316
Lake Butters, 110
Lake Crescent, 126, 408m
Lake Daphne, 53–4
Lake Dixon, 43–4, 47, 52
Lake Echo, 126, 408m
Lake Edgar, 222
Lake Ewart, 167
Lake Fanny, 118, 120
Lake Geeves, 150
Lake Gordon, 221, 408m
Lake Hermione, 44
Lake Highway, 276
Lake King William, 52, 221, 408m
Lake Mackenzie, 77, 221
Lake Margaret, 56, 217
Lake Maria, 141
Lake McRae, 150
Lake Meston, 124
Lake Mungo, 178
Lake Nameless, 120–1, 123
Lake Nutting, 114
Lake Pedder, xiii, 139–41, 153, 218 222, 308, 311, 346–7, 408m, *see also* Save Lake Pedder Action Committee
Lake Pedder National Park, 346
Lake Petrarch, 308–9
Lake Pillans, 118, 120
Lake Plimsoll, 220
Lake Richmond, 152
Lake Riengeena, 123–4
Lake Rodway, 250
Lake Rowallen, 149, 220, 281, 408m

Lake Sorell, 126, 408m
Lake St Clair, 26, 43, 45, 111–12, 126–7, 129, 145, 221, 250, 261, 292, 299, 302–3, 308–9, 311, 314–15, 320, 326, 338, 344, 408m
Lake Thor, 114
Lake Undine, 43
Land Care, 367
Lanterns, The, 67
Launceston, 23, 93–6, 136, 190, 217, 225, 234, 257, 284, 305–6, 313–14, 320, 322, 408m
Lawson Range, 27
Lawson, Will, 239
Lea River, 63
Lee-Archer, John, 236
Lee family, 149
Lefroy, 212
Legge, Colonel, 50, 202, 307, 309
Leith, William, 82, 88
Lemonthyme forests, 149, 350
Leven Canyon, 62–3
Leven River, 29, 41, 63, 75, 138, 192, 198
Liena, 316
Liffey Valley, 82, 101
Linda, 277
Linda Track, 48–52, 129, 293, 309, 311, 338
Linda Valley, 49–50, 215, 262
Ling Roth Lakes, 123

Little Fisher River, 105, 107, 110–11, 113, 122
Little Henty River, 75
Little Swanport, 302, 305, 408m
Livingston, Leonard, 339
Lobster Creek, 82
Loddon Range, 51
Loddon Valley, 167
Long, Frank, 256
Long Tarns, 110–11, 113–14, 117, 121
Longford, 24
Longleys, 266
Lorymer, Clement, 174
Low Rocky Point, 79
Lower Gordon Power Scheme, 348
Lower Plateau, 112, 117, 123–5, 127, 129, 145
Lyell Highway, 51, 205, 276
Lynch, Con, 256, 262
Lynchs Creek, 262

M

Maatsuyker Island, 170, 172
Mackintosh River, 154
Mackintosh Valley, 9
Macquarie, Governor Lachlan, 93
Macquarie Harbour, 18, 44–6, 54, 57, 76, 152, 154, 166, 214, 238, 253, 256, 261, 263, 265–8, 280, 317, 327, 408m
Macquarie, Lachlan (Boat builder), 239
Macquarie Plains, 134

Mangana, 212
Maria Creek, 141
Maria Island, 72, 170, 302, 305, 408m
Marion Valley, 111
Marlborough, 126, 129, 145
Mather, J.F., 319
Mathinna Plains, 26, 94
Maxwell Valley, 163
McAulay, Leicester, 339
McCarthy, Denis, 76
McCoy, Tom, 252
McDonough family, 256, 262
McKay, Alexander, 142, 253, 308
McKays Track, 142, 308
Meadowbank Lake, 132, 220
Meander, 81–2, 85, 89, 105
Meander Falls, 107
Meander River, 82, 85, 108m, 190
Meander Valley, 28, 82, 101
Melaleuca Inlet, 333, 408m
Melba Flat, 277
Meredith, Charles, 24, 256, 304, 306
Meredith, Louisa Anne, 24, 32, 192, 247, 256, 304–6
Mersey Crag, 113, 116
Mersey River, 24–5, 29, 59–61, 88, 108m, 124, 138, 148–9, 172, 190, 198, 219–20, 246–7, 250, 252, 280, 282
Mersey Valley, 9, 59, 61, 111, 120–1, 123–4, 131, 149, 220, 326

Middlesex Plains, 36m, 61, 63, 85, 167, 172–3, 247
midland plain, 23–4, 36m, 101, 189, 296, 298
Miena, 218
Miles brothers, 252
Miles, Ray ('Boy'), 122
Mill Creek, 67
Milligan, Dr Joseph, 47, 337
Mills Plains, 135
miners, 201–2, 213, 215, 259–61, 263–4
Mines Department, 339, 344
mining, xvii, 21, 27, 48, 56–8, 72, 78–9, 94, 150–2, 198–9, 201–3, 212–13, 215, 217, 248, 255, 259–64, 272, 275, 280, 284, 292, 309, 315–17, 323, 327, 329, 341, 344–5, 359–60
see also prospecting
Mining Department, 198
Mole Creek, 59, 98, 101, 121, 149, 172, 246–7, 277, 408m
Mole Creek Track, 221
Molesworth, 131
Montezuma Falls, 263, 275, 278–9
Moore, James, 50, 153
Moore, Tom B., 48–9, 51, 142, 255–6, 326
Mossy Marsh Tunnel, 282
Mother Cummings Peak, 88, 106
Mother Cummings Rivulet, 107
Moulting Lagoon, 135, 169

Mount Agnew, 75
Mount Anne, 13, 92, 139–40, 142, 144, 152, 339, 408m
Mount Arrowsmith, 36m, 43–52, 129–30, 292, 309, 314
Mount Arthur, 36m, 94–5, 136
Mount Barrow, 17, 36m, 90, 94–5, 276
Mount Berry, 76
Mount Bischoff, 94, 213, 257, 60, 264
Mount Bisdee, 143
Mount Black, 36m 55, 57–8
Mount Bobs, 142–3
Mount Byron, 309
Mount Cameron, 72, 212
Mount Cameron West, 178
Mount Charles, 129
Mount Dromedary, 131, 297
Mount Farrell, 264
Mount Field, 105, 147, 152, 316, 319, 343
Mount Field National Park, 327, 345
Mount Fortescue, 67
Mount Gell, 36m, 41–2, 44–7, 49–53, 55, 309, 311
Mount Gog, 82, 118,
  see also Gog Range
Mount Hobhouse, 127, 145
Mount Hopetoun, 142
Mount Housetop, 118, 172
Mount Hugel, 42, 127
Mount Ida, 128, 303
Mount Ironstone, 19, 88, 112, 117–18, 121

Mount King William I, 26, 42, 47, 50, 127, 309, 311, 338
  see also King William Range
Mount La Perouse, 143
Mount Lloyd, 315
Mount Lyell, 201, 213, 215, 262, 264, 318, 338
Mount Lyell Company, 255
Mount Lyell Copper Mine, 215
Mount Lyell Railway, 275, 277, 279
  see also North Mount Lyell Railway
Mount Maurice, 17, 90
Mount McCall HEC Road, 219
Mount Moriah, 118
Mount Mueller, 144
Mount Murchison, 13, 36m, 55–8, 63, 220, 277
Mount Oakleigh, 149, 316
Mount Olympus, 13, 36m, 55, 127–8, 202–3, 205, 303, 308–9
Mount Ossa, 123
Mount Owen, 215
Mount Pelion West, 36m, 55, 149, 316
Mount Picton, 36m, 58, 142–3
Mount Read, 36m, 56, 214, 264
Mount Rogoona, 110, 124, 252
Mount Roland, 17, 36m, 41, 59–62
Mount Rufus, 127, 205, 311
Mount Rugby, 76–7
Mount Solitary, 139
Mount Sprent, 141
Mount Strzelecki, 36m

Mount Stronach, 90
Mount Victoria, 14, 26, 36m, 98
Mount Wedge, 139, 309
Mount Weld, 144
Mount Wellington, 33, 36m, 55, 59, 92, 96, 105, 206, 238, 270, 276, 284, 300, 302, 337
see also Wellington Range
Mount Wright, 152–3, 329, 331
Mountain River, 92
Mountains of Jupiter, 110, 112, 122–4, 125
Mowbray Hill, 94
Moxon Saddle, 56
Munro Bight, 67
Murchison Highway, 57, 220
Murchison River, 57, 154
Murchison Valley, 311, 322
Murray, Cecil, 339
Murray, Jack, 339

N
Narcissus Valley, 111
National Parks and Florentine Valley Bill, 345
National Parks and Wildlife Service, 343
Navarre Plain, 45, 111
Needles, The, 88
Neika, 92
Nelson Valley, 293–4
Never Never, The, 124, 148

New Norfolk, 131–4, 297, 302, 408m
New River, 150
New River Lagoon, 79, 150
New Town, 304
New Years Lake, 118
Nicholls, Bert, 252
Nietta plateau, 61, 63, 277
Nile, 135, 169, 298
Nive forest, 303
Nive River, 47, 125–7, 108m, 129–30, 145–6, 298
Nixon, Bishop, 299, 306
Norfolk Bay, 71
Norfolk Plains, 24, 36m, 82, 135, 165
Norfolk Range, 27
North Bay, 71
North-East Dundas Railway, 275, 279
North-east Tribe, 26
North Esk River, 93, 95, 108m, 136, 169, 408m
North Farrell (Tullah), 56
North Heemskirk tin field, 248, 260
North Midland Tribe, 23–4, 82, 86, 134
North Mount Lyell Railway, 317
North River, 256
North Tribe, 24–5, 118, 173
North West Bay River, 238
North-west Tribe, 27, 171
Northdown Plain, 24
northern Plateau, 118, 121
Nubeena, 71, 408m
Nut, The, 98

O

Oakleigh ice-cap, 111
Oakleigh Plateau, 111
Ocean Beach, 75, 263, 338
Ogilvie, Albert, 217
Old River, 256
Olga River, 150
O'May, Harry, 239
Orr, Robert, 129
Ouse, 50, 129, 131–2, 408m
Ouse River, 22, 26, 120, 132, 145, 169
Overland Track, 326
Oxley, John, 77
Oyster Bay Tribe, 23, 29, 134–5

P

Paddocks, The, 148–9, 246
Paddys Lake, 62–3
Page, Joe, 78
Pallin, 'Paddy', 339
Pangaea, supercontinent, 5–6
Parangana, 220, 281
Parangana Tunnel, 282
Parsons Falls, 221
Parsons Track, 221
Paterson, Colonel William, 24
Patons Road, 149–50
Payanna Lake, 123–4
Payne Bay, 76–8, 265–6, 308
'Peak of Teneriffe', 53
    see also Wylds Craig
Pelion area, 150, 316, 320, 344
penal settlements, 70–1, 188, 266–7

Pencil Pine Tarn, 118
Permian rock band, 165
Permian world, 6, 106
Perrin, George, 197–8, 200–3
petroglyphs, 178
Philosophers Ridge, 262
photography, 313–14, 316, 319–20, 323–4, 366
Picton forests, 92
Picton River, 108m, 142–3
Picton Valley, 108m, 143, 145
Pieman Heads, 227, 327
Pieman River, 151–2, 154, 214, 219, 248, 256, 260–1, 265, 328–9, 338, 408m
Pieman tin field, 261
Pieman Valley, 108m, 201–2
Piguenit, William C., 16, 50, 52, 127–8, 135, 202, 299, 307–11, 314–15
Pillans drainage system, 110
Pillinger, 277
Pindars Peak, 143
Pine River, 125
Pipers River, 94
Plateau, Higher see Higher Plateau
Plateau ice-cap, 111
Pleistocene period, 7–8, 27, 43, 110–11, 155, 159, 162–3, 178, 348
Plenty, 134, 303
Poatina Highway, 276
Pokana River, 330
Port Arthur, 46, 67, 69, 71, 408m
Port Arthur Historical Site, 343

401

Port Cygnet, 91, 303
Port Davey, 18, 58, 65, 76–9, 142, 151, 205, 238, 244, 265–6, 307–8, 311, 316–17, 332–3, 335, 339, 408m
Port Davey Tribe, 76, 172
Port Esperance, 91, 98, 200
Port Frederick, 280
Port Latta, 217, 280
Port Sorell, 24–5, 82, 88, 296
Pot Boil, 73
Powell, Bill, 153, 329
Precipitous Bluff, 55, 339
Prinsep, Augustus, 32–3, 189, 236, 297
Prinsep, Elizabeth, 33, 297
Prion Bay, 79
prospecting, 27, 47, 56, 58, 63, 75, 90, 129, 149, 153, 155, 202, 213–15, 242, 254–7, 260, 264, 266, 286, 291, 320, 326–7, 329, 331, 333, 337, 339
see also mining
Prout, John Skinner, 72, 94, 128, 299–303, 306–7, 310

Q
Quamby Bluff, 36m, 84–5, 88
Quamby Brook, 82, 88
Quarter-mile Bridge, 277
Que River, 264
Queen River, 215
Queen Valley, 151, 215, 262
Queenstown, xiii, 51, 57, 205, 215, 262, 276–7, 360, 408m

R
Raglan Range, 202
Railway Exploration League, 342
Rats Castle, 119
Razorback, The, 308
Recherche Bay, 244, 270
Recherche district, 173
Recochet, Paul, 314
Red Hills, 56, 88
Redpa, 277
Reece government, 346
Reed, R. ('Dick'), 52
Regional Forest Agreement, 209, 351–2, 360
Renison Bell, 214
Repulse Lake, 220
Retreat, 85
Reynolds Neck, 220
Richmond, 24
Ridgley, 98
Ridgway, 238
Ring Valley, 58
Ringarooma, 26, 98
Ringarooma River, 90, 212
Risdon, 224
Risdon Cove, 166
Ritchie, Lieutenant Thomas, 82
Ritters Track, 120, 247
Roberts River, 143
Robinson, George A., 23, 61, 73, 76, 86, 161, 172–4, 176, 179
Rocky Cape, 18, 25, 74, 165, 205, 408m
Rocky Hill, 202

Roger River, 277
Rokeby, 225
Rolland, Captain John, 24, 59–60
'Rollands Repulse', 59
   see also Mount Roland
Rosebery, 56–7, 213–14, 264
Rossarden, 259–60
Rossbank Observatory, 301
Royal Ornithologists Union, 342
Royal Society of Tasmania, 316, 319, 342
Rubicon River, 25, 82
Rufus Canal, 52
Russell Falls, 345
Russell Falls Reserve, 342
Russell River, 142
Russell Valley, 144

S
Salamanca Place, 237
Saltwater River, 212
Sandy Lake, 122, 221
Sarah Island, 46, 266
   see also Macquarie Harbour
Savage River, 264
Save Lake Pedder Action Committee, 346
Scenery Preservation Act, 342–3
Scenery Preservation Board, 322, 342–5
Schnells Ridge, 142
Schouten Island, 72, 98, 170, 244, 305, 319, 408m

Scott, James Reid, 58, 77–9, 90, 142, 307–9, 337
Scotts Peak, 334
Scottsdale, 89–90, 408m
sealing, 72–3, 161, 244–5
Sedgwick Gap, 51
Sentinels, The, 309
Separate Prison, 70
   see also Port Arthur
Serpentine River, 139–41, 151, 222
Serpentine Valley, 222
Settlement Point, 76
Seven Mile Creek, 129
Shannon Lagoon, 282
Shannon River, 108m, 125, 145
Shannon Valley, 26, 54, 245
Sharland, William, 44, 167, 252–3
Sharp, John, 313
Sheffield, 277
shipbuilding, 78, 91, 239, 264–6
Sideling Ridge, 90
Sideling Track, 90
Simpson, Thomas, 82
Sisters Beach, 74
Sisters Creek, 165
Sisters Hills, 74
Sisters, The, 47
Skittleball Hill, 114
Skittleball Plain, 111, 119
Sleeping Beauty, 92
Smith, Captain Malcolm Laing, 82
Smith, James 'Philosopher', 63, 94, 213, 256, 260, 338

Smith, Ronald, 338
Smith, V.C., 339
Smithies, Frederick, 322
Smiths Cove, 268
Smithton, 26, 277
Smoko Creek, 106
Snake River, 144
Snowy Mountains, 9
Snowy Range, 14, 144
Solomons Jewels, 118
Sophia River, 167
Sorell, 24, 112, 225, 277, 305, 408m
Sorell, Governor William, 125
South Arm, 224
South Bruny Island, 19, 98
South-east Tribe, 179
South Esk River, 93–5, 136, 190, 408m
South Esk Valley, 14, 26, 93, 108m, 131, 134–5, 165, 169, 212, 259, 296, 298–9
South Heemskirk tin field, 261
South West Cape, 76, 79, 408m
South West Committee, 346
South-west Tribe, 27, 76, 171
Southern forests, xiii, 350
Southern Ocean, 5, 9, 65, 75, 78
Southport, 227, 270, 408m
Spires, The, 322, 339
Split Rock, 118–19, 121
Spode, Joseph, 134
Sprent, Charles P., 49–50, 128–9, 202, 254–5, 257, 309, 337
Spring River, 76, 78, 265, 308

Springfield, 90
Spurling III, Stephen, 311, 314, 319–20, 322, 338
St Clair Surface, 112, 123, 125–7, 129
St Davids Church, 236
St Josephs Church, 236
St Marys, 135
St Marys Pass, 276
St Pauls Dome, 135
St Valentines Peak, 36m, 17, 167, 296
Stacey brothers, 153
Stacks Bluff, 94, 134–5, 260, 299
  see also Ben Lomond
Stanley, 98, 280, 313
Staverton, 277
Steers, Basil, 252
Steppes, The, 330–3
Stirling Valley, 55–6
Stirling Valley Mine, 56
Stitt River, 56
Stitt Valley, 55
Stocker, William, 82
Stockers Plain, 17, 36m, 81, 85, 88
stockmen, 220, 241, 246–8, 252
Stone Hut Track, 106
Stoney, Captain H. Butler, 70, 91, 137
Stony Creek Tribe, 135
Storm Bay, 68–9, 280, 408m
Storys Creek, 259–60
Strahan, 262–3, 267–8, 277, 309, 338, 408m
Strickland Avenue, 225
Strzelecki, Sir Paul Edmund de, 47, 337

Styx River, 148
Styx Valley, 144, 360
Sunday Trampers Walking Club, 339
Sundown Point, 178
'Sunset Point', 88
  see also Western Bluff
Surprise Valley, 51
Surrey Hills, 25, 61, 85, 167, 172, 174, 208, 247–8, 257, 296
surveyors, 54, 58, 77, 142, 145, 149, 199, 252, 254, 263, 291, 296, 301, 307, 337, 343
Sutherland, Mr, 248
Swan Island, 73
Swansea, 98, 305, 408m

T
Table Cape, 17
Talbot property, 135
Tamar Estuary, 18
Tamar River, 24, 93–5, 108m, 136–7, 160, 198, 242
Tamar Valley, 14, 24, 83, 94, 131, 136–7, 189, 212, 225, 284, 296
Tarkine, 360
Tarraleah forest, 145–6
Tarraleah Plain, 111
Tasman, Abel, 27
Tasman Island, 36m, 68–9
Tasman Peninsula, 17–19, 65–7, 69, 72, 206, 408m
Tasmania Mine, 212, 260
Tasmanian Field Naturalists Club, 342

Tasmanian Government Railways, 322
Tasmanian Imperial Bushmen, 273
Tasmanian Wilderness Society, 347
Teepookana, 263
Teepookana Plateau, 268
Temma, 174, 248
Teneriffe Marshes, 54, 152
Tertiary period, 7
Throne, The, 141
Thumbs, The, 152–3
Tiger Range, 53, 147, 152
tin mining, 72, 75, 79, 90, 94, 212–3, 257, 259–60
Toombs, Thomas, 125
Totem, The, 67
tourism, 211, 218, 276, 282, 285, 317, 319, 324, 335, 342–3, 345, 349, 352, 361–2
Tourism Department, 322, 343
trappers, 52, 101, 113, 121–2, 149, 220, 242, 249–52, 264, 286, 326, 329, 337
Traveller Range, 112, 123–5, 127
Travellers Rest Lake, 123
Travellers Rest River, 129, 145
Trestle Mountain, 92
Trevallyn, 94
Triabunna, 208
Trial Harbour, 227, 261, 263, 338
Truchanas, Olegas, 154, 311, 323, 346
Trumpeter Island, 170
Tullah, 57, 220, 264, 277, 408m
Tully, William A., 47, 51–2, 129, 202

Turanna Bluff, 105, 110, 113
Twin Lakes, 53
Tyenna, 51, 132
Tyenna River, 148
Tyenna Valley, 270
Tyndall Range, 8, 13, 214, 220

U
Urquhart, Mac, 339

V
Vale of Belvoir, 61, 247
Vale of Rasselas, 51, 53, 108m, 151–3, 253, 309, 329
Van Diemen's Land Company, 25–6, 61, 82, 85, 98, 167, 172, 174, 192, 248, 253, 296
Vansittart Island, 73
Vansittart Shoals, 73
Victoria Valley, 54, 129, 293
von Mueller, Baron Manfred, 326

W
Waddamana Power Station, 218
'Waldheim', 327, 335–6
Walker, James B., 49, 128, 309
Walkers Creek, 67
Walls of Jerusalem, 110, 112, 114, 116, 118, 120–1, 148, 247, 252, 339, 408m
Waratah, 25, 260–1, 263, 277, 309, 338, 360
Wareen Cave, 164

Wargata Mina Cave, 164
Waterhouse, 212
Waterloo Point, (Swansea), 305
Wattle Grove, 138
Wayatinah Tunnel, 282
Wedge Bay, 71
Wedge, John Helder, 140–1, 152–3, 172, 252–3, 309
Wedge Plains, 153, 309
Weindorfer, Gustav, 61, 322, 327, 334–6
Weindorfer, Kate, 61, 335
Weld forest, 92
Weld River, 142, 144
Weld Valley, 339
Weldborough, 212
Wellington Range, 17, 71, 92, 131, 134
Wentworth Hills, 127
Wesley Vale, 206
Wesley Vale Pulp Mill, 350
West Coast Range, 9, 13, 27, 36m, 49–50, 55, 57–8, 110–11, 205, 220, 256, 262, 317
Westbury, 17, 88, 93
Westbury Road, 94
Western Arthur Range, 141
Western Bluff, 19, 36m, 55, 88
Western Creek, 88, 101, 106–7, 120–1, 247
Western Creek Track, 104, 106
Western Lakes, 112
Western Marshes, 82
western Plateau, 19, 118

'Western River', 82
  see also Meander River
Western Tiers, 82, 84–5, 87–90, 102–3, 105–7, 121, 123, 408m
'Westfield' property, 82
Whales Head, 248 see also Temma
whaling, 239, 244–5
Whitefoord Hills, 82
Whitlam government, 346
Wild Dog Tier, 119
Williamsford, 214, 264, 279
Wilmot Range, 140
Wilson family, 330–1, 333
Windermere district, 320
Windmill Hill, 93–4
Wineglass Bay, 18
Winnaleah, 98
Winterbrook Falls, 62–3
wolfram mining, 150, 344
Wombat Glen, 43, 50–1
Wooden Store, 50
Woodstock, 138
Woolnorth station, 26
World Heritage Area, 52, 79, 219, 360, 363
World Heritage Area Management Plan, 121, 219
Wurragarra Creek, 249
Wybalenna, 72
Wylds Craig, 36m, 41, 53–5, 127, 145–7

Y
Youd, Arthur, 252

Z
Zeehaen, 28
Zeehan, 213–14, 217, 248, 256–7, 263, 277, 279, 338, 408m

www.ingramcontent.com/pod-product-compliance
Lightning Source LLC
Chambersburg PA
CBHW061253230426

43665CB00027B/2925